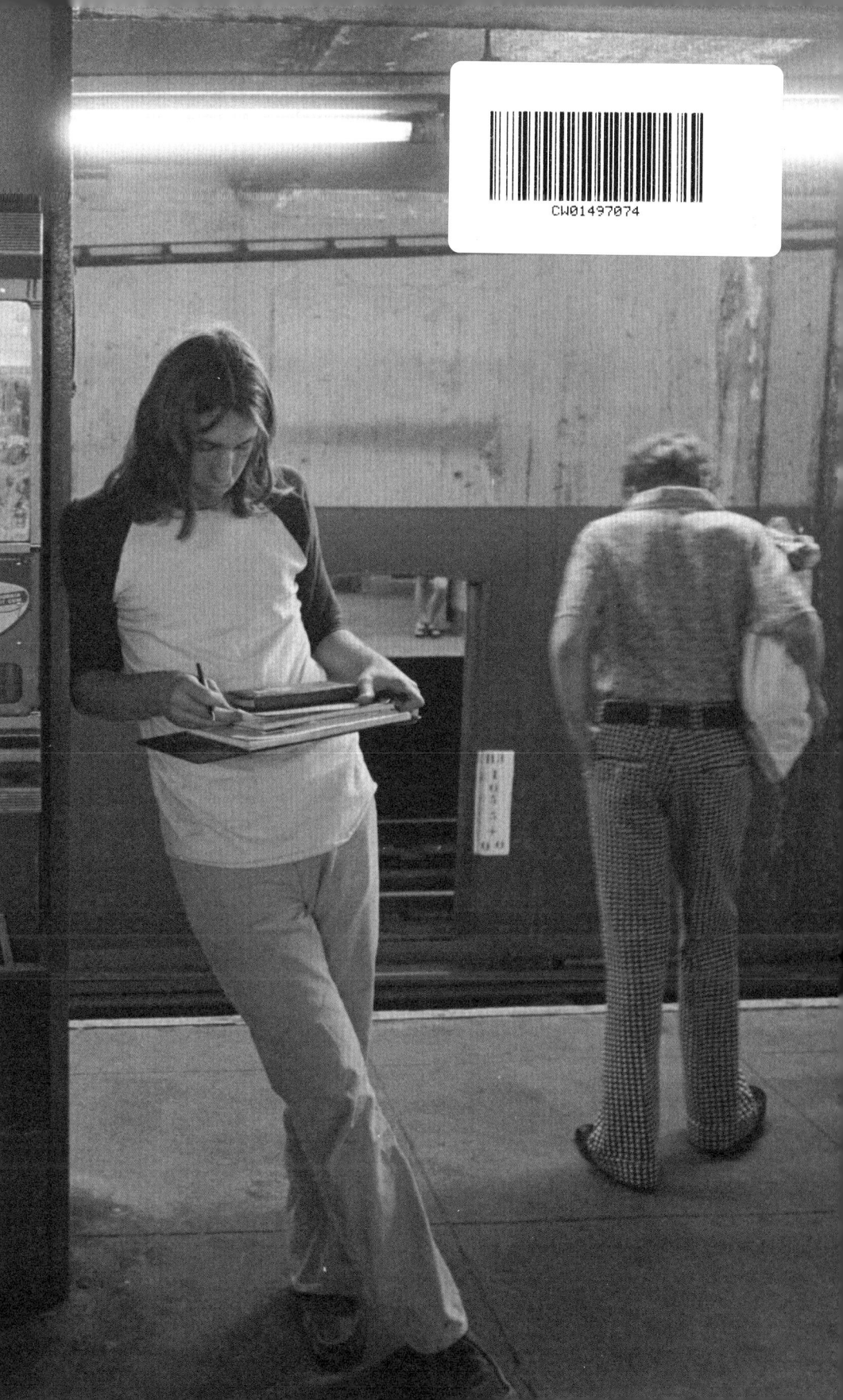

The Uncool

Also by Cameron Crowe

Conversations with Wilder

Fast Times at Ridgemont High

The Uncool

A Memoir

Cameron Crowe

4th ESTATE · London

4th Estate
An imprint of HarperCollins*Publishers*
1 London Bridge Street
London SE1 9GF

www.4thestate.co.uk

HarperCollins*Publishers*
Macken House, 39/40 Mayor Street Upper
Dublin 1, DO1 C9W8, Ireland

First published in Great Britain in 2025 by 4th Estate
First published in the United States by Avid Reader Press,
an imprint of Simon & Schuster in 2025

1

A catalogue record for this book is
available from the British Library

ISBN 978-0-00-869785-3 (hardback)
ISBN 978-0-00-869786-0 (trade paperback)

Image credits:
Courtesy of Cameron Crowe: 6, 8, 11, 24, 26, 32, 40, 41, 50, 54, 77, 115, 133, 160, 222, 223, 227,
240, 263, 271, 276, 293, 297, 311, 315, 319; Courtesy of Charles Phoenix: 33; Courtesy of Vince
Compagnone: 68, 94; Courtesy of Walt Disney Television Photo Archives/©ABC/Getty Images:
74; Courtesy of Black Sabbath and BS Productions Limited: 80; Courtesy of Gary Elam: 87;
Courtesy of Neal Preston: 103, 140, 145, 147, 161, 177, 180, 189, 232, 308, 317; Courtesy of
Kim Gottlieb-Walker: 111, 112, 245; Courtesy of Andy Kent: 220; Courtesy of Petty Legacy/
Paramount Plus: 306; Photographer unknown: 318; Courtesy of Robert Lewis: 320

Interior design by Carly Loman

Set in Granjon LT Std
Printed and bound in the UK using 100%
renewable electricity at CPI Group (UK) Ltd

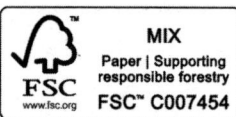

For Cathy

The Uncool

The only true satisfaction comes from doing good.

—ALICE CROWE

It was just after eleven at night. I was pacing around the darkened courtyard outside the Old Globe Theatre in San Diego, my former hometown. Eleven was the time I usually called my mom to check on her and say good night. She was still razor-sharp at ninety-seven, the gift of a life without smoke or drink. We were then less than ten days away from the first previews of *Almost Famous: The Musical*, the stage adaptation I'd written, based on my own autobiographical film. Inside the theater, a lively cast was still rehearsing. I could hear them singing as the sweet smell of gardenias wafted through the night air. It should have all felt so promising. But let's be honest. I mean, that *should* be our arrangement here. I knew the brutal truth. The play was not going to work, and I didn't want to talk about it.

"How's the play?" she asked immediately. It was more like a demand. My mother had never been a fan of small talk.

"It's like trying to speak in a different language," I said. "It's nothing I'm used to. It's—"

"It's going to be *great*," she declared.

I had to tamp down her expectations fast. Soon there would be live audiences, reviews, and more. "It's *not* going to be great. Good is the best we can hope for."

"Stop it," she said. "Mind is in every cell of the body! What you say will make it so." She lived on aphorisms. "Now, I want to hear you say, 'The play is going to be great.'"

She was *obsessed* with the play. And not just because the show-stealing part was the character based on her. For the last few years, every attempt at a conversation about other subjects had served only as a tiny distraction from the subject at hand—*How is the play?* The play! *Almost Famous*, the film, was an almost exact replica of our family life, particularly the difficult relationship between my sister and mother. The movie was never successful in the multiplexes, but audiences caught up to it later. I won an Academy Award for the screenplay. I'm still as surprised today as when Tom Hanks called out my name. It was a gentle story about music and family, not a blockbuster. But something about that intimate tale, and the way music can serve as an emotional guide throughout your life, caused people to discover and rediscover it over the years. The idea of turning it into a musical was a pipe dream that had gone from a possibility to a show booked in the very theater across the street from our old apartment. The whole unwieldy idea had been fueled by my mom's desire to see it on the Broadway stage.

It had not been a breeze. The director, Jeremy Herrin, was a flinty character who'd made some great theater back in England and also in New York, where we hoped the play would move after our run in San Diego. He'd not directed a musical before, but I trusted his musical taste. We cooked up a lot of good ideas, along with our celebrated composer Tom Kitt. Kitt's writing and arranging often lit up Broadway with a Brian-Wilson sense of emotion. Still, I grew up with Led Zeppelin and was worried that the play was summoning too much Billy Joel and not enough "Kashmir."

Then there was the case of the lead actor. He was a lively kid with a great voice. If you squinted you might even believe him as fifteen years old, despite the thick chest hair that had begun to sprout from under the neckline of his T-shirt. But with six weeks left until the first preview, he quit our musical to be the third lead on a cable TV show.

A whirlwind search had turned up a kid named Casey Likes from Arizona, a runner-up in a national high school musical theater contest. The more I explained these foreboding events to my aging mother, the more she defended her predictions of greatness like they were the beaches of Normandy. History had proven her strange psychic ability to see just around the corner. And so our conversations went round and round. I was the doomsayer, and she blasted me with rah-rah enthusiasm. As long as I didn't interrupt her nightly appointment with Rachel Maddow, she was fine to continue our usual tradition.

"It's going to be great!" she declared again. I could picture her in the grand reclining chair in her apartment, just a few miles from where we were rehearsing. "Opportunity favors the prepared mind!" She added one more aphorism, because she always did. "I've seen it in my mind, just get out of the way. The play"—she paused dramatically—"will be great."

"I have to go." I actually didn't, except I really did.

"Doubt is the devil!" It was another one of her favorites.

This was the point when, I'm ashamed to admit, I erupted. "I'm telling you the truth! I don't know why I'm here! I thought it would be a good idea! But all I can think now is that the only thing worse than embarrassment is *embarrassment in my old hometown.*"

"Stop it," she said.

I couldn't downshift. My own ridiculous voice was echoing off the walls of the courtyard. It felt so good to say it, to *proclaim* it. "I WANT MY OLD LIFE BACK!" I shouted.

Immediately, I felt a creeping sensation that I was no longer alone. I turned slowly to behold the play's costumer, Abby, quietly smoking a cigarette in the darkness ten feet away. She nodded to me with her cigarette. I nodded back darkly. She'd heard everything. Suddenly we knew each other too well.

"I have to go," I said to my mother. "Let me talk to Ruthie." Ruthie was her friend, her hairdresser, and lately her caretaker.

"I told her to go home. I needed a break."

"Ruthie should be there. You shouldn't be alone."

"Ruthie makes too much of a fuss," she said. "I can take care of myself. I'm worried about *you.*"

"Why are you alone?"

"Because you didn't want me to come live with you!" Now we were on to another issue, far less blissful to her than the promise of the play. "I've outlived my welcome," she said. "Nobody wants me anymore. And you want to put me in a nursing home!"

She'd just separated from her second husband, Gary, a few months earlier. He was seventeen years younger than she was, but they had a chemistry only they truly understood. How anybody could leave their wife at ninety-seven, I still didn't know. The play had become her obsession, followed only by her fear of being put in an assisted-living facility.

"I'm not trying to put you in a nursing home," I said.

"No, you are," she said quietly. "I've *seen* it."

My earliest memories involved her mysterious gift of prophecy. She could often predict events long before they happened. Of this she was sure: her life would be a battle against the weakening of the American spirit. All around her, she could see the signs. America was lacking in moral values. The similarities were shocking to her. It was only a matter of *when*. Just around the corner was the fall of the Roman Empire.

"Be positive," she said. "There's enough negativity in the world! Stay focused on the light. That's what people love about your work! Stay positive and you'll *attract* positivity."

"I wish you were right," I said.

"Relinquish your fears," she said. "Thoughts are actions!"

Nearby, Abby crushed out her cigarette and left me alone to argue with my mother. Her sneakers slapped against the concrete courtyard.

"I'm hanging up now," my mom said. "Do the play for me, and for your sons. Get out of the way or you'll ruin everything."

I hung up and stared at the flickering lights on the edge of the still-lit marquee. It was the best of Southern California at night, a lush late-summer evening. The scent of our old neighborhood. Suddenly it all came back in a blast. I was fifteen again. Except I wasn't. I was now decades older, trying to figure out my life in the shadow of a musical about me being fifteen, trying to figure out my life. If only I were as diabolical a writer as life itself.

Put some goodness into the world before it blows up.

—ALICE CROWE

"Tell me a secret about how to play this character. Something nobody else knows."

We were in New York, a month earlier, trying to save the musical with our new lead actor, Casey Likes, and he was asking me for help. He was seventeen and struggling with the part. I was impressed by his question.

I told him a story I hadn't told anybody else. The secret to *Almost Famous* was the empty chair at the dining room table. Understanding that involved knowing our family story, a story that began years earlier in another time and another country.

They met in an elevator in Kyoto, Japan. James Crowe was a rising star in the military. He was from Stanton, a small town in central Kentucky. His acceptance into the West Point Academy was celebrated on the front page of his local newspaper, *The Clay City Times*. Jimmy, the hometown hero, blazed through the tough four-year program in only three years. Stationed overseas, he was destined for service in the Korean War when he met a dark-haired schoolteacher from California. She was in Japan on a teaching assignment. She had a striking figure and a consequential nose. She was a seeker who collected the best ideas of all the philosophers she'd studied and brewed them into her own blend of strong-minded positivity. She had a shatteringly loud sneeze and a skittish, hyperintelligent mind. He was a soft Southern charmer, a mint julep in summer. They married the next year, and all the hometown girls shed a tear. They still carried a torch for the charming young man with a quick laugh and a winning smile.

Alice George was the opposite of those girls, the ones with names like Bitsy or Anna Sue. The Southern way was rife with the unspoken. *Bless your heart* usually meant just the opposite. *Look at you*, while said admiringly, was a suggestion you were overweight. My mother found such nuance a waste of time. Straight-up bluntness was her default mode.

"Why come in the back door," she would say, "when the front door is open?"

As a young elementary school teacher, the long-limbed Alice George had decided to teach her way around the world. A strange sense of intuition had ruled her life. She called it a "third sense." The only reason she was even in Japan was because she'd demanded a transfer from the 'Iolani School in Honolulu, Hawaii. 'Iolani was an exclusive school, proper, with a regular tea service. She and a girlfriend taught preteens. They also shared an apartment near the beach. One day Alice developed

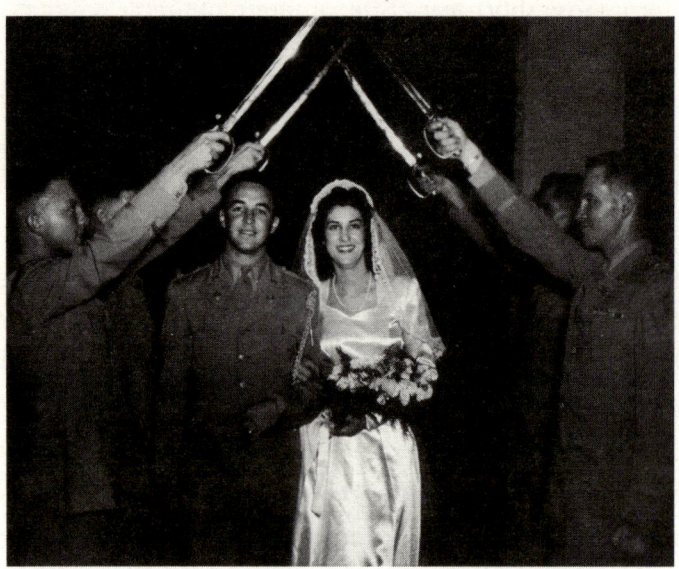

James and Alice Crowe get the full military wedding. Miyako Hotel, Kyoto, 1952.

a sudden sense of doom. Trouble was coming. Her roommate dismissed the premonition as mere worry. Alice hurriedly arranged to be sent to another school, in Kyoto. Two months later the largest tsunami in Hawaiian history killed 150 people, destroyed hundreds of homes, and left my mother with a lifelong ache. Her skeptical (disbelieving?) roommate was swept out to sea.

After their marriage in 1947, my father landed a choice assignment. He was sent to Governors Island, in New York, to serve as aide to Major General Roscoe Woodruff, commander of the I Corps overseeing the Pacific Theater. They lived the social life for a time, helping the general and his wife with their events and exploits. Once he was admonished by Woodruff's wife for the stale peanuts at their cocktail party. My mother chafed at such ridiculousness. The Stale Peanut Incident loomed large in our family's mythology. Soon pregnant with their first child, my mother and father came to a crossroads. Alice was not built for the cookie-cutter role of military wife. It was family vs. the military.

Jimmy Crowe asked for an honorable discharge from the 40th Infantry, where he'd been activated in the Korean War. It was a company known for intense short-term combat skirmishes. We never discussed the specifics of his service. Only once did I pop the question: *Did you ever kill somebody?* He laughed softly at the question. I took it to mean military discretion. *Probably yes.* Or maybe it was just the way I phrased it.

Many years later I found a yellow Kodak box of color slides in his belongings. Some covered his time staging near Kyoto, preparing for deployment. Others were taken by a fellow officer on the front lines of the Korean War. The photos were spectacular. And there was my father, arms pulled behind him, in front of command bunkers, at the 38th Parallel, the main line of resistance, the tip of the spear. You could almost hear the gunfire. He'd seen the best and the worst of the war. He'd clearly seen the victories and the bloodshed. All I'd imagined and more. All of it, just behind the gentle laugh at my question. It was all there in Kodachrome slides, rich with color, vivid portraits of a time long before he'd decided to move to California, a time when a single gunshot would have made the decision for him.

I often felt a phantom limb for the glittering military future that my father left behind. I can sometimes imagine him with a chest full of medals and the same perfect posture, hands clasped behind his back. The same pose I see in every photo of him. I was the result of Jimmy Crowe leaving that glittering life behind and becoming a full-time family man. I was the last child. If it weren't for the Stale Peanut Incident, I wouldn't exist.

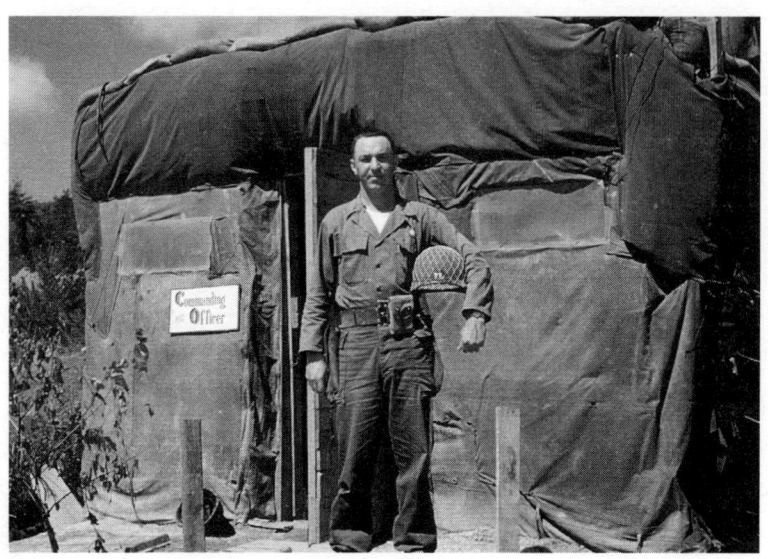

Commanding officer's bunker. Korea, 1953.

Opportunity favors the prepared mind.

—LOUIS PASTEUR

I was raised in the desert. My father came to Palm Springs in the late fifties and staked his claim on civilian life as a real estate man. We lived in a small house with a rock garden for a lawn. The local businessmen embraced my dad and his military record. It was a city on the rise, a sunbaked town with a thousand swimming pools and the constant hum of air conditioners. I'm one of the few people you'll ever meet who was born there. Mostly, Palm Springs is a place people visit and leave.

In 1970, when I was thirteen, we moved to San Diego. My dad stayed in the desert as a real estate man. He also owned an answering service business in Palm Desert. There were some ghosts left behind in the desert; I'll tell you a little bit about that later. My father commuted from the desert on the weekends to be with us, while my mother and I lived in a basement apartment next to the I-5 freeway entrance, just across the street from Balboa Park.

Tucked into the park was a local landmark—the Old Globe Theatre. It was a stirring replica of Shakespeare's original populist theater in London. I was just starting to fall in love with music, from Marvin Gaye to Led Zeppelin, but my mom, a beloved professor and counselor at the nearby inner-city San Diego Community College, was adamant about one thing. She hated rock and roll. It was all about brain cells. Rock was inelegant and, worse, obsessed with base issues like sex and drugs. The intellectual excellence of theater was much more her style.

The casts for the Old Globe Theatre productions often roomed in our apartment building. I would hear the actors going over lines while washing their clothes in the laundry room next to our basement apartment. Years later, I learned that a particularly expressive skinny guy in a paisley shirt who was always pacing and acting out scenes with an invisible partner was Christopher Walken.

One day my mom announced, "We're going across the street to see *Henry VIII*."

"I don't want to go."

"One day you'll brag about it."

"I will never brag about it." I wanted to stay home and secretly listen to rock radio, which she had banished from our home.

I could rarely say no to her in any way she understood. And so we trudged across the bridge to the theater, where men in tights took the tickets and spoke to us in crisp British accents, and we watched the meticulously rendered words of William Shakespeare. I was bored . . . until the elixir of the characters began to kick in. Afterward we talked about the nature of good and evil, yin and yang, and how Shakespeare rarely strayed from examinations of entertaining but flawed characters.

Chances are, if you were quiet around my mom for any length of time, she'd soon be teaching you a lesson or quoting a Greek philosopher. Watching the evening news, she would study Richard Nixon with squinting eyes and a deep sense of history. To her, American politics had become a Shakespearean play still in search of its tragic ending. "'Envy no man until he is safely dead,'" she might cry out. "*Herodotus said that!*"

Richard Nixon was the enemy. Ralph Nader, Cesar Chavez, and JFK were the heroes. Rock music, especially the kind that was sexually provocative, was the enemy. The slowness of the American educational system was also an irritant. By the time I arrived, the youngest of three children, my mother had streamlined her teaching approach. She skipped me through kindergarten and put me in first grade when I was just five.

"Kindergarten is just babysitting," she said. "In Europe they don't even *have* kindergarten." When my school later mistakenly skipped me over fifth grade, she convinced me to stay in sixth. "Nothing happens in the fifth grade," she confided. *"Maybe fractions."*

What she didn't warn me about was that skipping grades in these key adolescent years would create serious land mines in my life, and they weren't academic. They were physical.

"You have no pubic hair, you little cunt." I had drawn the attention of a tall demon of a schoolkid named Tom Tobin. I'd been trying to turn away in the locker room showers, so my schoolmates wouldn't see I hadn't grown any, uh, hair down there. *"Where are your pubes, little cunt?! Where are they?!"*

To my horror, more kids gathered. My lack of pubic hair had become a subject for study and now ridicule.

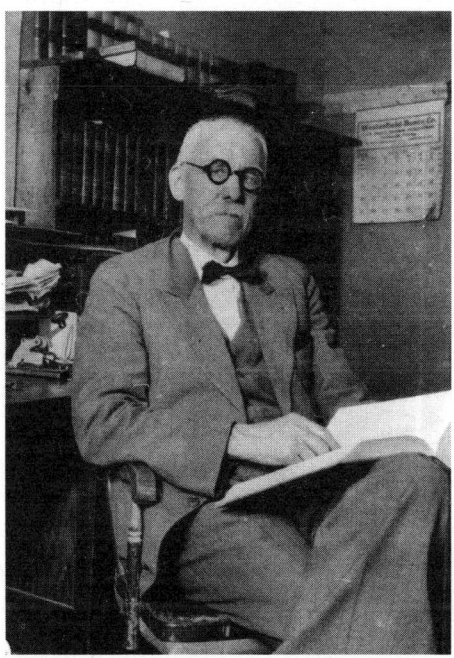

J. D. Atkinson: the youngest and oldest lawyer in the country. Lexington, Kentucky, 1956.

"Yeah," demanded another kid. "Where are they?"

"He's a little baby girl!" Tobin shouted at me, twisting his head to the right and left like a fun house clown. He was wearing large Clark Kent glasses and nothing else. "WHERE. ARE. YOUR. PUBES?!"

"I had 'em," I said. "I *shaved 'em off*."

The strangeness of my reply weirded Tom Tobin out. Frankly it weirded us all out, even me. I escaped with my dignity, but just barely. Humor was my best shot at deflection. Privately I was haunted by the rejection. I would disappear into the world of music, where my favorite songs were often written from the hearts of similarly rejected songwriters. For two or three minutes, I felt understood. Only time could solve my physical issues. In the meantime, I was stuck with the demonic presence of Tom Tobin and his Clark Kent glasses.

"Put on your magic shoes," my mom would say. "Just get through it. One day you'll be a great success, and those kids will be in the dustbin of your memory. They'll be stuck in town, and you'll be like your great-grandfather, who was both the youngest and longest-practicing lawyer in the country. How about *them* apples?"

Life is 10 percent what happens to you
and 90 percent how you react.

—CHARLES SWINDOLL

Even back when we lived in the desert, my sister Cindy was a neighborhood icon. In the middle sixties, we'd moved to Indio, a smaller town nineteen miles up the I-10 freeway from Palm Springs. Down the street was a wild-eyed kid who'd been to juvenile hall and back. He was seventeen and lived alone with his father. The word was he'd been arrested and kicked out of school in another town for an incident involving arson. Our neighborhood criminal was also known to have a crush on my sister. There was a fleet of them with crushes, really. Cindy had a smoky, independent persona. In other words, she was *cool*, and to hear some of the other kids talk, she was *bitchin'*.

Sometimes on a Saturday night, a car might slow down outside our house, and some heartsick kid would call her name and speed off. Her boyfriend, Steve Dagnan, was a star on the Indio High swim team, and even in my neighboring grade school, he was the stuff of legend.

Steve Dagnan had blond hair cut like Prince Valiant and heavy sideburns trimmed sharply at his jaw. He looked like summer and smelled like chlorine. Dagnan stood out in any crowd. I first spotted him on our lawn, from a distance. He was with a group of my sister's friends. He whispered in her ear like I did. It was always strange to see your older sibling with *her* friends, the mysterious people you were not meant to know as the goofy younger brother. They were from *her* world, and she liked it that way. My dad was often busy doing fieldwork, "sitting on houses," real estate slang for hosting an open house. I was usually surrounded with women. I didn't even know it, but I was harboring a pang for an older brother, someone I could talk with after-hours, perched on the edge of his bed, like Chip from *My Three Sons*.

My sister Cindy yearned for a normal life. I was sure she'd have given anything for us to only live one street over, on Bliss Avenue. Yes, that was the name. Bliss Avenue was where the upper-middle-class neighborhood began. One block away, where all the families were more cheerful and complete. Bliss Avenue, where the kids all seemed to live freely without parental supervision. If only we lived on Bliss Avenue.

Once, when my sister arrived home from a swim meet with Steve Dagnan, my mom was waiting for her. She stepped forward and carefully studied my sister's lips with curious precision, like a jeweler examining a suspicious diamond.

"You've been kissing," she announced.

"No I haven't."

She studied her lips for a moment. Just in case. "Yes you have."

"How can you tell?"

"*I can tell.*"

My sister changed tactics. "Nobody wants to come to our house because there's never anything good in the refrigerator!"

"The fact that I'm not a good cook has nothing to do with you making out in cars with Steve Dagnan."

It was moments until I heard my sister's door slam. I often wondered how my mother was able to detect lips that had been kissing. Was it an extra ripple in the lips? Or was it the guilty defiance on my sister's face? My sister had too much pride to lie well. And there was also the curious case of our mother's ability to sometimes read minds, as well as predict the future. *Slam!* All I really knew was that my cool sister couldn't wait to get out.

There was another sister. Cathy was three years older and no longer lived with us. Sometimes we would visit her on weekends. She lived in a special place an hour and a half away, just past all the car dealership billboards in Covina, down a long lane of trees, inside a gray building that looked like a hospital, except for the barbed wire at the top of the gates that surrounded the place.

Sometimes the thing you worry about most doesn't come about.

—ALICE CROWE

"Mom has her hooks in you," Cindy said. It was too hot to stay indoors, so we were sitting underneath our grapefruit tree. Across the street, the neighborhood kids were playing Slip 'N Slide. "You'll never be cool if you're trying to perform for her, always showing off, always trying to butter her up."

"What if making her happy makes me happy?"

"She wants you to be a lawyer." Cindy stared at me. "Do you want to be a lawyer?"

"Maybe. If it makes me happy."

"You don't know what makes *you* happy. Not yet." She leaned forward with a hushed voice. "She doesn't even let you have a bike."

It was true. The lack of pubic hair was nothing compared to the scarlet letter of not owning a bike. All around me, the kids had Schwinn Stingray bikes, with swooped handlebars. They weren't even that expensive; it wasn't that. It was a symbol of freedom. With a bike, you could go anywhere. But my mom had had a premonition that I would be in a terrible bike accident, and of course, after the Hawaiian tsunami, she held firm on her premonitions.

Only begin and the mind grows heated.

—GOETHE

Our house in Indio smelled like woodchips, hamster pellets, and wilted cabbage. My passion for raising these friendly and wildly horny rodents—the golden hamster—had spilled out of my bedroom and now occupied part of the kitchen. Hamster cages lined the wall. No wonder Cindy wanted to escape. There was no kissing, nothing delicious in the refrigerator, and no rock music allowed in the house. Just the wheezing sound of my hamsters trotting on their treadmills in the kitchen. Cindy, my cool sister, was in teenage hell.

Tending to my menagerie, pretending not to listen to my parents talking in the kitchen late at night, I heard them fretting about my sister's relationship with Steve. Cindy and Steve Dagnan had already discussed marriage.

"If they get married," my mom said, "she'll be stuck in the desert forever."

"You can't tell her not to be involved with him," my dad parried. "You'll drive her into his arms even more."

"She doesn't realize all the world has to offer past Steve Dagnan," said my mom. Nobody ever just called him Steve. He had a brand name, like James Bond or Paul McCartney. "That's the power of sex!"

My mom would often blame problems on sex. The sex drive. The corruption of a society that used sex to sell everything. Sex in songs. Sex on television. If there was a problem, sex was never far behind as the cause.

"How do you know they've had sex?" my dad said.

My mom narrowed her eyes, as if picking up the information from a distant radio tower. "They've had sex," she said.

"But you don't know—"

"She needs to see the world," my mom said. "That's what I did. And that's how I met you."

I could feel that Steve Dagnan was up against powerful forces. My sister felt unloved at home, and Steve took all that time to get to know her, to hear her problems, and to offer his own family as a refuge. When Steve looked at my sister, it was with the gaze of a surfer on an endlessly perfect wave. Plus, he was nice to her hamster-loving little brother, me. I sadly listened as my parents hatched a plan to pool their resources and send Cindy on World Campus Afloat, the college on a boat. She would visit Shanghai, Hong Kong, Manila, Bangkok, Bombay, Haifa, Venice, Gibraltar, Lisbon, and Oslo.

Steve Dagnan stood next to me at her graduation. He vowed to wait for her, and she for him, but we both knew what might happen out there in the world beyond the desert. Shanghai, Hong Kong, Manila, Bangkok, Bombay, Haifa, Venice, Gibraltar, Lisbon, and Oslo. She might become a different person. He would still be the swim team captain with the perfect sideburns. And I would lose my first potential big brother.

Mind is in every cell of the body. Thoughts are everything.

—ALICE CROWE

We were on our way to see Josephine Kellerman, the renowned psychic. My mother brought me along for the early-morning drive. Mrs. Kellerman lived in Yucaipa, a colorless city an hour up the road from Indio.

Yucaipa was known as "the jewel of the Inland Empire," but I wasn't buying any of it. Even at ten, I was suspicious. No one looked young in Yucaipa. I was sure that people automatically aged fifteen years just crossing the city line. As we grew closer on the I-10 freeway, the billboards grew more deeply conservative. We passed one sign that shouted: SAVE OUR REPUBLIC—JOIN THE JOHN BIRCH SOCIETY!

"The Birchers," my mom rumbled. She was never one to squander an opportunity to teach. "Watch out for the John Birch Society. One day they'll take over. They'll disguise themselves as Republicans and put all the teachers in jail!"

She was a nervous driver who hugged the steering wheel and seemed to be surveying all of the other cars as if looking for a sniper. She'd asked me to create a homemade sign for freeway-intensive drives like this. One side read: THANK YOU. The other side said: YOU BASTARD. Depending on the kindness (or lack thereof) of the fellow drivers, my mom might instruct me to "hold up the sign."

It was 1967, a troubled year for our family. My mom saw dark clouds on the horizon. She collected psychics like baseball cards. Many were quacks; some seemed more authentic. The authentic ones spoke highly of Mrs. Kellerman, the shy Hungarian woman who was a connoisseur's psychic. She was a seer. She could hold someone's hand or even a piece of their clothing and—*bam!*—she'd start receiving urgent messages from the beyond. Her popularity was all word-of-mouth. On the several days of the week when she accepted visitors, a line of cars was waiting outside her home by 6:30 a.m., when she conducted her first reading.

Most of her clientele were average people, but some were celebrities. Nancy Reagan, wife of then-governor Ronald Reagan, was a frequent visitor. So were Bob Hope, Liberace, and Gomer Pyle himself, Jim Nabors. An original Bob Hope painting hung above her small piano, the only decoration in her austere living room. The painting was signed with his catchphrase: *Thanks for the memories.*

Kellerman's advice and predictions were nearly 100 percent accurate, according to a study made by a group of experts from Redlands. She'd been born in a veil, which meant she was delivered in a completely untouched embryonic sac. This happens in one out of every eighty thousand births. A veiled birth was supposed to be extreme good luck, a sign of someone remarkable. Kellerman, it was said, had the Gift. She asked only for a three-dollar donation.

We arrived at our scheduled time and Mrs. Kellerman ushered us into her tiny sitting room. She had ten cats that scurried underfoot. She took my mother's hand as they sat at her table. Kellerman shut her eyes. Almost immediately, her strong Hungarian features erupted in shock. Her eyes popped open.

"You have my gift," she said.

"I know!" my mom said. "I've known it most of my life."

"It's a burden, but it doesn't have to be," said Mrs. Kellerman. "Think of it as an angel on your shoulder."

My mother nodded.

"Come work with me," said Kellerman.

"I can't. I just got my teacher's raise."

"Please think about it." She was studying my mom like a football coach who'd just discovered a future Heisman Trophy winner. "You can live here and work with me."

"I'll think about it."

Kellerman began her reading. "The first half of your life will be painful," she told my mom as she rubbed her hands. Visions were coming to Kellerman. "The second will be spent helping people." She paused and then continued. "You will outlive two husbands. One of your children makes up stories. He's a liar." I was instantly mortified. "Another child feels neglected, and the third is a karmic child."

"How will my husbands die?" my mother asked.

"I don't see it clearly," said Kellerman. "But death is just a passage. We pass into another realm. Our loved ones are all still with us. Just on the other side."

Afterward, Kellerman followed us to our car. "You have the gift," she repeated to my mother. "Think again about coming here. I'll teach you, and you can take my business when I retire."

"I'll come back," she answered. "But I can't leave my family."

My mom climbed in the car, and now Kellerman had me alone for a moment. She fixed me with her gaze. "Start telling the truth and you won't break any more bones."

I hadn't broken any bones yet. That came later.

My mom drove us home in near silence. I could tell she was concerned. *What is a karmic child?* Suddenly she realized she'd almost missed our exit, and as she quickly tried to change lanes, she was blocked by a driver who angrily leaned on his horn, loud and long.

"Give them the sign," my mom instructed.

"Which side?"

"The bastard."

If it wasn't this, it would be something else.

—JAMES CROWE

My dad found comfort in sayings. An aphorism is meant to cheer you on, to summon greatness. *A saying* is different. A saying usually carries this gentle message: *Just deal with it*. Sayings kept my father's rudder in the water. They kept the ship going forward. In all his photos he looked the same, the rigid posture that came from West Point topped off with a cheerful can-do smile. I wondered how he was able to keep the same expression, whether sitting on a tree stump in the Korean brush or wearing a sweater in the hot desert air, posing for a family photo. He had a sunny disposition, with a wide Irish forehead like the actor Gene Hackman. People liked my father, and if one of the kids needed their allowance early, or if an air-conditioning repairman was leaving the house after fixing one of our units, he'd press a five-dollar bill into their hand.

"Here's that money I owed you," he'd say. And for a second there would be a slightly confused but happy look on the receiving end. Then they'd get it. And in that moment, well, that was the delighted look that lit up the faces of friends and family whenever they saw Jimmy Crowe coming their way.

I guess I always knew there was more to my dad than the infectious laugh and the easygoing manner. Years ago, I read a book about the hidden fishing streams and lakes of the Northwest. In it was a sumptuous description of a deep, turquoise-green watering hole, lined with lush low-hanging branches. The exact spot was hard to find but worth searching for. It was filled with fish. "But beware if you swim," read the description, "the dark shapes below are the bigger anadromous fish." I often think about that line when I encounter unexpected darkness. My mind can't shake that one memorable description. There they are. *The bigger anadromous fish.*

I once sat next to a psychiatrist on a flight. He was pissed off that he'd lost his seat in first class. He was churning with nervous energy, trying out innumerable positions in the seat, until he finally surrendered to the discomfort. He was stuck sitting next to me in coach, and somewhere after his second Jack Daniel's and soda, he told me the secret to the world.

The *secret*, he said, twisting toward me in the seat. The secret *to the world*. Is simple.

"None of us," he said, "are that special." He went on to elaborate. Everybody fell into one of five different categories. Once you knew that, you could free yourself. You're not the first person in the world to go through this or that, to feel agony or joy. No. You were just one of *five people*.

I asked him how quickly he could determine which kind of person someone was.

"Within three minutes," he answered.

"Do you know what kind of person I am?"

He nodded. "But *you* don't. And that's what you get to spend your life figuring out."

He was, of course, full of shit. The nuances within the five types—if there really were only five types—were everything. But don't we all secretly know that we are absolutely unique, one of a kind, never to be duplicated? Anybody who denied it was wrong, because the fact is we are all born unique and worthwhile.

But did Cathy know that?

Silence is golden.

—THE TREMELOES

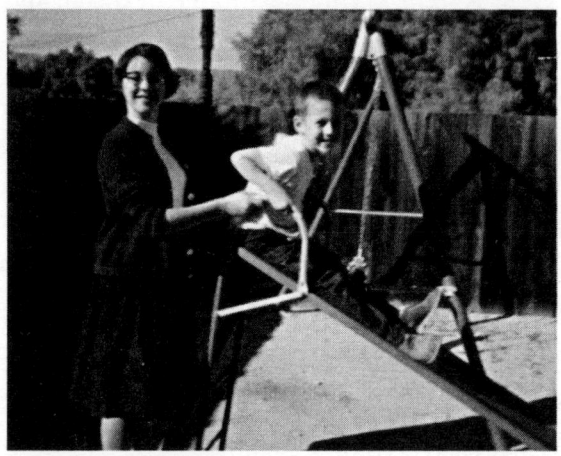

Slidin' in the backyard: Cathy and me.

I'm not sure when things began to reveal themselves with Cathy. She was born in a military hospital in upstate New York, where my father was stationed. There was a backlog at the hospital that day. There was a theory that the doctor was to blame. He'd shot up my mom with a heavy tranquilizer to delay the birth. There was another theory that Cathy had slipped from the tall steel hospital table, hitting her head after being born. All my parents knew was that she was an emotional kid, and somewhere around first grade Cathy came home with the words that changed everything.

"The kids are teasing me about not being normal," she said.

At that moment, all their lives would change. My father's career in the army had been a mostly glittery ascent. With the first child came the sense that all would be storybook excellent. Then came the high-flying moods, the outbursts, the despair, and finally the words that leave a parent feeling helpless.

"Am I not normal?" Cathy asked.

The world of happy/sad soon permeated our life in the desert. In the summer of '67, radio supplied the soundtrack. My oldest sister, in her glasses with the butterflies in the corners, fell in love with "Yummy, Yummy, Yummy" by Ohio Express. "Silence Is Golden" by the Tremeloes spoke to her happy/sad soul. Her favorite was the undisputed king of sweet teenage melancholy, Brian Wilson, and the Beach Boys. "Surfer Girl" gave her two and a half minutes of a blissful life she could only visit. Perhaps she dreamed of running into the waves, a shiny blue surfboard under her arm.

The year before, my mom had gone to the mailbox and seen the cover of *Time* magazine: "Is God Dead?" She yelped when she saw it, an involuntary shout. Everything she suspected was coming true.

"It's the dark ages," she said. "They're coming."

My parents' lives had become a quest for Cathy's diagnosis. Her emotions could swing wildly from sweetness to deep sadness. Her fellow students were cruel to her. The cruelest blow was just around the corner. Her own grade school rejected her midsemester. Cathy was asked to take special classes in a trailer. She longed for the kind of romance she loved in all those deep and innocent pop songs. She loved Motown too. Always, the songs were her touchstones. We often went to Custom Classics, the only store in our little desert town that sold records. As songs like "Apple, Peaches, Pumpkin Pie" ran through her head, she'd order the records she'd heard on the radio. Her life was a serenade of sunny classics, but her inner struggle was mounting.

My mother wrestled with her own emotional equilibrium. The desert was a petri dish for her anxiety. My two sisters were increasingly hard for her to manage. One day I noticed that my mom and dad now had separate bedrooms. I had asthma, and a weak immune system, but figured I could help out by working on a jokey personality. I could learn magic tricks. I could come up with funny routines. I could be a class clown, right in my own home.

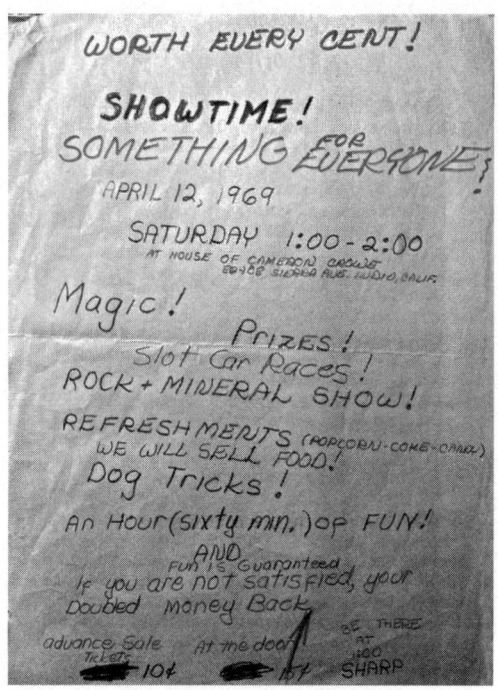

"Doubled money back!" Magic in 1969.

Sometimes we'd travel up to Los Angeles, to one of the big medical operations in Westwood. I'd race around the cool clinical hallways of the big hospitals while my mom and dad would disappear into a room. I slid around the shiny floors and waited for them to exit, stooped with worry. It felt scary to me, like a space-age purgatory where small-townish people like us were told whether we went to heaven or elsewhere.

The ride home usually started off with silence. My mom would soon pull out something from a plastic bin where she carried teaching materials. She might read a story about the hereafter, or a tale from Greek mythology, or passages from Carl Jung's *Memories, Dreams, Reflections*.

"Why waste time looking out the window," she'd say, "when you can learn?" My dad listened with a pleasant smile. Years later, I have a better idea what he was thinking. I didn't see the complexity in our family's struggles. I didn't have anything else to compare it to. I was loved. Wherever I turned, I felt it. And wherever there was stress, I would just work harder on my jokes.

"I bought us tickets to see a kid named Bob Dylan," my mom an-nounced one day. Tickets were $1.50. The ad in the college news-paper had a small picture of young Dylan, with the description "Singing Folk Poet in Concert." Several weeks earlier, he'd released an album called *The Times They Are A-Changin'*. It was April 1964.

I was seven, Cindy was twelve. On our way to the concert, my mom pointed out the Barry Goldwater campaign posters that hung on the lampposts. "The John Birch Society finances all those posters," she noted. "I worry that I brought you into this world."

Bob Dylan was clearly an intellectual's delight. My mom carried a blanket, and we camped out on the cold gymnasium floor. The gym was a little over three-quarters filled. It was still the early sixties, and the audience was mostly curious types still stuck in the fifties. But the college kids, the ones with the growing beards and the solemn sense of simpatico, were the ones who made me feel . . . older, cooler. We sat on our blanket on the outskirts of the main floor. There was no "show," no screen projections, barely any lights. Just a microphone at the center of the stage.

After a few minutes, Bob Dylan, then just shy of twenty-three, took the stage in jeans and a white work shirt. He had an announcement to make. Minutes before the doors opened, the young underdog Cassius Clay, later to be Muhammad Ali, beat the heavyweight champion Sonny

Liston in a sixth-round decision. Dylan, swaying and often looking down at his boots, dedicated his first song, "Who Killed Davey Moore?," to Cassius Clay.

I loved his sense of humor. Dylan had an impish persona; he bobbed and weaved as he played his political songs, mixed with a few wistful tunes about girlfriends back home. Soon we were all on his side. The chilly gymnasium had become a gathering of a tribe. It was that rare feeling that we were all exactly where we all belonged. *So, this is what a concert is like.*

Sometimes I think about an alternate reality. What if someone from the future had taken me aside and shared the scenario of what was to come? That I would become a music journalist. And that twenty-one years after that night on the gymnasium floor, Bob Dylan would be sitting in my small living room at a red table, scanning his memory to answer my detailed questions about some of his greatest songs. He'd arrived on a motorcycle, looking like the cover of *Highway 61 Revisited*. All for the liner notes of his upcoming box set, *Biograph*.

"You are a part of everyone else's sixties experience, including mine," I said. "Did you feel like you had one of your own?"

It was then the summer of 1985. He'd just performed at Live Aid a few weeks earlier. Dylan looked down into a cup of tea and answered the question with that same impish smile I recognized from my first concert experience with my mom and sister.

"In the sixties," he said, "it could have been the twenties. Nobody really figured it out until the late sixties that something had happened. I remember Joe Strummer [from the Clash] said that when he first heard my records, I'd already been there and gone. It was like a flying saucer landed. You were there, but you didn't see it. That's what the sixties were like. Everybody was there, but only a few people saw it."

On that night in 1964, I wouldn't have been able to wrap my head around such a scenario. I was seven years old, and I was going to be a lawyer, like my great-grandfather. Like Atticus Finch in *To Kill a Mockingbird*. But I did know this: I sure wanted to go to another concert.

"Did you enjoy Bob Dylan?" my mom asked as we filed out of the gymnasium.

"It was so good!"

My sister agreed.

"Well, someday the Republicans are going to ruin all of this," my mom said, "for *everybody*."

Who killed Davey Moore, why an' what's the reason for?

—BOB DYLAN

"What's wrong with Cathy?" I asked.

My parents, who were probably as confused about her condition as I was, would struggle to explain it to me. They used the phrase "emotionally disturbed."

There were other names bandied about for her so-called condition. None of them carried the kind of empathy you might hear today. The message was clear. Cathy had to be careful out there in the world. She'd get looks of sympathy mixed with ridicule whenever she stepped outside the bubble of our family. Our family had been hit by the crack of a dark whip.

She had a big heart to go with her roller-coaster moods, but like my other sister, her relationship with our mother was not an easy one. Alice Crowe was skittish about the domestic stuff, never comfortable with the traditional fifties stereotypes of June Cleaver from *Leave It to Beaver*. Cathy's despair increased until one day she cut her wrists, crosswise not lengthwise. The doctors called it a desire for attention. Cutting your wrists *lengthwise*, they said, usually meant the patient was truly suicidal.

"A cat scratched her arms," was what I was told. Not too long after that, she was sent to the place with the barbed-wire gate. I was overjoyed when she came home for the summer of 1967. I was nine years old and ready to soak up all the wisdom she had to offer. Our age difference was a plus for both of us. I felt older. She felt safe.

This being the late sixties, the concept of mental illness carried a lot of luggage. My mother was a perfectionist. She had her own issues with emotion and anger. She was headstrong, and so was Cathy. I could feel the jagged rhythms between them when Cathy was in the house. It was hard for me to fathom how deep the problems went because whenever I saw Cathy in the hallway she stroked my hair and purred like a cat. I loved seeing her without the butterfly-cornered glasses. She looked thoughtful and beautiful, like the chorus of a Brian Wilson song. Music and fantasy gave her joy, they were her protection, and she loved the faraway world of romance.

"Do you have a crush on anybody at school?" she asked one day.

I admitted that I did.

"Who?"

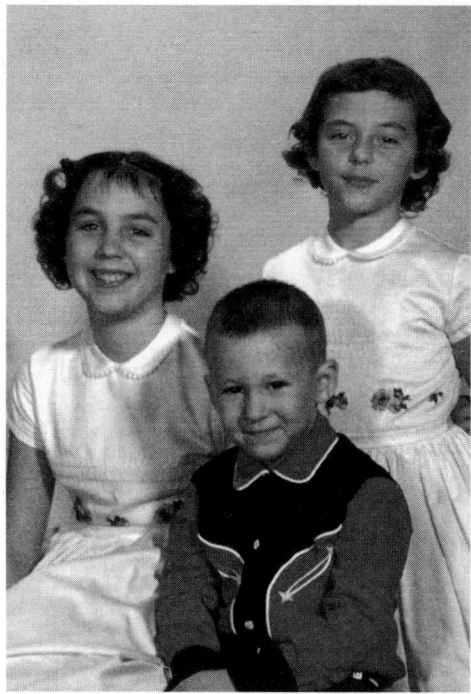

"Should we trust him?" Cathy and Cindy and me. Palm Springs, 1962.

I told her about Brenda Zeckley, the funny girl in my class who wore cool floral muumuus. She had bobbed hair with bangs that swooped across her forehead. She was also two years older than me, like everybody, because my mom had skipped me.

"You should dedicate a song to her," said Cathy. "And later, maybe even ask her to the Date Festival."

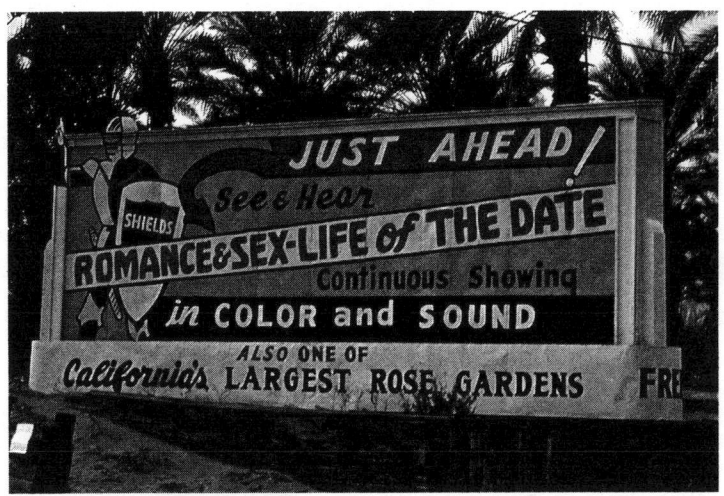

The Date Festival was the social event of the season, an annual carnival-like celebration held at the Riverside County Fairgrounds. Dates were the fruit the town was known for. They grew on date palm trees that lined the streets and flourished in the blinding heat. Everything in Indio was tied to that sticky-sweet missile-shaped fruit. Dates made me squeamish. They were the exact color of the American cockroach, a fact that seemed to bother no one in Indio but me.

Cathy and I went to Custom Classics after school and tried to decide the perfect song for me to buy for Brenda. "Sunshine Girl" by the Parade was a possibility, as was "Yellow Balloon" by the Yellow Balloon.

Cathy had a special feeling about "Silence Is Golden" by the Tremeloes. She also liked the Grass Roots' "Let's Live for Today." Plus, there was "Georgy Girl," the wistful song by the Seekers. We decided on "Silence Is Golden." Feeling like bandits, we bought the single for eighty-seven cents. Cathy also ordered some Beach Boys records the store didn't stock. She'd heard them on our local station, KREO, which she listened to on a turquoise transistor radio she loaned to me so I could listen late at night under my pillow.

"Give her the record and tell her, 'I've been thinking about you.'" Cathy instructed me to do it after school the next day, so Brenda Zeckley could go straight home and play it. "And down the line, you can ask her to the Date Festival."

I was nervous about the choreography of all these big-league moves. Luckily, I felt fortified by my sister's romantic sense. She'd experienced plenty in her eighteen years, even if a lot of it had been spent shuttling between unsympathetic doctors.

"Brenda," I said the next day, "I've been thinking about you."

Her face lit up. I handed her "Silence Is Golden."

"How sweet of you!"

"And I want to go to the Date Festival with you." I knew instantly that I'd overreached, but it felt defiant. It felt good. I couldn't wait to share this moment with Cathy. And it was exactly then that Boyd Hansen materialized beside us. Boyd was the wickedly good second baseman on our school's middling baseball team.

"What's up?" he asked Brenda.

"Cameron asked us to go to the Date Festival."

"Sure, man," he said, finally noticing me standing right in front of him. "Come with us."

I watched as he slipped an arm around her shoulder.

"And he gave us a record," she told Boyd. "Wasn't that nice of him?"

"We'll have to listen," said Boyd. Before they walked away, Brenda turned and gave me a warm wink and a smile. Suddenly the disappointment disappeared. I felt like a hero, even for losing. It was another instance of my favorite emotion, courtesy of my big sister. The song I'd given Brenda would always take me back to that exact emotion, like an anthem.

The happy/sad.

Well, it's been building up inside of me
for I don't know how long.

—BRIAN WILSON

The records arrived after her death, and my dad went down to Custom Classics to close out the account. Among the Beach Boys records she'd ordered were two of their finest, "California Girls" and "Don't Worry Baby." Listening to them made me feel like she was still with us. It always has. For a long time, my mother wouldn't discuss the details of how she died. Cathy's death certificate was much more definitive—suicide by barbiturates.

They had removed her body from the house while I was asleep. It happened on a Wednesday night, less than two weeks after her nineteenth birthday. My mom found her. We were now living in *the house where it happened*. Cindy was devastated. Her best friend was gone. She sobbed for weeks, a distraught fifteen-year-old girl in the desert. As I write this, I know that Cathy is still at her shoulder, every day. Procol Harum's solemn "A Whiter Shade of Pale" was a big hit that summer. It played everywhere and it felt like a requiem.

I sat on the playground wondering how all this anguish had erupted over my awkward but sincere sister who loved "Silence Is Golden." Knowing I'd never see her again, I rewound back to the last moment we'd been together, in the hallway, right by the turquoise painting of a flower. She had rubbed my head affectionately. She was already fading away in my memory. *Was it my fault? No, it couldn't be. Did I make too many jokes?*

"She was in pain," my father told me. It was the only time I'd ever seen him cry. He reached to hold on to the side of the bed, but there was nothing to hold on to. I folded my arms across my chest, like an adult. In some ways, they're still folded. Soon the cloak of denial whooshed around us, and we forged ahead. I wondered why Cathy hadn't left me a message of some kind. Not even a suicide note. And then I remembered the records she'd ordered. My California Girl sister was telling me not to worry, baby.

"You're my last chance to be a good mother," my mother told me a few years later in a rare conversation about Cathy. "When you lose a child, you seek purpose and reason."

The Empty Chair

Her turquoise chair, the one where Cathy used to sit, was still at the kitchen table. Her room had been cleaned out. Some of her clothes had been given away. Removing that turquoise chair from the kitchen felt like injustice. And so it remained there. The empty chair. Nobody wanted to be the one to remove it.

Late at night I'd listen to my sister's transistor radio. Tucked under my pillow, everything coming out of that tinny speaker sounded deep and important. The flatness of the desert was fantastic for picking up radio stations from as far away as Chicago. All kinds of music bubbled up from under my pillow. The songs were sometimes long and mysterious. I would ride a song like the Moody Blues' "Nights in White Satin" or the extended version of Buffalo Springfield's "Bluebird" as far as it could take me. Sometimes it would send me all the way into the ether of unknowing.

I wondered why I often felt invisible and got all mixed up with the idea that maybe my Catholic school teachers didn't have it right. What if there was no God? I'd just be a void. I wouldn't even be around to laugh about being a void. I'd just be nothing. I wouldn't even know if my own empty chair was still at the table. Or if it might finally get tucked into a corner of the garage, where someone like me would sometimes go sit in it and listen to happy/sad anthems.

Music was already more than music. It was a door that opened for three minutes. Sometimes way longer. In the forbidden world there was no judgment. Only your own thoughts and secret desires, slashing through the atmosphere. And when the song was over, the door clanged shut again. There was no choice but to scramble back to the beginning. Sometimes I would listen to one song twenty or thirty times in a row. There had to be other people like me. I just hadn't met them yet.

A year after Cathy left us, my mother and father had both thrown themselves into work. Alice went headlong into public service, often taking me on long bus rides to Thermal, California, where she worked with troubled families as a regional director of the Head Start program. My father tended to his real estate practice and his thriving business on the rise, Answering Services. Somewhere in Palm Desert was the main exchange, where a team of women operators plunged telephone cords into a phone bank and took messages for doctors and lawyers, and sometimes even me, in warm, honey-coated voices.

On weekends, we were all under one roof again. Not everyone understood the odd chemistry of our family, but I did. My father often let my mom take the lead in public. He shared his own quiet wisdom at home. Her love of the metaphysical fascinated him, but his approach to human conversation was far more down-home. He could talk to anybody about anything. He knew the names of the postman's kids. My mother was, of course, famously unable to chitchat. A simple question about the weather could flummox her. *Why should we talk about the weather? There's nothing we can do about it. What about world hunger?*

One Thanksgiving we sat in the living room of my aunt and uncle's home on March Air Force Base in Riverside. I was in my accident-prone phase then. I had been banned from playing sports at school after a concussion playing catcher and breaking my clavicle playing second base. Uncle Bob, also a retired air force officer, held a drink and raised the subject of lawn color.

"So, Alice," he asked my mother, "how green do you like a lawn?"

My mother stared at him with haunted eyes. Her mind had been somewhere else. She'd been examining the windows and doors of their home, and the lack of locks. She had a fear of intruders. I'm not sure she'd even heard his offer of holiday chitchat.

"Is this house burglar-proof?" she asked, leaning forward with urgency.

"I like a green lawn, freshly mowed," answered my father. "That's the smell of summer."

I treasured time with my dad. For the first five years of my life, while my mom battled various illnesses, including depression, he moved my crib next to his bed and watched over me. On weekends we'd sometimes hit golf balls or go fishing. He'd discuss the state of his businesses and the colorful clients he worked with. There was Dr. Elmer Carson Rigby, a pioneering cardiothoracic surgeon who'd treated Nat King Cole. Another was Dick Cosette, the barrel-chested Canadian raconteur who schooled my dad in the ways of Palm Springs real estate. ("Always collect the money while the client's tears are still hot," he advised.) Cossette was also secretly a bodyguard for Howard Hughes. He'd recently been made the head of Hughes's day-to-day business in the desert. Cosette was promoted because Hughes loved the way he cooked a steak—deeply charred on the outside, pink on the inside.

Companies like Answering Services were the future, my father said. Businesses needed to know that someone could answer their phone calls at any hour. A live twenty-four-hour operator meant no call would go

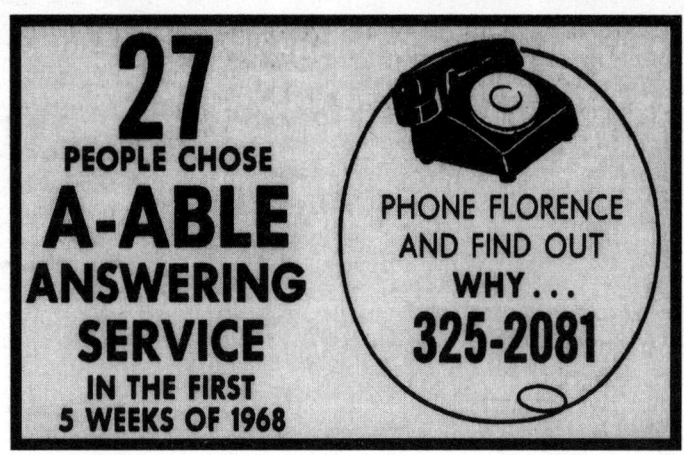

unanswered. The flagship operation was named A-Able Answering Service, chosen because it would be the first listing in the business pages of the phone book. I had come to know the operators by their silky phone voices and warm personalities. There were Sandy, Dorothy (a.k.a. Dot), and Veronica. Each could make a simple phrase like "I'll see that he gets that message" sound like an invitation to a Tahitian adventure.

"I have to swing by the answering service and pick up some mail," he said one afternoon after we'd gone fishing. "You want to meet the operators?"

We entered the darkened A-Able headquarters, and the busy phone bank of operators erupted with joy. The night shift was ending. A tray of snacks lined the wall, and a TV flickered in the corner. It was their clubhouse. There they were. Sandy, Dot, and Veronica. These butterscotch voices belonged to stout women with curlers in their hair, wearing colorful muumuus and housecoats.

"It's you!" cried Sandy. She wrapped me in a hug. That unmistakable pixie voice was coming from a woman three times my size. "It's Jim Crowe's son!"

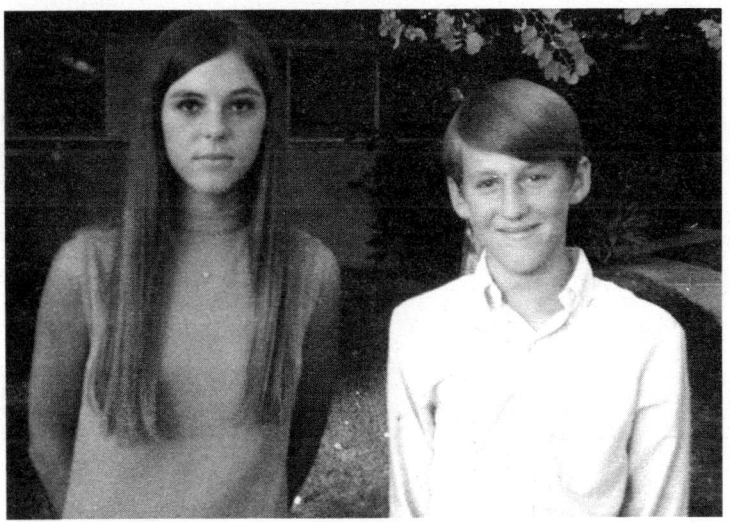

"Great! Now Mom is going to get rock banned from television." My sister and me in front of the house in Indio.

They loved their boss. He knew the names of all their kids and looked after them with health plans and decent salaries. It had been a busy Saturday night, and they had lots of gossip. One doctor had received many important calls, none of them from his wife or patients. They were a community unto themselves, twenty-four-hour warriors with a personal touch.

As we drove home, my dad explained that in business, you must create a need and then fulfill it. A missed call was a missed opportunity. Every phone call was an invitation to a relationship. Only positivity came from such a personal connection. The future of Answering Services was blazing and bright.

"Nothing," he said, "beats the sound of the human voice."

If I can dream.

—ELVIS

One summer night in 1968, I grandly talked my parents into giving rock and roll one last chance. I convinced them to watch Simon & Garfunkel on *The Smothers Brothers Show*. I was sure that the literary quality of Paul Simon's songs would win over my mom and dad. I was certain it would be a success. Soon they would be giving us money to buy records by Jimi Hendrix, Cream, and the gloriously high Beatles on the cusp of their *White Album* era.

We sat as a family, bathed in the blue glow of the television as Simon & Garfunkel hit the *Smothers Brothers* stage. Looking clean-cut and super earnest, they began "Mrs. Robinson." Of course I had picked the night that Paul Simon, suspiciously glassy, apparently decided to chuck the whole "clean-cut and earnest" thing right out the window. Eyebrows arching with false sincerity, Simon smirked through his then-controversial lyrics, *"Coo coo ca-choo, Mrs. Robinson / Jesus loves you more than you will know."* Looking out from the television, he seemed to find my mother's face, knowing somehow that she'd spent all that hard-earned money sending us to Catholic school. With each mention of the word *Jesus*, Paul Simon's mocking tone grew more lacerating. We shrunk into the sofa.

Finally, my mother switched off the tube, threatening to write CBS and all the show's sponsors. (She did.) Later that evening, I sat in Cindy's room studying her smuggled-in copy of Janis Joplin's *Cheap Thrills*.

"Great idea," she said dryly. "Now Mom's going to get rock music banned from all of television too."

On World Campus Afloat, my sister found romance with a dashing young man from Chicago. Steve Dagnan handled it with stoic nobility. He still held a mighty torch. Cindy would soon leave us again, to visit friends in San Francisco and return with a cache of albums by the Doors, the Byrds, Janis Joplin, and more. My parents and I still had great dreams of me becoming a lawyer, but music was constantly whispering in my ear about other things.

I still had that turquoise transistor radio I kept under the pillow. The local station had begun to draw name concert acts to the Indio fairgrounds, and I listened sadly as Aretha Franklin and Iron Butterfly passed through town, playing great shows while I sat home in a cultural prison hearing all about Carl Jung. My sister and I were electrified when Buffalo Springfield announced a show in Indio. It didn't even matter that the group had already broken up and the drummer was illegally using the name. Clearly this was the biggest band anybody would ever talk into playing our town.

Who would ever imagine that thirty-plus years later, the Coachella Valley Music and Arts Festival would land at that exact spot and bring huge waves of glamorous fans and artists from the Rolling Stones to Beyoncé and Billie Eilish to our windswept fairgrounds. All I knew back then was I had to get to a concert. If only there was a way to break down the wall between me and my family and rock.

In 1969, we left the desert and *the home where it happened* and moved to San Diego. At thirteen, I finally had a breakthrough. I began to compete in radio station contests; you know the kind—*"Be the first caller and win!"* My scheme was simple. Using two phones side by side, I kept one line ringing constantly, tying up the radio station's request line. When a contest was announced, I would already be on the line. The disc jockey would then pick up my call and hang up again, clearing the line for the official first caller. Boom! I already had the number mostly dialed on the other extension. Dialing one last digit, I slipped in as first caller. The method worked! I won tickets to a movie. But my eye was already on a much bigger prize.

Right about this time, local disc jockeys began to hint that a very big star was coming to the San Diego Sports Arena. Soon it was announced. Sadly, it was not Creedence Clearwater Revival, as I'd hoped. It wasn't even someone from my generation. I couldn't imagine what the big fuss was about when ads featuring the music from *2001: A Space Odyssey* announced with great importance that the concert event of the year was none other than . . . Elvis Presley.

To me, Elvis was a jokey figure, an oddly bronzed gentleman who showed up in afternoon movies like *Paradise, Hawaiian Style*, goofily singing to dogs and strange women in jet-set bikinis. Years later, I would come to appreciate the Technicolor kitsch of those movies, but at the time Presley was at best a guy John Lennon praised in interviews as being a genius before he entered the army. Regardless, drunk with contest-winning prowess, I easily won four tickets to see Elvis at the San Diego Sports Arena. At school, I traded two of the Elvis tickets for a pair of seats to a concert I was much more interested in—Eric Clapton's Derek and the Dominos at the San Diego State University gymnasium.

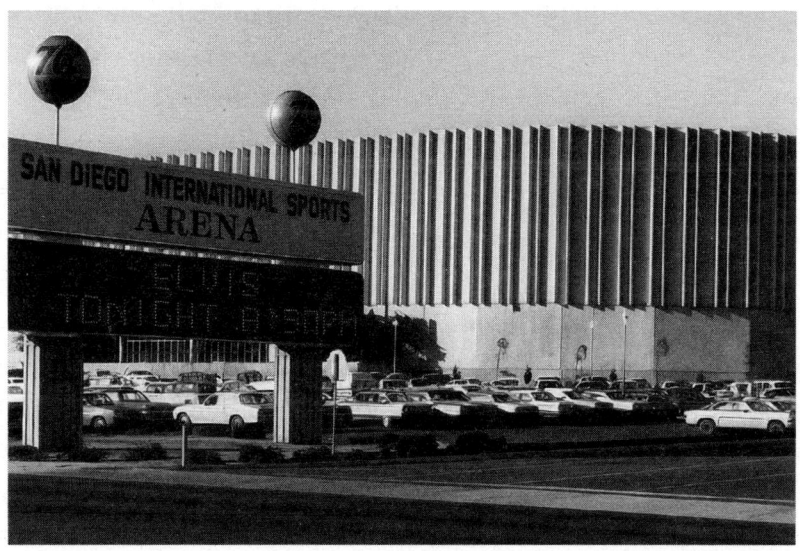

My pleasure was soon mixed with horror. Good news: my parents approved my going to both concerts. Bad news: my date at both concerts would be my mom.

When the day arrived, I sheepishly dressed for my date with Mom. I chose a pair of bell-bottoms, clothes I hoped would scream, *Please know I'm so much cooler than I appear to be, going to a concert with my mother.* On the way to the show, my date discussed the scholastic view of the King. Elvis the Pelvis, she said, had brought smut to national television, and *The Ed Sullivan Show* had been forced to show him only from the waist up. I couldn't quite figure out how he could be so subversive.

"What was he doing that was so awful?" I asked.

She answered the question clinically. "He had an erection."

"Wow," I said.

Now I *really* didn't know what to expect. I had seen only part of Elvis's 1968 comeback special, on a television in a Radio Shack, and all I remembered was his noble pose as he sang "If I Can Dream" against a bank of red lights blinking E-L-V-I-S. No doubt about it, this guy was one serious mixed message. One day communing with God, the next appearing on *Ed Sullivan* with a boner.

I dreaded how unhip we were. Me in my desperate bell-bottoms, her in a smart academic-looking pantsuit with scarf. But as we turned the corner to the Sports Arena parking lot, I saw something that immediately lightened my load. Stretched out before us was an endless sea of jolly blue-haired ladies, most of them old enough to be my grandmother. Where did these people come from? I had seen none of them on our city streets. Perhaps they flew in for the show. I did know this: my mom and I were clearly the coolest customers in sight. We settled into our free bleacher seats, halfway back and on the right.

I watched as the spectacle began. First onstage was an emcee who began hawking scarves and special show programs with frightening fluency. This was a hard sell like nothing I'd ever imagined at a concert. This was circus-level hucksterism. The emcee's routine was clear: men-

tion Elvis's name every ten seconds. Each mention drew a war cry from
the audience. Then came the Sweet Inspirations, Elvis's backup singers.
They performed in the still-lit arena. They too mentioned Elvis's name
in between each of their few songs. Then the emcee returned, telling us
that Elvis's plane was on the way to San Diego right now. Then came the
comedian who preceded Elvis, Pat Buttram. The response was riotous.
This was Mr. Haney from *Green Acres*. I remember none of his jokes,
save for a comment that the success of his television show was nothing
compared to the greatest gift of all, his friendship with Elvis. Pause for
thunderous cheers.

 In between jokes, Buttram tracked Elvis's travel, as if describing
Santa Claus or a missile heading for its target. It worked, majorly. After
a few minutes, he received a note from a stagehand. Elvis's plane had
just landed in San Diego. Pause for mayhem. "In fact," said Buttram,
"Elvis loves San Diego. He told me last night!"

 The arena shook. *Elvis loved San Diego!* And this being a full two
years before Watergate, we believed him. Pat Buttram wrapped up his
routine, and I must confess I felt a strange sensation. Now even *I* was
psyched for Elvis.

 The emcee returned to announce that Colonel Parker had *just now*
released some new scarves, right now, just for San Diego. A few minutes
passed for more scarves to be sold, and then the lights finally dimmed,
all the way. Mind-warping, bloodcurdling screams rose up all around us.
Not the endearing Beatlemania screams of adolescents, no. These were
the unsettling screams of mothers. The kind of scream you associate
with, say, a murderer entering your house at midnight.

 Suddenly, "Thus Spake Zarathustra," the theme from *2001: A Space
Odyssey*, pumped over the loudspeakers. Elvis's band took the stage.
They were some of the greatest session players ever, and as James Bur-
ton strapped on a shiny Telecaster, the band blasted into the beginning
vamp of "That's All Right." They were a loud, large, lumbering Elvis
machine. And from our seats, I could see into the backstage of the Sports
Arena. The metal gate opened, and in swished a line of limousines. This

was truly wild, I thought. Even in the city he loved, San Diego, Elvis didn't arrive until after his opening song had already *begun*.

Finally, Elvis Presley appeared from stage right in a glittering white jumpsuit. For a couple minutes he strode back and forth, striking karate poses, kicking and laughing with band members, all while the intro to "That's All Right" continued in an endless loop. The band seemed crouched and ready to respond, watching his every move, should Elvis approach the microphone to sing. But Elvis didn't want to sing. Not yet.

Less than a year after the comeback special, gone was the man supposedly repentant for the many years spent playing hooky in Hollywood. In his place was a wandering white speck moving back and forth. And it wasn't as if he were troubled by the artistic compromise; in fact he seemed very very very *very* relaxed with the whole idea. I was not yet an Elvisophile, schooled in the subtleties of the King, but I recall thinking: *He really really likes San Diego.* The place was filled with hysterical appreciation as Elvis finally took the microphone. "Well, that's all right, mama," he sang, and then he abandoned the mike again for more photo opportunities and karate poses.

Elvis laughed at the rapturous women in the front row as the Sweet Inspirations fiercely continued singing their parts, whether Elvis joined in or not. Occasionally, he returned to the mike to add the words "That's all right." Finally, signaled by a specific karate move, the song stopped. Over screams, the King solemnly thanked the crowd for coming and then offered, if I remember correctly, an imitation of John Wayne.

Soon the band snapped into "Polk Salad Annie." Halfway through, Elvis crouched down low on the stage . . . then lower . . . then lower . . . until he was on his back. He continued kicking, into the air, flat on his back, chatting to the audience and singing. He even tried out a few more impressions, including, I swear to you, then-president Richard Nixon. Rising to his feet, Elvis wandered the stage and struck more poses. The band swerved and vamped with his every move. From time to time, Elvis, who was clearly having a very good time, would toss in the words "got your granny." My mom and I exchanged a long look. Elsewhere in this arena, everyone seemed to get the joke. We shrugged and continued watching the increasingly riveting spectacle.

Calming down a bit, the King announced his next song, "Bridge over Troubled Water." For a handful of minutes, everything shifted. Suddenly he was committed to the words he was singing, shutting his eyes and rising with the emotions of the song. The heartbreak of a squandered career disappeared. For this one number, he performed some lingering artistic duty to himself. When it was over, he left the stage for a long break.

Elvis returned and began "Love Me Tender." The King sang the first line of the song as his onstage sidekick Charlie Hodge timidly appeared next to him with a cache of scarves. As the Sweet Inspirations continued, Elvis abandoned the song entirely, and Hodge began the curious gesture of simply passing each scarf behind Elvis's neck before Presley then bequeathed it to one of the cardiac-arrested women in the front row. Some he kissed, some he didn't. The song lumbered on for many minutes.

I looked over at my date. "What's going on?"

My mother had the look of a social scientist, studying a cultural moon rock. "I'm . . . not . . . sure," she managed.

Around us, women wept. Another handful of songs followed, and all were sung in his special blend of photo-op haiku. After "Can't Help Falling in Love," Elvis bowed reverentially and said good night. The lights rose instantly. The famous words were spoken: "Elvis has left the building." After an important pause, the announcement continued, "But if you didn't get a scarf, there are a few still available at the concession stands if you act quickly!"

Elvis had been onstage forty-seven minutes.

We drove home in stunned silence, still not quite sure what we'd seen. Many years later, with proper sociological perspective, it's easier to judge. He had already jammed with the Beatles, sung with Sinatra, married Priscilla, made thirty-three movies, and rocked the world. Perhaps he had been on his best behavior in the bigger markets of this mini tour, but in San Diego he let his hair down completely and simply mocked the whole spectacle. This was the beginning of Elvis's third act. Comeback Elvis was already dead and in his place was the unmoored karate King, kicking and laughing and finally embracing the bars of his pop culture prison.

A week later, my mom accompanied me to the Derek and the Dominos performance. Now, this was a real rock concert, still one of the best I've seen. A riotous crowd, unable to get in, broke the huge glass pane at the front of the hall while Eric Clapton, barely moving, burned through some of the great guitar rock of the coming decade. *Layla and Other Love Songs* was only two weeks old. Audiences were just catching up to the bounty of new material. By the next year, the album and title song would be considered Clapton's brokenhearted creative peak, and that blistering band would have already broken up in a haze of ego and drugs.

As Elvis Presley had proven a week earlier, a musician can only play at that level and depth for a finite number of years before the law of attrition kicks in. Some die, some survive, some homogenize. I can still feel that night, the private thrill of a committed audience linking up with a committed performer. Clapton was on fire, and everyone knew it.

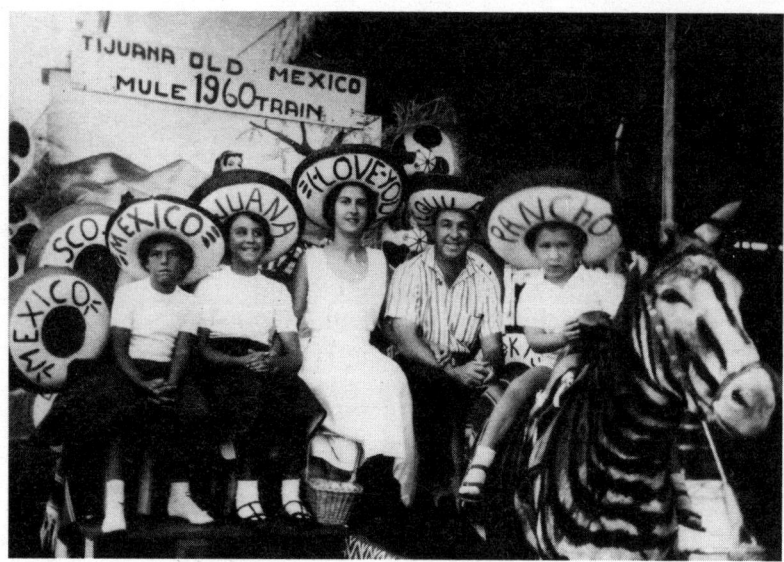

The family in Tijuana, 1960.

That night, my schoolteacher mother succumbed to the power of rock and roll. And even when a tie-dyed Romeo in front of us offered her a spoon of cocaine, she chose to ignore it. It was an unforgettable night, if only for what she said quietly as we walked to the car.

"I understand your music," she said. "It's better than ours."

Seek out heroes and role models. Most will not disappoint you.

—ALICE CROWE

Summer 1971. As long as I could remember, I was sent to summer school. The idea was that it was an easy way to amass extra units. Going to summer school meant you would have the freedom to graduate high school early. Perhaps there was some magical trip to Europe ahead, or an amazing way to spend the extra three or four months when everybody else was still in school. Honestly, I wasn't in a rush to go to the big social events. I was younger than any of the others. Who wants to be the guy who goes to senior prom alone?

At least my summer school was near the beach. Walking home meant strolling down Newport Avenue, a street rich in counterculture cool. There were two head shops, a place that sold waterbeds, a theater that always seemed to be showing *Harold and Maude* or *King of Hearts*, and best of all, a record store called Soundsville. The place had no curtains, and the hot sun would pound into the record store. For some reason, nobody brought up the fact that *the sun warps records*. In the brightly lit display window was usually something exciting, maybe even a forbidden Bob Dylan bootleg.

One summer afternoon while passing the store, I noticed a new record they'd given a place of honor in the front window. It was a square block of blue, with a handwritten card just below it. "New Joni Mitchell," was all it said. I was thrilled. Joni Mitchell's "Both Sides Now" had been the rare song from the rock era that had eased around my strict schoolteacher mother's ban of "promiscuous music." Mitchell, the engaging young Canadian composer, had been a striking guest on *The Dick Cavett Show*. I'd loved Mitchell's first albums, along with her graceful persona of deep feeling and out-of-this-world musicianship. But for a young person still learning about passions and the mysteries of romantic love, *Blue*, her newest album, was a manual on the depth charges of real romance. Once again, music was at my shoulder, guiding the way.

We'd moved to Friars Village, a just-built condominium complex about ten minutes from downtown San Diego. We were right across the street from USD, "the best law school in Southern California." It was all part of the original plan. I was going to be a lawyer, like my dad's grandfather J. D. Atkinson. He'd been the youngest and oldest practicing lawyer in the country. That dream was also a tribute to my dad. Just as he did, I would be carrying the Kentucky traditions of his family and planting that flag in California.

Suddenly we were out of the basement apartment and into the new world of condo living, a place with two floors and at the top of the hill a vista that looked out across the San Diego Bay and the San Diego Sports Arena itself. My future alma mater, University High School, was two blocks away.

San Diego was a city of the future, a breezy change of pace from the desert. It was an interesting mix of sailors, surfers, and retirees. For any concert that came to town, the local surf culture turned out in full force. Many rock tours began or ended in San Diego. In San Diego, the pressure was off. They'd already faced the critics in New York, Chicago, and Los Angeles. Now it was time to party.

Meanwhile, Alice Crowe had become a big hit in San Diego. San Diego City College became her domain. She was hungry to be needed, I think, and the world of community college students suited her. She taught several classes and served as a counselor, an advisor to students unsure about the curriculum of their life and education. They were always grateful to unburden their hopes and dreams to Alice Crowe, who was endlessly fascinated with the lives of others.

My mom's persona as an inner-city college professor was a reinvention that suited her offbeat style. The school was on the outskirts of Logan Heights, now known as Barrio Logan. One of her classes was Chicano Studies. She was made head of the Chicano Studies Department, and even began calling herself Alicia, the original name given to her by her Spanish grandmother, Audelina Sanchez.

She often dressed in a red blazer too heavy for the heat, and a bowler hat. Her classes were always filled. She was light on homework and heavy on personal interaction. The lively conversations often continued after hours, in the living room of our small condo. It wasn't uncommon to come home to a house filled with passionate students, heavy thoughts, and political diatribes.

The walls of her class were covered with aphorisms, of course. Her new favorite came courtesy of the French priest and theologian Teilhard de Chardin—"Joy is the most infallible sign of the presence of God." The prediction of Mrs. Kellerman, the Yucaipa Prophet, had come true. The second half of my mother's life was filled with laughter. She had found purpose and reason in helping others.

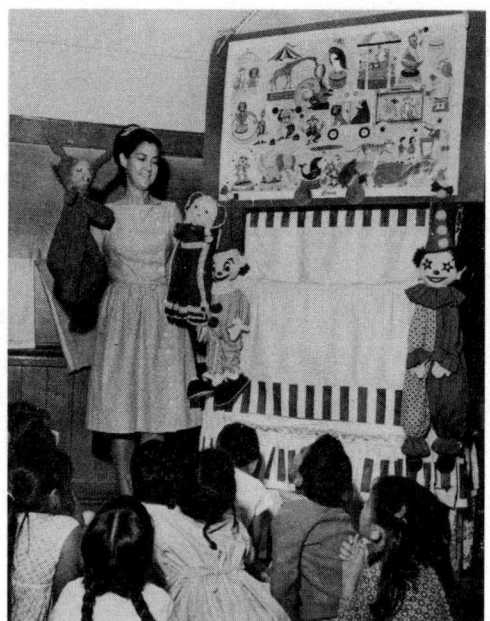

Sometimes she'd wear clown ears: Alice Crowe teaching HeadStart classes, 1967.

One day when I was fourteen, she invited Cesar Chavez, the farm-worker and political activist, to speak at one of her classes. Chavez showed up in a faded denim work shirt and loose pants, wan from fasting but charged with commitment. There was twinkle in the button-brown eyes that shone brightly on his creased, solemn face, leathered from the sun. He took to the podium and clipped on a little microphone. You had the feeling of someone who was *of his time*. Nobody took a breath as he spoke about his cause—better conditions for the farmworkers who were the spine of California labor. *Viva la huelga!*

"I want you to meet my son," my mom told Chavez when he'd finished. His eyes flashed as I shook his hand. They were tough like worn-out baseball mitts.

"Your mother's been talking about you," he said. "I hear you're a writer."

It was the first time I'd heard myself characterized that way. Somehow it felt right. And it was true. I loved writing. I'd already started reading *Rolling Stone* and contributing stories to my high school news-paper. I could feel those law school dreams slipping away. I just hadn't broken it to my parents yet.

"He's also going to be a lawyer," she added.

"Good," said Cesar Chavez. "We can use you!"

I promptly blurted out something that would become a constant and a passion for the rest of my life. I wasn't even sure where, or why, or how, I'd use what I was about to ask him for. I just did.

"I'd like to interview you."

Cesar Chavez waved off the cohort who was waiting to whisk him away and we sat down on two wooden chairs in my mom's classroom. I was almost fifteen and had just taken a step into the world I wanted to live in.

"Ask me anything," he said.

There are two paths you can go by . . .

—ROBERT PLANT

In the fall of 1971, my cool sister Cindy moved into a mission-style courtyard apartment two blocks down the street. It was enough to give her breathing room from my mom. She was flourishing in her new freedom. She was a flight attendant for Western Airlines, with a robust schedule and a sparkling red and yellow uniform.

She'd also taken on a roommate, a fellow flight attendant named Leslie. Leslie had a mop of unruly blond hair and a worldly sense of mischief behind her blue eyes. Her room was populated with open suitcases. Mostly the apartment seemed to function as a waystation between adventures. I liked listening to Leslie's salty stories about far-flung characters and cities. I dreamed of traveling and open suitcases of my own. Looking at her open suitcases, I sometimes felt sentimental about adventures I hadn't even had yet.

Sometimes my sister would overhear and with a flurry of hand motions behind my back, Leslie's R-rated stories would end before they turned X. When Leslie pulled out her shoebox of weed to openly and shockingly prepare a joint, I didn't partake, but more important, I didn't report the incident to my mom.

We were growing closer again. Clearly, Cindy found me more tolerable when not in the presence of our mom. The two of them in the same room together was still a pins-and-needles affair. The smallest comment could turn into an explosion, and always with the same punctuation. *Slam!*

I always felt caught in the middle.

When Elton John announced a September 18 show at the San Diego Civic Theatre, I thought I'd invite Cindy. The Civic was just down the street from us, and I scooped up two great twelfth-row seats for a whopping seven dollars. It was the *Los Angeles Times'* Robert Hilburn who'd championed the arrival of Elton John as a majorly important artist the year before. Hilburn was that rare mainstream journalist who wrote about rock with respect and excitement. He was correct in placing a big early bet on Elton John, who still credits Hilburn for his early success in America.

I gobbled up every new Elton John release, and there were many. From *Elton John* to *Tumbleweed Connection* to the wonderful score for a UK movie called *Friends*, he'd already built a hefty body of work. John and his lyricist Bernie Taupin had the opposite of writer's block. This was writer's *Vesuvius*. They'd even wedged in the live album *11-17-70*. By the time Elton John hit San Diego, he already had *another* album in the can, called *Madman Across the Water*. The title seemed apropos. John was already known as an explosive live performer, and San Diego was a near-final stop on his third American tour in less than a year.

Cindy and I took our seats. Just after 8 p.m., Elton John slipped onto the stage with no fanfare. He nodded to the crowd and sat down at the piano for a starkly beautiful "Your Song." A few songs later he announced a track from the upcoming *Madman* album. It was a wistful new song with a shimmering opening: "Tiny Dancer." We shared a look; the song moved us both. My sister and I were becoming a team.

The concert built to a strange, unresolved finish. The final encore, "The King Must Die," had spun into a ferocious haymaker of a jam, and all three members of the band were playing at full-tilt power until suddenly drummer Nigel Olsson flopped off the drum kit, unconscious. Olsson was pulled offstage and a panicked Elton John spoke to the crowd in a quavering voice. "I don't know what's happened," he said. "Nigel's in a bad way." Many of us waited in our seats long after the house lights had come up. For days, I checked the news to make sure Olsson hadn't died at our concert.

Many years later, I happened to meet Nigel Olsson. He pleasantly listened to my description of the show, the details of his collapse, and the concern that filled the theater as we worried for his well-being. He nodded as if combing through the mists of many shows, many cities, and many versions of "The King Must Die."

"Oh yes," he finally said. "I remember. That was the show after Las Vegas, and we all know how that goes . . . *The show after Las Vegas.*"

I tried to nod nonchalantly, like *Of course, we showbiz types* all *know what "the show after Las Vegas" means.* Demon alcohol, road fever, all that. But really, all I was thinking about was what happened later that evening, and how it changed everything I thought I knew about the future.

Tin soldiers and Nixon's coming . . .

—NEIL YOUNG

We walked home from the Elton John concert that September evening, and Cindy rewarded me with a thrilling invitation. Her roommate, Leslie, had invited Cindy to join her in taking on a tantalizing part-time job at a local underground paper, a free giveaway called the *Door*. They'd recently shortened the name from *San Diego Door to Liberation*. You'd often find their free issues in red dispensers downtown, or blowing across Broadway Avenue unread. It was a mostly political paper, but they also printed record reviews and sometimes interviews with musicians.

Downtown San Diego was then in need of a cleanup. Sailors and prostitutes congregated at the bars and strip clubs near our home. Across the street from the bus stop that took me to summer school was the gloriously run-down Spreckels Theatre. Next to the Spreckels was a hippie head shop that reeked of patchouli oil. A speaker above the door would play music like Grand Funk Railroad's *Closer to Home*. The Trip was an eighteen-and-older store. It used to be a porn shop, but the bespectacled middle-aged owner, Eugene, had changed with the times. Now he sold bongs; Dennis Hopper posters; incense; *Zap Comix*, the X-rated showcase for cartoonist Robert Crumb; and various underground magazines.

Eugene let me wander in one day and even slipped me a copy of a magazine called *Rolling Stone*. Mick Jagger was on the cover, wearing lipstick, a still from his then-new movie *Performance*. I was hooked. I ordered back issues and read interviews with all the important musicians, like David Crosby, who gave their writer Ben Fong-Torres a spectacular unguarded interview. Their regular feature the Rolling Stone Interview was my favorite. Even John Lennon sat down for a lengthy, no-holds-barred conversation. Everybody said *fuck* a lot. Janis Joplin posed nude. *Holy shit.* Reading *Rolling Stone*, I felt older, cooler, and in the know.

Sometimes Eugene sold me the latest issues of *Creem* magazine, a music magazine out of Michigan even more irreverent than *Rolling Stone*. The editors were Dave Marsh and a particularly exciting music writer who'd migrated to Detroit from none other than San Diego. Lester Bangs was his name, and his record reviews were scholarly about music but always reckless and hilarious. His rants about the latest records by Iggy Pop or Van Morrison spun dizzily through my head like crazy jazz.

Reading the *Door* at my bus stop one day, I was amazed to come across several record reviews from Lester Bangs himself. How could it be that my rock-writing hero was also published in our tiny local give-away paper? Which brings me back to Fifth Avenue and that September evening when we walked back from Elton John worrying about the possible, probable death of their amazing drummer.

"Do you want to come with us to a staff meeting for the *Door*?" my sister asked. My lack of tattle-taling to Mom was clearly paying dividends. My head nearly exploded right there on Fifth Avenue. *Holy shit, of course I want to go!*

"Sure," I said coolly.

The *Door*'s main staff lived and worked together in an unkempt three-story mini mansion just a few blocks from us. Our neighborhood was under the flight path of Lindbergh Field. San Diego then had the dubious distinction of being home to the most dangerous airport in America. Planes had to make a steep descent, threading through a slalom course of high-rises, to touch down on a landing strip just off downtown. It was a miracle there'd been no flight disaster. (That happened about seven years later when a PSA jet collided with a small Cessna plane over North Park, killing 135 passengers. "Ma, I love you," were the last words on the black box.)

People living under a flight pattern learn to adapt to the regular thunder of the planes overhead. It's no big deal. Soon the noise disappears. It's only when someone visits and suddenly panics, looking for a table to crawl under, that we remember. Oh, it's just a part of life in downtown San Diego. I already felt a kinship with the ramshackle *Door* house in our very own neighborhood.

"Try not to talk too much," my sister advised me as we walked up the steps. "I don't really know them that well yet."

"I won't embarrass you." I could already hear a buzz of voices and cool music as we hiked up the steps to the thick Victorian-style front door.

She patted my back and rang the doorbell. A tall rail-thin man pulled open the thick wooden door. Sam Martin was the *Door*'s political cartoonist. His untamed hair was parted violently in the middle. He looked like a character straight out of *Zap Comix*, one of those stoners who'd stuck their finger in a socket and now his bloodshot eyes were telescoping out of his head. Next to the pleasing hipness of my sister was an overly excited kid wearing a short-sleeve plaid shirt and a wacky grin. Sam looked concerned.

"Who's this?"

"He's my brother," Cindy stated valiantly.

He swung the door open. The scent of cheap Mexican weed and tomato sauce wafted through the large living room. The windows were outfitted with dusty red drapery. Chairs were being assembled in a semi-circle. Sam's wife, Susan, was ladling vegetarian stew from a large pot in the kitchen. I told Sam I liked his artwork. He was pleased. To my sister's horror, he offered me a roach clip and a nub of a joint. I declined.

"The meeting will start in ten minutes," Sam told me. "Grab some grub."

It was late afternoon, when the planes were stacked up and landing every few minutes at Lindbergh Field. Their engines roared above as the staff gathered and sat in fold-out chairs assembled in the red sitting room. A serious man with John Lennon glasses took the first seat. He was followed by several women with pages of notes, men with facial hair that I longed to be able to grow myself, and a few others who were already talking about an unnamed political event that had to be addressed, and *soon*. I sat at the end of the semicircle, next to Leslie and my sister.

Last to arrive was a bearded, burly man who descended from a creaky staircase. He had a healthy girth, an open shirt with a silver pendant, and rippling brown hair. He looked like a besotted English baron. The kind of character Richard Harris used to play, most of the time with a goblet in his hand.

"That's Bill Maguire," Cindy whispered. "He's the editor and the publisher." She added the next fact with a touch of wonder. "He's got a big *waterbed* on the third floor."

"How'd he get it up the steps?"

She shook her head. It was unknown. Maguire was filled with mystery. He seemed much older than the others. He'd lived a lot of life and already had serious counterculture bona fides. He'd hung out with Dennis Hopper in Taos, New Mexico. He was said to have dated Linda Ronstadt, then famous from "Different Drum," her hit with the Stone Poneys. His spicy interview with Janis Joplin for the *Door* was infamous. ("Just trying to have a good time. Get laid and get stoned, that's all I'm trying to do," she told him. "That's my three ambitions in life, and I'm doing good at all three.") He had severe dyslexia, which he kept mostly hidden. He was passionately political, also a bon vivant who often drove his colorful VW van up to Los Angeles, where he had *connections*. He'd even been a beekeeper. He was still only twenty-six.

The meeting began instantly. Maguire ticked through the serious topics at hand in a dramatic voice, sometimes interrupted by a tiny giggle. The friendly hippie halfway house soon turned into a hotbed of political conversation. The staffers were united in their desire to uncover the many levels of corruption of then-president Richard Nixon. Nixon was a polarizing politician, of course, and the paper had lately been stirring up controversy by investigating the shady business deals of a local businessman, Nixon's best friend, C. Arnholt Smith. Nixon had famously declared San Diego was his favorite town, his "Lucky City."

Now, let's stop right there. To a struggling antiwar, antiestablishment underground paper in 1971, nothing could have been more galvanizing than hearing that Richard Nixon, King Lear himself, had claimed your town as his *Lucky City*. And now came the coup de grâce. Nixon was planning to bring the Republican National Convention, his reelection coronation, to our own San Diego Sports Arena. This August! *Nixon's coming!*

A sense of unity and purpose swept through the living room. The *Door* would be the fly in the ointment of Richard Nixon's Lucky City. One by one each staff member offered to contribute a journalistic sword to the battle. One staff member offered to write a searing exposé of C. Arnholt Smith's finances. Another writer, an earnest young woman named Paula Tharp, mysteriously revealed that suspicious and threatening letters had already been coming to the *Door* from a right-wing outfit called the Secret Army Organization. Surely it was funded by Nixon's reelection committee, she said, or the CIA, or both. My sister reported on the Calendar section that she and Leslie had been curating, which included planned protest events.

The meeting was just about over. I was the only one who hadn't spoken. It wasn't my place. I had barely even been invited. I decided not to say what was on my mind. Better to shut up in the company of this extremely cool and *purposeful* gathering of fledgling revolutionaries, journalists, stoners, and hippies. I wasn't about to shoot my mouth off and blow my promise to my sister about not embarrassing her with any unscripted little-brother behavior. *No.* But then again, there was that small voice inside that wouldn't go away. It said: *Do it.*

"I'd like to review the new James Taylor album," I said.

There was silence. The serious man in the John Lennon glasses, the *Door*'s political editor, let out a sigh. "I have an issue with the music coverage in our paper," he said.

"Well, let's talk about it," said Maguire. "Bring on the dialogue."

"Do we want to be a *music* paper?" the political editor asked. "Just another corporate shill in the business of selling the counterculture back to itself? Or do we want to be a serious publication jousting for the future of this country? We're the paper that Nixon, and the CIA, are already trying to destroy!" He looked at each of us. "Why should we review a James Taylor album when James Taylor records for Warner Bros., who are owned by Warner Communications, who produced the movie *Woodstock* but also manufacture *napalm*?" He was wrong about the napalm connection, but nobody dared question him. "Babies are burning in Vietnam because of Nixon's bombs, and yet *we bend to it*. For a James Taylor record?"

All eyes now turned to Maguire, who shifted his weight in the chair. "James Taylor is not the enemy," he said. "Record company ads are what we need to survive. When I go to Los Angeles and try to sell ads, all the record companies tell me there's not *enough* music coverage in the *Door*. If we have no paper, we have no voice at all."

"I think music should be free," Sam Martin offered. A large passenger plane stormed overhead. "Wouldn't *that* be groovy?"

"Look," said Maguire, "I'm not trying to be groovy; I'm trying to pay the bills. Those motherfuckers in Escondido want more money than ever to print the paper. I'm always haggling with them. The music labels are the only ones who put money in our pockets. They send us free records to review. We gotta write about 'em or we get no ad money." He turned to me. "Write about James Taylor if you want. There's also a bunch of promo records leaning against the wall. Take a few. Write a few reviews. If we print your review, you can keep the record."

I felt the earth move, ever so slightly. *Free records!*

Bill Maguire's conundrum was an early rumbling of all that would come later—the battle of deeply held progressive principles vs. the lucre

of pop culture. It was the onset of the boomer generation, a generation ready to demonstrate in the streets for racial equality and women's
rights, and to rail against Nixon and the war in Vietnam . . . *but* they
also dug rock music, and they liked movies and they liked cultural stars.
And there sat Bill Maguire, the publisher of the *Door*, at the crossroads,
feeling hopeful that the mild corruption of begging for record company
ads from the Man might also help pay for the revolution. (Along with
the weed he sometimes sold on his trips to Los Angeles.)

The meeting ended and Maguire ascended to his waterbed on the
third floor. Staffers feathered off in other directions. The editor in John
Lennon glasses came over and gave me a conciliatory soul shake. Sam
Martin took me to the records, and I finally asked him the question.

"How did you get the great Lester Bangs to write for the *Door*?"

"He used to come around here a lot," Sam said. "He lived in El Cajon
and wrote for *Rolling Stone*. Jann Wenner fired him over a Canned Heat
record review. So he moved to Michigan to work at *Creem*. He still sends
us reviews. We don't have room for most of 'em. They're very . . . long."
Sam pointed to the green cabinet by the wall. "They're in there if you
want to read 'em."

Right there in the rusty green cabinet was a treasure trove of Lester
Bangs's unpublished record reviews. He'd sent reviews about all kinds
of music, from acid jazz to rock to comedy records. They were rife with
x-ed out sentences and filled with long late-night jags about life and love
and music. It was a wealth of Bangsian magic, wild and beer-stained and
beautiful. Unsolicited bursts of inspiration, sent to a tiny underground
paper in San Diego where they sat mostly unread. I've often wondered
what happened to all that writing. More than anything he ever published, it was that green cabinet bounty that made me want to a) meet
Lester, b) shake his hand, and c) write.

I left with an armful of records and a whiff of the very thing that had
been so elusive: a sense of camaraderie. Here was a group of people I
could maybe even call buddies. It didn't matter that they were all older
than me. I dreamed of dropping by often, saying hi to Sam and the oth-

ers. One day maybe I'd even see my name printed in their paper. What would *that* be like?

Walking down the steps of the *Door* house, my sister looked at me with a sweet sense of pride and relief. "You did really good, honey."

"Thanks, Cin."

"Don't let Mom smell pot smoke on you."

Doubt is the devil.

—ALICE CROWE

February 1972. The *Door* had begun publishing my record reviews with some frequency. The paper's main priority was still taking down Nixon, of course. The typesetter was clearly less meticulous with the music coverage. Carole King could become *Casole Kirg*. Jethro Tull could hit the paper as Jethro *Tubb*. Fine with me. I had an insatiable appetite to keep writing. I was a regular visitor to the *Door* house too. One day I followed Maguire all the way up to his bedroom on the third floor. I had an important request.

We stood together in his room, surrounded by thick crimson drapes. The bedroom had the heavy scent of sandalwood candles mixed with the chlorine from a large, roiling waterbed that dominated the center. There were numerous framed photos of distant hippie gatherings populated by willowy flower children. Against the wall was his Marantz stereo system, crates of records, and a fresh batch of promotional albums that he'd kept for himself. It was my first look at Todd Rundgren's new album *Something/Anything?* Also leaning against the crates was the first Raspberries album, the one with a scratch 'n' sniff sticker that smelled like raspberries. He had Neil Young's *Harvest* and Jackson Browne's debut album, *Jackson Browne*, the one with a canteenlike cloth cover. They were all records that would become important to me.

Maguire often told stories that playfully polished his ladies'-man persona. His sparkly eyes held the promise of shenanigans as he talked about his friends and travels in the music business. Yes, Janis Joplin had flirted with him. He still held a candle for Linda Ronstadt, but she had rebuffed him. Allen Ginsberg, his pal, would soon be contributing poems to the *Door*. It was true of many of the colorful characters I was meeting. I was never sure how much was bluster and how much was truth. He thanked me for the increased music coverage and said it had helped the paper. I went out on a limb and told him I was ready to move on from record reviews to begin writing interview pieces for the *Door*. He agreed.

I'd never forgotten my interview with Cesar Chavez. I'd made sure to listen, and if Chavez paused, I didn't cut in with a story about myself. Chavez spoke candidly in our interview. It was more of a conversation, really, like the ones I'd watched on *The Dick Cavett Show*. I loved the process.

Recently my mom had invited the celebrated comedian Dick Gregory to speak at her humanities class. Gregory surprised us by accepting.

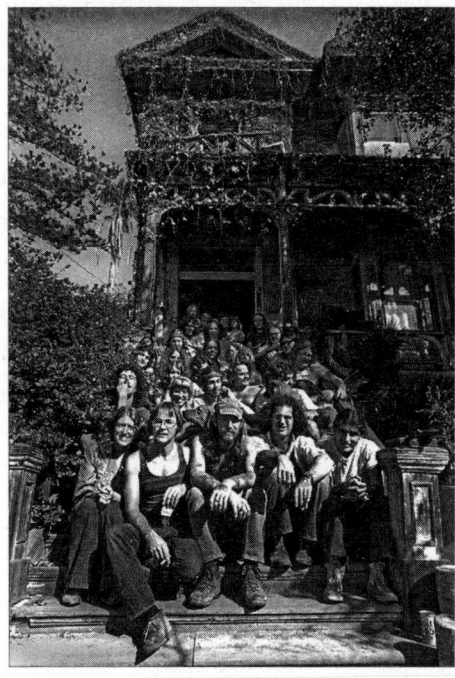

The *Door* house and staff pose for one last photo before evacuation, 1974.

Recently he'd changed his mainstream act to include personal politics. His work as a monologist was a big influence on Lenny Bruce and Richard Pryor. Lately Dick Gregory had become an anti–Vietnam War activist. He was on a fast for peace when he arrived, sallow faced and electric, at City College. Once again, my teacher urged me to meet my heroes.

"Go talk to him," she said. "You'll regret if you don't."

I told Dick Gregory I was an aspiring writer. Gregory invited me to go running with him in Balboa Park the next morning at sunrise. He also invited a fellow student named Bob Brown who lived near us, on Sixth Avenue. Bob Brown had recently introduced me to the thoughtful, politically based new album by Marvin Gaye, *What's Going On*. We met Gregory at the El Cortez hotel at six the next morning. He was already in the lobby and ready to go. We looped around the park. The morning ended with us all listening to Gaye's album at Bob's place, talking about the war, and singing along with Marvin. I wrote the story for the *Door*, and it was enormously satisfying, even though I was sent to detention for being late to school.

There was another writer, Danny Sugerman, who contributed to the *Door*. Danny wrote record reviews with more swagger than I ever did. He lived in Los Angeles, that faraway kingdom just up the 405 freeway. Only three years older than me, he already had a foothold in the record business community.

One afternoon Danny called the *Door* and we talked for hours. Danny was overflowing with stories about his close friend the late Jim Morrison of the Doors. Sugerman first met Morrison when he was twelve. His Little League baseball umpire was a roadie for the Doors. He promised Danny, a struggling player, he could meet the band if he hit a home run. Danny smacked a grand slam. He was put to work at the band's Cal State concert in 1967. With an increasingly angry crowd waiting, it was young Sugerman who finally coerced Morrison, hours late, into taking the stage, where he opened the show with "Soul Kitchen."

Befriended by Morrison, Danny was soon working in the Doors' office answering fan mail. The extent of their bond depended on the

degree to which you allowed yourself to believe Danny's wildly entertaining stories. They were the closest of pals! They hung out at Barney's
Beanery! They drank together, talked about women, and wore each
other's leather jackets! Jim was *Dionysus, man*! Danny's love of rock and
roll was boundless, he was filled with purple prose, and I loved every
dangerous minute of his spectacular tales. And that was just our first
phone conversation.

Perhaps we'd meet one day, Danny said, but he had to hang up now.
He was headed to a Rolling Stones tour rehearsal.

With sputtering regularity, I was able to talk my parents into letting
me take the Greyhound bus to the kingdom up the road. Sugerman
promised me a place to stay for a couple of days. I had two hot tickets to
see David Bowie at the Santa Monica Civic Auditorium. Glam rock had
become the latest trend. T. Rex, led by the ringlet-haired Marc Bolan,
had been the first to land a big hit with "Ride a White Swan." Bowie
then blew the door off its hinges with his futuristic concept album *The
Rise and Fall of Ziggy Stardust and the Spiders from Mars*.

Danny was waiting at Union Station when I arrived. In person, he
had a hungry hustler's look. His chest was always thrown out. He could
go days in the same tight jeans and half-unbuttoned shirt. His hands
forever on his hips, he looked like he was always posing for an album
cover. We boarded his yellow Pinto and headed for the Sunset Strip.

"Bowie's in town," he announced. "We're going to find him, and
we're going to *interview* him."

It was pure fantasy, of course. Bowie did no interviews. Not even
close. His manager was a British Colonel Parker type, Tony Defries.
Defries was a well-known proponent of *mystique*. He allowed no press
near his artist. Bowie was visible only in concert, or in a flurry of photos
from his mayhem-filled British shows. One of the more famous shots
featured him on his knees, miming fellatio with guitarist Mick Ronson.
Defries' management style was working. Bowie was clearly on the fast
track to legendary status. Everybody was talking about him, including
us, but we all knew the truth. *Nobody gets near Bowie.*

The Strip was Danny's playground. Sugerman's Jim Morrison stories flowed as always, along with his continual monologue that sounded like our mutual writing hero, Lester Bangs. Rock was his savior. His father had ties to the Mafia. ("I can't say any more about it.") His uncle Louis controlled all the crime business west of the Rockies. *Maybe.* I could never figure out what was bravado and what wasn't. I was too fixated on the passing billboards on Sunset Boulevard that featured *album covers.* This was Disneyland for a young rock fan.

"Where *is* Bowie?" I asked.

"Let's try Rodney's," said Danny. "He was with Rodney last night."

Rodney was Rodney Bingenheimer, the Hollywood scene-maker who sported a British rock star bowl cut and a tiny voice that sounded like a sigh. Rodney was an important early proponent of glam rock, a West Coast Andy Warhol who was famous for being semifamous. He had a flair for discovering artists early and escorting them around town, including Bowie. He'd also just opened his own British-themed bar on Sunset, Rodney's English Disco. We arrived to hear the Sweet's "Little Willy" playing at earsplitting volume. The place was all mirrors. Rodney was decked out as if he'd just stepped off the set of *Top of the Pops.*

"Oh, hi," he said, elegantly bored. "It's all happening."

Rodney Bingenheimer glanced at my large brown chukka boots and never looked at me again. He spoke only to Danny Sugerman, and while they were good friends, neither turned to the other as they spoke. Both were trained to always check the door for anybody who might be more happening.

"David was here earlier," Rodney offered with his trademark nonchalance. "And you just missed Elvis and his friends, the Memphis Mafia crowd. They stayed for a couple pints and moved on. Elvis liked the Gary Glitter record."

It was hard to even fathom. The King of Rock and Roll had just been in this tiny room, downing a Guinness in this sea of mirrors, shaved eyebrows, and platform heels, listening to *glam rock*? It was just a year ago that he was rolling around on the stage of the Sports Arena, imitating Richard Nixon!

Elvis and I were both a long way from home.

"Try the Riot House," said Rodney. A pack of glitter girls arrived in their tallest platforms, and Danny had suddenly unbuttoned two more buttons on his shirt, even though he was holding drinks in both hands. It was some kind of magic trick.

Soon we were on our way to the next hot spot, looking for Bowie. The Riot House was the code name for the Continental Hyatt House. It was already well-known to me as the hotel in Hollywood for rock's luminaries. Their lenient way of tolerating rock stars had made them a haven-away-from-home for visiting bands like Led Zeppelin and the Who. Next door to the Riot House was a newly opened comedy club, the Comedy Store. The lobby was a hotbed of fans, disc jockeys, roadies, groupies, and all sorts of rock riffraff. It was a gathering of the tribes, and a petri dish for people like me. I noticed the same look on many faces. We were wide-eyed new arrivals.

Danny entered the lobby like a king. Everybody knew him. He introduced me to the photographer Richard Creamer and his friend Michelle Myers. Both were in their early twenties, with a world-weary affectation way beyond their years. Danny gave me a look—*Michelle is important*. Michelle knew everything about everybody. She helped book acts at the Whisky a Go Go. Behind tinted aviator glasses, she had the same tart sense of humor as Rose Marie from *The Dick Van Dyke Show*.

"Welcome to the Dog Hustle," Michelle said, and sighed. Michelle had the *definitive* seen-it-all voice. Her world-weary affectation made Rodney's look like mere child's play. A moment later, when Michelle uttered the phrase that opened all doors, the "open sesame" of the scene, I instantly knew exactly where it had all come from. She was the Picasso, the queen, the only one who added four layers of meaning to the three words that came next: "It's all happening."

"It's all happening," agreed Richard. "Who's this?"

Danny introduced me as Cameron from San Diego. They looked vaguely disappointed with everything about me and my unimportant city. "We're looking for David," Danny explained.

"David just left," revealed Michelle. "He's going up to see Wolfman Jack. He's in the hills now. Cherry Vanilla says he's in a good mood." Cherry Vanilla—real name Kathleen—was Bowie's friend and publicist. "It's all happening."

"It's all happening," Richard added in a slightly different tone than he'd used for his earlier version of the same phrase. I judged the subtext—*It's a good crowd tonight.*

"It's all happening," repeated Danny. I heard it as *It's good to see you guys.*

"It's all happening," I agreed. They stared at me. I hadn't yet been given clearance to judge what was happening or not happening.

"It's all happening," said Danny, and now it sounded like an apology. "Hey, I'm starting my own fanzine," he told them. "It's called *Heavy Metal Digest.* Everybody's writing for it. Lester Bangs, John Mendelsohn, Greg Shaw . . ."

The glam-rock crowd swelled, and Danny greeted all with a similar brew of bravado, Jim Morrison stories, and gossip about the Hollywood Trash he called friends. "Hollywood Trash" was a badge of honor, code for outsiders who'd been rejected by the cool kids in high school. Here, we belonged. It was, indeed, all happening for a certain type of person who finally felt appreciated under the semi-fluorescent lights of the Riot House lobby. And when the elevator doors opened and Alice Cooper exited for a night on the town, he passed through the lobby like a wrestler approaching the ring. *It was all happening.* And I didn't want to go home.

I soon spotted another bona fide star. Leonard Barr was a vaudeville comedian who was a favorite of Johnny Carson and *The Tonight Show*. He was a living room favorite in our home. Barr was in his seventies with a craggy face like a beagle, a rumpled suit, and a porkpie hat. His act was that of a lovable loser. He barked out punch lines and we howled at his deadpan delivery. Barr looked wildly out of place passing through the world of young rock fans and was probably headed back to the Comedy Store. I caught up to him, touching his shoulder just as he was exiting the lobby.

"Hey," I said. "I know you from the Johnny Carson show. You're great."

Leonard Barr immediately turned and snarled like an angry dog. *"Blow me, you fuck!"*

He hustled out of the exit. I stood there, haunted by the sheer force of his anger. Such was the power of television. Because he'd been in our living room, I saw him as family. It was a lesson in celebrity. I had diminished him. The casual permission I gave myself to actually touch him had set the old comic off like a neutron bomb. I was ready to leave the night circus when Danny arrived at my side. He'd watched the strange encounter with Danny-vision.

"You're fitting right in!" he chortled. "He's a comedian, man! They're all fucking tortured." Danny slapped me on the back. "He invited you into his pain! Don't you see?!" Sugerman was ecstatic. *"He loved you!!"*

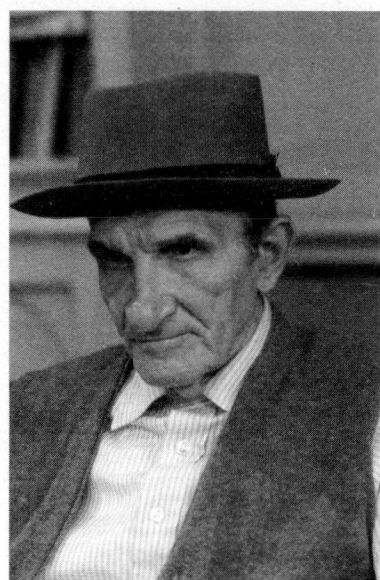

Leonard Barr: A strange lesson in celebrity, 1973.

That night I stayed on the sofa in Danny's room. He lived at his mom's house in a suburb near the airport. In the darkness, we mourned all the opportunities passing us by while we committed the sin of sleeping. Danny whispered more stories in the night. About *Jim*, about his father with vague ties to Cosa Nostra, and more about Jim.

In later days Danny would come down to San Diego, where my mom and I would pick *him* up at the bus station. Danny crashed on the roll-out sofa in my bedroom, which was now packed with records. I'd built shelves on either side of the room and lived in the oxygen-deprived space in between. We talked endlessly about shared heroes like Lester Bangs and we cherished our adventures in music.

My mom was aghast that Danny smoked, but even more so that he often went barefoot in the house. He regaled her with tales about how he looked after me in Los Angeles, but in her eyes she knew. The half-buttoned shirt and bare feet were the giveaways. Danny Sugerman was Eddie Haskell, my favorite TV character, the teenage con man from *Leave It to Beaver*. She knew Danny's parental flattery was a smokescreen hiding a world of temptation: drugs, drinking, women, the coming of the Antichrist, all of it.

I was often defending him. Yes, he paraded his aroma-challenged bare feet. Yes, he had a penchant for bending the truth into grand narratives about the power of rock. *Yes!* But in his own passionately fabulist way, Danny made me trust in my wildest dreams.

Danny would go on to officially manage the legacy of the Doors. His idolatry of Morrison would be immortalized in the book *No One Here Gets Out Alive*. It was a huge bestseller. Little did Jim Morrison know when he still walked the earth, beer in hand, that his enduring presence on T-shirts, on posters, and in rock history would largely be cemented by the hyperbole of the worshipful kid who sorted his fan mail. Maybe we're all just one Little League grand slam away from immortality. Danny would indeed make his mark and he'd sadly check out early like his hero, but to my mom he was always just "the kid with the smelly feet."

Last Press Agents Before the Freeway

It was a time just before the mainstream media fully caught up to the power of rock and roll. Writers like Danny Sugerman and I had our small outposts to write about the music we loved, but publications like *Time* and *Newsweek* had barely covered the growing wave that was rock culture. Soon that would all change. Two Hollywood press agents with long hair and an eye to the future spotted it early. Bob Gibson and Gary Stromberg started a publicity company dedicated to rock, and before long they represented everyone from the Rolling Stones to Michael Jackson to T. Rex and Jethro Tull and many more. *Time* and *Newsweek* would soon be begging to put rock stars on their covers.

Their office was in a small pink building at the crook of Sunset Boulevard and Halloway Avenue, right next to the Old World Restaurant. Just up a set of steps was a nondescript door with a sign: GIBSON AND STROMBERG—LAST PRESS AGENTS BEFORE THE FREEWAY. It was an early lesson in rock and roll mystique. Just behind that bland door was an explosion of color, flash, thumping music, and an irreverent team of fourteen young publicists, mostly passionate women who walked the walk and talked the talk. They loved this music too. It was a long way from the hard-bitten world of sweaty and desperate press agents like Sidney Falco, the publicist played by Tony Curtis in *Sweet Smell of Success*.

The offices were a haven for up-and-coming rock writers like Danny and me. Emerson, Lake & Palmer's "From the Beginning" might be blasting from Patty Farallas's stereo. Bobbi Cowan, the nurturing queen of the Gibson & Stromberg publicists, might nab you in the hallway and pull you into her cubbyhole to introduce you to Cheech and Chong. No one could sweep you up into a state of life-or-death fan passion like Bobbi. Or you'd spot Stromberg himself, in a long-sleeve baseball shirt, with T. Rex's Marc Bolan at his side. Stromberg toured with the Rolling Stones and looked the part. If you peeked inside his office/conference room, you wouldn't even see a desk. Just the longest puffy sofa I'd ever seen, and it circled the room.

Freelance journalists who lived for choice interview assignments quickly learned the quid pro quo of Gibson & Stromberg. To interview one of their big acts, it helped if you'd written about some of their up-and-coming clients. I'd always loved Jethro Tull, the hard-rock art band led by Ian Anderson. Anderson had a unique rock persona; he looked like a character from *The Lord of the Rings*. He often played and was photographed with a flute.

Bobbi Cowan, who'd become a cheerleader for my nascent life as a young freelancer, knew that it might help me land an interview with Ian Anderson if I wrote something about the up-and-coming band that An-

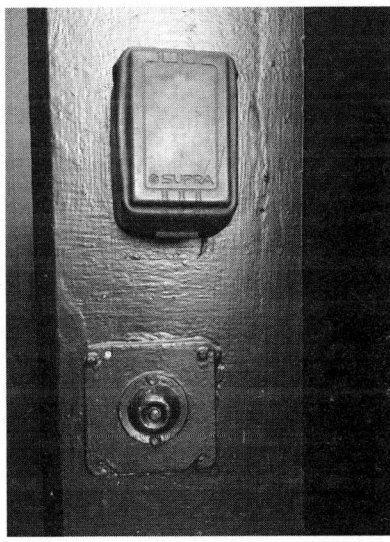

The backstage buzzer of the San Diego Sports Arena. I asked for it before they tore the place down in 2026. They gave it to me early.

derson was championing at his own record label. The band was called Wild Turkey, featuring Glenn Cornick, a former member of Tull. They were headed to San Diego for a high-profile appearance opening for Yes and Black Sabbath. Bobbi arranged for me to interview Wild Turkey backstage before the show. I'd never been backstage anywhere, much less at my favorite venue, the site of all my favorite concerts, the San Diego Sports Arena. My pass would be waiting at the backstage gate, she said, and I should ask for the band's manager, Terry Ellis.

Act like you belong.

——PROMOTER LARRY VALLON

I was fourteen. I decided to stash a collection of my articles from the *Door* in my orange shoulder bag, so I could prove that I was a semi-seasoned professional. I wore a brown corduroy sport jacket, like the reporters I'd seen on television. I was ready for my first big field adventure in the world of journalism.

It was still daylight when I arrived, dropped off early by my mom on show day. I could hear Wild Turkey sound checking their song "Butterfly" in the empty arena. They sounded like Jethro Tull but with a different singer. At the bottom of a steep loading ramp was the backstage door. I pressed the buzzer to the right of the backstage door. The door was answered by an angry, scrawny man in a loud yellow jacket. His name was sewn above his pocket. Not that I would remember the name forever or anything like that, but . . . *Scotty* was a dick of gigantic proportions.

"You're not on the list," he told me, shutting the door.

I pressed the buzzer again. Scotty appeared again.

"I'm supposed to ask for Terry Ellis."

"You're not on the list," he answered. "Go to the top of the ramp with the other girls."

There were indeed two girls at the top of the ramp. I went to join them as the limos of Black Sabbath and Yes whooshed by. The girls were soon escorted inside, met by roadies from Yes who lavished them with laminated passes and whisked them past Scotty. Finally, I returned to the buzzer. Scotty opened the door.

"Could I just talk to Terry El—"

"Don't press this buzzer again."

He slammed the door with great relish. I returned to the top of the ramp. I knew it was the end. One of our family mottoes had always been "Wear magic shoes." There was no more magic in my shoes. The doors opened and sixteen thousand fans filed inside. The evening had begun for them, but it was over for me. I turned to head for a phone booth, to call home for a ride. Then came a little bit of magic.

Boom. The backstage door clanged open. A lanky man stood in the light, like John Wayne in *The Searchers*. He spotted me and beckoned. I ran back down the ramp. Larry Vallon was the show promoter.

"How can I help you?" he asked. He had an avuncular, curious manner. Someone had already told him I'd been out on the ramp for hours. I told him about my instructions from Gibson & Stromberg to find Terry Ellis, to interview Wild Turkey. I fished out some of my articles. He chuckled briefly.

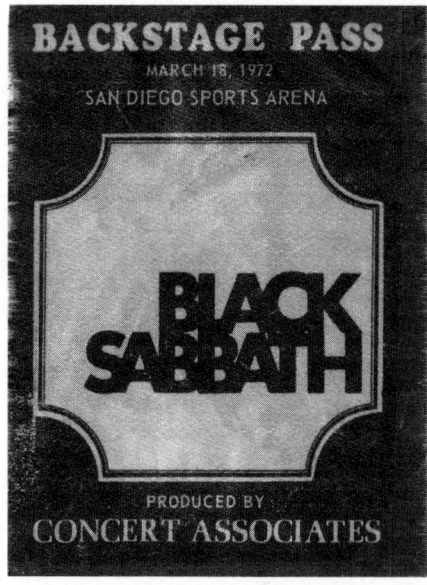

"Put it on your pants, never your shirt."

Vallon explained that Terry Ellis hadn't come with the band today. "He's probably hobnobbing with Jethro Tull," he said. Then he smiled and withdrew an enormous wad of backstage passes held together with a rubber band. He peeled one off and handed it to me with great aplomb. He knew it was a key to the castle, and he offered me some simple advice I never forgot.

"Act like you belong," he said.

Scotty was scowling as Larry pulled me past him and pointed me to the dressing rooms. I immediately felt a part of the circus. Cases were rolling, camaraderie was everywhere, nobody (except Scotty) was excluding me. If you were there, you belonged. I asked a muttonchopped roadie named Black Rudy where Wild Turkey might be. Black Rudy led me to what had to be the smallest dressing room in the complex, where they were waiting.

After interviewing Wild Turkey, I slipped into the dressing room next door. This one belonged to Yes. I found *their* road manager and asked for an interview. They obliged, and I interviewed their singer, Jon Anderson, and then their keyboardist, Rick Wakeman. As they prepared to perform their set, I ran into my old buddy from the backstage gate.

"Have you interviewed Black Sabbath yet?" Larry Vallon asked. "Let me introduce you to Ozzy."

So I interviewed them too. I would have interviewed the arena's Zamboni machine if I hadn't run out of cassettes.

A few days later, feeling courageous, I sent a letter to Lester Bangs and his coeditor, Dave Marsh, at the Birmingham, Michigan, office of *Creem* magazine. I included copies of some of my articles. I even asked for an interview assignment. A week later, a jolting surprise arrived. It was a letter from *Creem*, and in the upper right corner of the envelope was the same hasty penmanship I recognized from his green filing cabinet collection of record reviews. It read simply: "Bangs."

I sat in my small, airless bedroom filled with vinyl for a good twenty minutes, savoring the envelope. Would it be a rejection or a ticket to the future? I sliced open the corner so as not to disturb any part of this hallowed piece of communication.

"Your writing is damn good," Bangs wrote. "Why don't you give us a thousand words on Humble Pie?" He added: "Call me and we'll discuss."

I waited for a couple hours and dialed the number at *Creem*. A garrulous voice answered after two rings.

"Bangs," he said.

We discussed the *Door*, and we laughed about Bill Maguire, his waterbed, and his VW van. Lester mentioned that he was coming back to town sometime near Christmas. His mom still lived in El Cajon, he said, as well as his ex-girlfriend. He also wanted to visit a DJ friend who worked at KPRI, the FM station just down the block on A Street. We made loose plans to maybe get together.

Creem printed my Humble Pie story, and it took me some time to come down from the surreal mountain where I'd seen my name printed in a national magazine. The same one I'd read at my school bus stop.

"Don't get intoxicated by it," my mom warned. "Don't forget your dream. We moved across the street from California's finest law school *for a reason*. You wanted to be the youngest lawyer in the country, like your great-grandfather." She paused for effect. "There's no room in the world for a *thirty-year-old rock critic*."

Back at the *Door*, politics had taken center stage. The Republican National Convention was now just around the corner. Anti-Nixon demonstrations ramped up, as did the force of the rhetoric in the *Door*'s articles. Soon a dark shadow passed over the mini mansion where my earnest fellow staffers flew their journalist freak flag. The *Door* house was burglarized; typewriters were smashed and machines were taken. One morning a gunman fired bullets into the Ocean Beach home of the San Diego State professor-activist Peter Bohmer. His girlfriend, Paula Tharp, my friend and ally from the *Door* staff, was shot in the elbow. When Tharp was released from the hospital, we all gazed at the scar.

It was now a war. A group called the Secret Army Organization took credit for the incident. The *Door* blamed Nixon's henchmen for the incident. The anti-Nixon movement in San Diego grew even stronger.[*]

One day, a package arrived at the *Door* house. It was sent from none other than the poet Allen Ginsberg. He'd sent us a cassette with a handwritten title: "Going to San Diego." The song was a call to political action, written and recorded by Ginsberg. Bob Dylan himself accompanied Ginsberg on guitar. *"Come to San Diego, the whole world's gonna swing . . ."*

The *Door* was never more seized with purpose. All the counterculture superstars were headed for our town! The *Door* even acquired new political eloquence with the sharp editing and reporting of writer Bill Ritter, who would later go on to be a star television reporter in New York. Our little paper with the ramshackle mini mansion under the flight pattern had become the national voice of the opposition. *The Door versus Nixon hisownself!*

---

[*] Mainstream media scoffed at the *Door*'s accusations that the activity was coming from the highest levels of Nixon's White House. Many decades later the ACLU successfully unsealed documents that showed the *Door* had been correct. Donald Segretti, head of the Committee to Re-Elect the President (CREEP), had approved the plan with Nixon himself. Nixon personally ordered Segretti to "get rid of" anybody who'd planned to disrupt his Lucky City convention. There was even a foiled assassination attempt, complete with a plan to shoot Peter Bohmer during a visit to Mexico.

We may lose, and we may win . . .

—GLENN FREY, JACKSON BROWNE

A nd then it was all over. In early May of 1972, the Republican Party voted to switch plans and move their convention to the kinder city of Miami Beach. The cultural spotlight swung away from San Diego. Watergate moved to center stage. The *Door* continued, but the fever had lapsed. All that was left was that handwritten cassette from Allen Ginsberg.

"Take It Easy" hit the airwaves a few weeks later, like a blast of California sunshine. The band was called Eagles. (You were not supposed to call them *the* Eagles back then.) The song was instantly memorable, a potent stew of the stuff I'd loved. I always felt that a favorite song has a mind of its own. It arrives just when you need it, and that arrival memory remains for the rest of time. Every time you hear the song, you can remember the feeling, like you're reading a diary entry. It's one of music's great gifts. I bought a used electric guitar, turquoise of course; learned to play the song; joined a band called the Masked Hamster; rehearsed with the Masked Hamster twice in my schoolmate Russ Schumacher's garage; was told the band had broken up; walked by Russ's house a few days later; heard the Masked Hamster practicing with a new guitarist; and decided my instrument was the typewriter. All to the soundtrack of "Take It Easy."

The Eagles were coming to San Diego's Golden Hall for a show on July 5, opening for Procol Harum. Procol Harum's "A Whiter Shade of Pale" had been a sad anthem just five summers earlier. I called their label's publicist, a woman named Lita Eliscu, and asked to interview Eagles for the San Diego *Door*. She was as laconic as I was enthusiastic but left me tickets and gave me the name of Paul Aherne, the band's promotion guy. Aherne would set the whole thing up. I'd already learned that "the guy who will set the whole thing up" is usually the guy who never shows up. I mentally prepared to improvise.

I invited my high school paper's photographer, Gary Elam. We arrived backstage early on the day of the show. I'd stuffed a lot of cassettes, and even more questions, into my orange shoulder bag. The Eagles were already performing their sound check.

They were working on "Take It Easy." Guitarist Bernie Leadon was fiddling with an effect that would allow his electric guitar to duplicate the song's memorable banjo part. The group seemed cocky and almost smirky in the best way. These guys had come to *play*. Their leader and singer was Glenn Frey, then twenty-three, in a black shirt and perfectly faded jeans like I'd always sought but never found. He had long straight hair that somehow fell perfectly, like mine never did, and a cauliflower nose not far from my own.

Nobody seemed to know who or where Paul Aherne was. I was ready for this. I found a friendly-looking road manager in a straw sunhat. His name was Richard Fernandez. Aherne, he said, wasn't coming and nobody had mentioned an interview. Fernandez would help me through many journalistic adventures over the next forty years, from the Eagles to Tom Petty & the Heartbreakers to Steely Dan, but neither of us knew that yet. I told him I was from the *Door*. I showed him my press pass and gave him a few copies of the paper.

"Let me try to set you up after the show," he said. "I can't promise anything."

Before long, the lights dimmed in the hall. "We're the Eagles from Los Angeles," announced Glenn Frey. The band began with an a cappella opening that led into "Take It Easy." Though none of them was actually from my home state, the band sounded like the clear, cool sound of California. They ripped into their forty-minute set with take-no-prisoners efficiency. The band was rawer and more stripped down than their debut album. They ended the set to a rousing reception. I headed for the Eagles' dressing room to begin the interview.

"I can't find Glenn, but go on in," said Richard Fernandez.

Guitarist Bernie Leadon, bassist Randy Meisner, and drummer Don Henley were positioned around their tiny dressing room, cooling off from the show. Henley sat in a metal chair and looked like a student who'd been called into a teachers' meeting. The others surrounded him. I introduced myself and turned on my recorder. They were just at the dawn of a career. They answered my questions with verve but often ended with "Glenn can tell you that story." Glenn, they said, was "probably chasing some girl."

Fifteen minutes later, the door opened. Frey had a waggish grin and two fingers curled around the tip of a longneck bottle of Budweiser. He was slightly buzzed, he said, and apologized for being late. Two girls had rebuffed him. He had a slight drawl that came from Jack Nicholson and a personable swagger that came from Detroit, and the interview *took off*. Soon Frey was talking about his band with the fervor and charm of a player-coach. The room was filled with his hopes and dreams for the Eagles, and he seemed to know exactly how to achieve them.

"We've got four voices to sell our records," he said. "So instrumentally we're free to get better playing the music we want. It's like the yearly modifying of a V-8 engine. You make basic modifications on it every year, or, analogically, every album. So we'll just keep changing the stage and the music, with the vocals being the main entity." He added: "American bands break up. British bands stay together. We're going to defy that theory."

Thumping through the walls of the dressing room, I could hear the headlining band, Procol Harum, playing "Conquistador." But the real show was in this tiny dressing room. Something in my head clicked.

This was how to set your course for the future. This was *no looking back*. It was exhilarating, and I couldn't help but believe in all Frey was planning for the band. If someone had told me a secret that night, that this little band with big dreams would one day sell more records than the Beatles, I would not have bet against it.

I asked the Eagles to pose for a group photo that might accompany my article. They happily gathered by their road cases, arms around each other. Gary, my high school photographer friend, snapped the shot. Looking back, it might be the only photo of them with their arms wrapped around each other. Famously volatile, the Eagles would define a generation (or three) with the simple motto Glenn Frey often wore on a T-shirt: SONG POWER.

Procol Harum was still onstage playing "A Whiter Shade of Pale." Once that mournful song had been a trigger for sadness, an anthem for the empty chair. Now it would also remind me of my first great interview.

"Send me your article," Frey said, tearing off a piece of paper from my notebook full of questions. "We're going to do the next album in

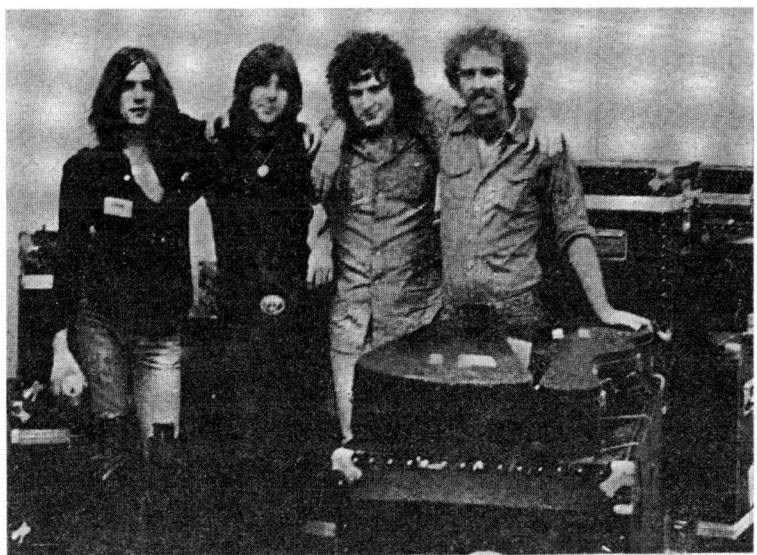

The Eagles in the San Diego *Door*, November 1972.

England." He wrote down his address and phone number. "When we're done with it, let's talk about that too." Before he disappeared, he gave me a nickname too, based on the hit by Mitch Ryder and the Detroit Wheels. "See you later, C. C. Writer."

Being the youngest person in the room was something I often felt insecure about. There was a lot to learn from Glenn Frey's surefooted confidence. His enthusiasm was infectious. You wanted to be on his team. It felt like a clue on how to survive on this path that was sure to deliver hard knocks. Lead with your optimism. Maybe this was *my* V-8 engine upgrade.

The only problem is that I was still too young to drive without a permit.

Gary Elam dropped me off at my home. Still elated from the events of the evening, I let myself in the iron front gate and immediately sensed something was wrong. There was a heaviness in the air. I could see a room full of students and some faculty through the screen door. My mom was sitting facing away, in her usual chair, with many of her inspirational books within reach. When she heard me at the door, she turned and I saw her face.

She was crying. My father was sitting nearby. There had been an attempted coup d'état at school. The "movement" Chicanos had tried to oust her from her position as head of Chicano Studies. They were questioning her background—she was half Spanish—and calling her a "closet Anglo." Some of her closest students, people she'd counseled or even given money to, had turned on her and come to demand her removal.

I escaped to the vinyl vault of my bedroom. One thin floor above me, my mom was feeling crushed and betrayed. Alice Crowe was fighting for her academic life. I could hear her defending herself with righteous indignation. Just yesterday she'd been one of the most sought-after teachers at City College. Now she faced the pitchforks of the very people who'd often told her that she'd given them respect and purpose in their own lives.

Alice Crowe would keep her job as professor but soon resigned as head of Chicano Studies. The betrayal turned into a personal plus. The politics of the department had weighed her down. She was now free to be an even more committed teacher and counselor. Long after her detractors had moved on, she remained as the school's most popular figure.

You never know good luck or bad.

—ALICE CROWE

In October of 1972, the singer-songwriter Kris Kristofferson was headed to San Diego's Civic Theatre. Kristofferson was appearing with his fiancée, Rita Coolidge, the star vocalist from Joe Cocker's *Mad Dogs and Englishmen* tour; the album and concert documentary featured a ragtag band of rock veterans, led by pianist Leon Russell, who managed to outshine Cocker himself. Coolidge's solo performance of the song "Superstar" stole the show from coast to coast.

Rita Coolidge had also just released a new solo album, *The Lady's Not for Sale*. I called A&M Records in Los Angeles and became phone friends with her sunny-sounding label publicist, Dorene Lauer. I asked to interview Coolidge for the *Door*. Dorene agreed and told me she'd be traveling to the hotel with Rita. She'd be there to make sure the interview happened on the afternoon of the show. I was ecstatic and stayed up several nights honing my questions.

My mom and I had seen the concert documentary *Mad Dogs and Englishmen* the year before. Like *The Dick Cavett Show*, the film sailed past my mom's now-melting rock prejudice. It came masked as *culturally significant intellectualism*. My mom had also developed a little crush on the film's unexpected star, bandleader Leon Russell and his long silver hair.

As the concert approached, I began to hope that I'd get lucky and maybe even get a shot at interviewing Kris Kristofferson, who rarely did interviews. He was too busy being legendary himself. He'd already been newly minted as the most revered songwriter since Bob Dylan. His achingly personal songs, like "Sunday Mornin' Comin' Down," "For the Good Times," and "Me and Bobby McGee," were already classics. The movies had come calling too. Kristofferson's rough-hewn good looks and striking blue eyes were already landing him leading roles in films by Sam Peckinpah and Paul Mazursky.

The afternoon before the show, I waited in the lobby of the downtown Westgate Hotel holding on to my shoulder bag packed with questions, cassettes, and copies of the *Door*. Coolidge appeared first, alongside Dorene the publicist. Coolidge had her own smoky rhythm; she moved through the lobby like someone about to slide up to a microphone. Dorene helpfully set us up for the interview in Coolidge's hotel suite.

Kris was coming from another city, she said, and was going to meet her at the show. She answered all my questions, spoke candidly about her music, and shared warm inside stories about her collaborations with Joe Cocker, Graham Nash, Stephen Stills, and others. She blushed when talking about Kristofferson. The relationship was still new and clearly electric. Some of Rita's family were coming to the show to meet him that night, she said. The two of them had just returned from Mexico, where she and Kristofferson had been filming a movie with Sam Peckinpah, *Pat Garrett and Billy the Kid*. Kris played Billy the Kid. Their costar, who played a character called Alias, was the most elusive interview of them all, Bob Dylan.

"Do you think I could ask Kris some questions?" I ventured when we were finished.

"Oh, you'd love Kris," she said. "I don't see why not."

Several hours later, I stood backstage as Kristofferson's band members gathered to take the stage. Backstage was still a new thrill to me. I looked at the floorboards and thought about how Elton John, Ray Charles, Frank Sinatra, and many others had stood in this exact spot. *The spirits were still in the air!* Rita arrived nearby, smiled, and squeezed my arm. Suddenly, Kris Kristofferson was standing next to us. He was slipping on a vest, holding on to a beer, joshing with his bandmates. He was more than tipsy and more than happy about it. It wasn't Hollywood, it was *music*.

Rita pushed me toward Kris with a look—*Take your shot*. He shook my hand and flashed a private smile. The kind of smile that made you want to tell him all your secrets. For the length of my interview pitch, the singer-songwriter-actor sincerely tried to focus on exactly who was talking to him. Nodding vaguely, perhaps consenting and perhaps searching for meaning, he lurched onstage and worked through a bottle of tequila during the two-hour set with Rita Coolidge. A man having a playfully tough time remembering some of his own lyrics wouldn't soon be remembering an interview with the San Diego *Door*.

Kristofferson's show was more revue than concert. Rita sang a handful of songs, guitarist Stephen Bruton or keyboardist Billy Swan might sing a song or two, and Kris sang his hits. Kristofferson played more the role of unassuming host than someone who craved the spotlight. You just *liked* the guy.

After the show, Kristofferson was surrounded with well-wishers and a few disc jockeys. I waited quietly for the promised interview, gripping my orange bag, trying not to look like a pest. Kristofferson walked right past me, heading for the exit, then stopped. He turned and looked at me. He scratched his head. Then he remembered.

"Rita's folks are here and . . ." Kristofferson's voice grew more gravelly and his chin dropped to his chest. "I've never met 'em and . . . I'm supposed to meet 'em at this cantina across town. How 'bout if we do it there."

He wrote down the name and address. El Torito. A Mexican bar-restaurant in Mission Valley. My friend Vince Compagnone, the *Door*'s photographer, drove and we raced to the location so we could arrive before Kristofferson. We pulled up just in front of Kris and his entourage of his soon-to-be-wife's friends and family. Kristofferson motioned for Vince and me to stay close.

A hand reached out to stop me. It was the maître d'. He had a bushy mustache and wore a red bullfighter's vest. Once again, my age had become my enemy.

"Excuse me," he said. "This is a bar. You can't come in."

"He won't drink," said Kristofferson, immediately pulling me forward.

The maître d' stepped between us. "No, my friend."

Kristofferson then changed tactics. "I'd really appreciate it if ya made an exception," he said, deploying the movie-star smile. "My wife's family is here and—he's, uh, writing a story and . . . Maybe there's something I can do for you."

He reached for his wallet. The maître d' stopped him.

"Amigo," he said. "It's the law."

"Aw man," implored Kristofferson. "*Really?*"

It was all my fault. Kris Kristofferson had already lived a life or two. He'd landed a helicopter on Johnny Cash's lawn to sell him a song. Emptied ashtrays for Bob Dylan during the sessions for *Blonde on Blonde*. Taught literature at West Point. Hell, he'd just played Billy the Kid in a Sam Peckinpah *western*. Two days earlier he had probably been twirling six-shooters and doing tequila shots in Mexico with Warren Oates, for Chrissakes! Now he was stuck with me and my orange bag, scolded by an angry faux bullfighter maître d' in a red vest. My sister would have told me this was all my mom's fault, skipping me those three grades. Of course it would all end up here, with me humiliating Kris Kristofferson, author of "Me and Bobby McGee," at the Mission Valley El Torito.

And then the maître d' finally relented.

"Okay, amigo," he said. "You can sit out here in the lobby. With no bar service, of course."

He pointed to two large red leatherette chairs. I thought about one of my mom's favorite aphorisms. I'd heard it a little *too* much growing up. *Out of the depths of despair now came the invincible summer.* Less than an hour after coming offstage from a sold-out show at the Civic Theatre, with his future in-laws waiting in the next room, Kristofferson agreeably sat in the lobby, nodding hello to all the tourists and customers, all to make good on his promise of an interview for the *Door*, a local giveaway paper. With no bar service.

"Okay, let's do this, hoss," said Kris Kristofferson.

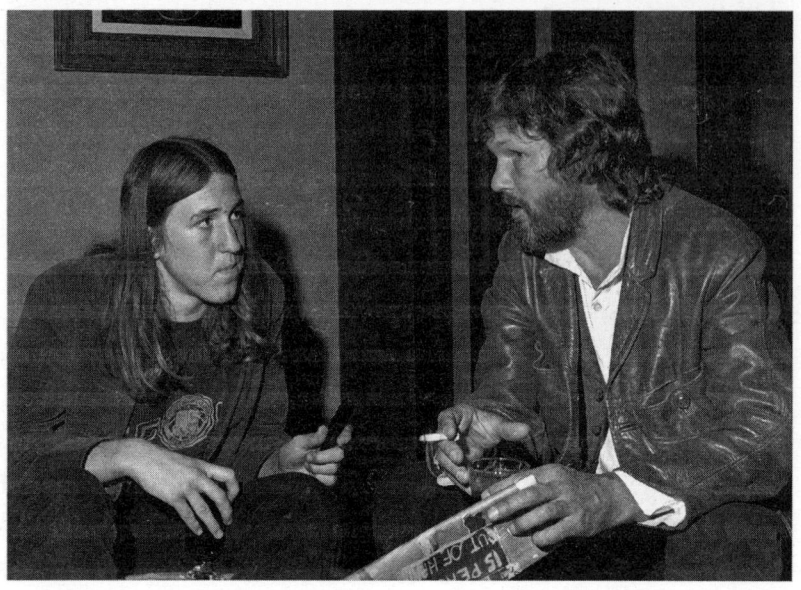

I fumbled through my questions. In the photos Vince snapped that night, you can see me trying to be professional with a forlorn face, longer than usual, like a painting by El Greco. Patrons of the restaurant would pass, take a few steps, and then turn around to gawk at one of Hollywood's brightest stars, right there in the big red chair. I sat knowing he'd soon want to bail to the more protective bar environment inside. Except he didn't.

My first question was about whether he preferred playing live concerts or making records. It earned a short answer and a lengthy silence. I battled the urge to fill the quiet with something, anything, but chose to shut up. We were now in the Siberia of Silence. Finally, Kristofferson jumped in and began confessing fears about the rigors of constant touring and the toll it had taken on his personal relationships. The more I didn't speak, the more he enjoyed our conversation.

Kristofferson was already a master at writing plainspoken, unsentimental songs about sadness. I asked him if he needed to be sad to write a sad song. He sparked to the question.

"I write sad songs when I'm happy." He laughed a little. "I guess because when I'm sad, I'm too sad to write a good song!"

Kristofferson, once a Rhodes scholar, was soon talking with me like an intellectual equal. He began quizzing me about books we'd both read. He discussed Kurt Vonnegut's *Slaughterhouse-Five* and Joseph Heller's *Catch-22*. Then he pivoted to movies. We talked about director Peter Bogdanovich and *The Last Picture Show*. I was amazed at what was happening.

"He's got some kind of wild imagination," Kristofferson said appreciatively. "And how 'bout that soundtrack!"

"How *about* those tunes," I chirped.

"When you're painting a picture or writing a song," he said, "you're trying to move somebody emotionally. It's a feeling either of sadness or whatever, but in a *movie*, you can use it all. You get two shots, the music and the visual trip too. You're right there, you're not even conscious of who's sitting next to you. You can be scared or shocked, and then you got Hank Williams, and you know it's going to strike a chord."

I didn't know it yet, but Kristofferson had flagged the very passion that would guide the rest of my creative life. The marriage of film and music would soon be my favorite part of writing and directing films. All I knew then, sitting in the big red chair, was that I'd discovered a blissful place in the world. I liked asking about things I wanted to know. I liked listening even better.

One of Rita's relatives soon came to check on him, with a *How long* look, and I knew my time was coming to an end. Then, just as our conversation was winding down, something truly surprising happened. He started to talk about Bob Dylan.

Kristofferson proceeded to uncork stories from the secrecy-laden set in Durango, Mexico, where he'd been filming the Peckinpah movie with Bob Dylan. Dylan, the favorite child of *Rolling Stone*, the man who did no interviews at all, the man who revealed nothing. I silently prayed for no interruptions from margarita-slugging fans. Kristofferson's memories were fresh and he couldn't stop listing the thrills, chief among them that he'd just finished recording an entire album of new material with Dylan down in Mexico. Dylan hadn't recorded new material in years. *And nobody knew it yet.*

Kristofferson had given a young freelance writer from San Diego a very important scoop. I checked my cassette recorder. Still rolling. This was fantastic. This was *news*.

Finally, he leaned forward and pleaded for mercy. "I'm going to get divorced before I've even gotten married," he said. "I gotta spend some time with Rita's family." I was sure I'd never see him again, but he added an invitation for more. "Could we finish this in Los Angeles tomorrow?"

"Absolutely!"

I poked my head into the illegal bar area. Rita was still sitting patiently with her family. I waved *Thank you* from afar. She laughed. I was delirious with the Dylan scoop that Kristofferson had placed in my lap. Then, as he passed into the bar, Kristofferson threw *another* bonbon my way.

"Hey, I'm playing the Troubadour tomorrow night if you want to go," he whispered. "It's a 'contract' gig. I agreed to three more shows when they booked me for the first fuckin' time. So if you have a guest or something . . . lemme know."

"I'll see you in Los Angeles."

Kristofferson told me to call him at the Continental Hyatt House tomorrow. His voice was a commanding rumble. "We'll finish the interview at the hotel and I'll put you on the list at the Troubadour." He was finally headed inside to hang out with his future relatives. "I'm under the name Colonel Hijinx."

I was still new at the job, of course, and blissfully ignorant of the cues I'd learn later. In the free-flowing world of musicians, particularly ones in the whirlwind of early success, every day is a new beginning, a day free of the memory of any previous commitments made the day before. "Call me tomorrow," I would later learn, usually meant "Goodbye." But Kristofferson had opened the door and I didn't think twice about barreling through it.

The next day I called Judith Sims, the Los Angeles editor of *Rolling Stone*, and introduced myself. I'd been sending the music editor Ben Fong-Torres tear sheets of my work but hadn't yet gotten a reply. Now I had something juicy for the magazine. Sims took down my information and put me on the phone with a fact-checker. The news checked out. I was promised a blurb in the next issue of the magazine. I'd kicked the door open at *Rolling Stone*.

"You're not going to Los Angeles," my mom said. She explained that what I thought was journalism was actually just about making managers rich.

"Mom," I implored, "Kris Kristofferson *taught at West Point*."

Nearby, my West Point–graduate father perked up.

"He invited me to his show," I said. "I have to finish the interview we started at El Torito. Give me a chance." I paused. "'Me and Bobby McGee.' *Busted flat in Baton Rouge, waiting for a train . . .* He wrote that. And Janis Joplin sang it. And you loved it."

She melted. In another fortuitous turn of events, Bill Maguire, the *Door*'s publisher, was heading up to Los Angeles with his new girlfriend that very day. It was set. I called the Continental Hyatt House and asked for Colonel Hijinx.

"I'm sorry but he's not taking any calls."

"Could you tell the colonel it is Cameron Crowe from San Diego, and it will be me and two others coming to the show?"

Bill Maguire's girlfriend, Sharon, was a youngish lawyer. On paper, it was a relationship that seemed sure to fail. Maguire was a large and robust presence, a burly bon vivant type. Sharon looked like a wispy-thin and slightly aloof coed from an expensive East Coast school. Maguire smoked pot on the way; she opened the window and fanned her face. When we got to Los Angeles, I called Colonel Hijinx again. This time he picked up.

"Come on over, let's do some more interview!" Kristofferson said. It couldn't have been because he sought publicity from a tiny underground paper that perhaps nobody read carefully except the FBI. It was clearly Rita Coolidge who was still shining her well-known mother-hen beacon of empathy my way.

Bill Maguire dropped me off and went off to sell some ad space, which was also code for weed, and squire Sharon around Los Angeles. I finished the interview with Kristofferson in his small hotel room. He was happiest talking about artists other than himself. We talked more about Bob Dylan. He told stories about Johnny Cash. He laughed about recording an entire early album while he had pneumonia, and then he confessed he'd been touring a year and a half straight. He was overbooked. And then there were the movies he'd agreed to make. Colonel Hijinx yearned for a break.

This time I read the room. I shut off the tape recorder. He bid me goodbye until the show. In an afterthought he asked, "Do you have a place to stay?"

"Not really."

He flipped me his key. "Stay here, hoss. I'm leaving after the show anyway. Room'll be empty."

You have no idea how happy this made Bill Maguire when I told him later. "That is *great*." He clapped me on the back. "Kris Kristofferson gave you his fucking hotel room!"

I basked in his approval for a moment.

"How many beds in the room?" he asked.

"Two little beds."

"Sharon," he crowed, "we got a place to stay!"

I was curious how this was going to work but didn't think about it much during the intimate show Kristofferson put on at the Troubadour. Maguire downed several drinks. Sharon had one or two. Or maybe three or four. I said goodbye to Kristofferson and thanked Rita. She was still laughing about the night before.

"Enjoy my hotel room," said Kristofferson. "And if I left anything behind you know where to find me. With her!"

Bill, Sharon, and I arrived in the hotel room around two in the morn-ing and agreed that it was lights out. We were all exhausted; it had been a long day. I settled down in my bed and Bill and Sharon took the other one. It was my first time bunking down with adults, but my head was filled with quotes and the promise of getting into *Rolling Stone*.

"Good night, you guys."

"Good night."

The Continental Hyatt House certainly knew their clientele. The drapes at the Hyatt House were *blackout* dark. It was a mecca for late sleepers. Darkness enveloped the room. Silently, I flipped through the many victories of the night. This life! These people! My silent reverie was soon interrupted.

It was the sound of the bed creaking next to me. Then came the hushed grunting. That mismatched couple was getting busy, and only three feet away. Soon, Sharon joined the carnal symphony with bird-like chirps of delight. Perhaps the flat mattress felt like an aphrodisiac to them; this never could have happened on Bill Maguire's waterbed without someone getting seasick.

Staring at the ceiling, listening to them in the dark, I suddenly felt sad. Sad that I was invisible in the next bed. Sad for the world outside the blackout curtains. Sad for my family. Sad for my older sister who barely made it into her teens. Sad for poor Bill Maguire, who sold weed to try to save the world from Richard Nixon while snaking a hotel room on someone else's dime where he could seduce Sharon in the tiny twin bed of the man who wrote "For the Good Times."

It was an elemental, human ache. I wasn't sure why this feeling of existential dread also carried an intense feeling of . . . *this is life*. Some-times the record, or the person, that pisses you off the most becomes your favorite, your best friend, your obsession. It was a strange itch of not belonging that my favorite music scratched. This was the world of the happy/sad. For the rest of the night, life felt like a great song by Todd Rundgren. Part ache, part exhilaration. Would I ever get a girlfriend?

Nobody in that room slept a wink.

Do not let your actions be based on your fears.

—ALICE CROWE

A few days away from turning fifteen, I'd grown my hair long and taken to wearing Pendleton shirts like the ones I'd seen Neil Young wearing in photos. There was an exciting show coming to a popular local club, Funky Quarters. The headlining band was Looking Glass, fresh off their big hit "Brandy." I knew I'd have trouble getting in to see the show. Funky Quarters was an over-twenty-one place that served beer and wine. I was six years short of being legal. Still, I'd set up an afternoon interview with Looking Glass. They were represented by Bobbi Cowan, my champion from the world of Gibson & Stromberg. She lived in the San Fernando Valley with my soon-to-be best friend, the photographer Neal Preston.

The opening act on the show was a Chicago singer-songwriter named Jim Croce. He'd had a minor airplay hit with the jaunty title song of his album *You Don't Mess Around with Jim*. Croce had a bushy "working-man" mustache and a face that reminded me of someone you'd see on a can of tomato paste. I'd given the album a bad review in the *Door*. Another song from the album, "Operator," was starting to take off too.

Looking Glass, the headliner, was a New York–based band with a loose pop style. They'd released an album early that May and the first single hadn't done much. As it sometimes happens, a regional DJ discovered a different song on the album and started playing it. By mid-July, "Brandy," a kind of sea-shanty ode, was a big summer hit.

I met up with Elliot Lurie, the writer and singer of Looking Glass, outside the club. He struck me as a friendly, sharp East Coaster. We decided to do the interview after the show, but as I headed inside with him to watch the sound check, I knew it might be the same old story. A bouncer would surely see me and have me thrown out. It took about thirty seconds for that exact thing to happen.

"He's underage!" The club's bouncer was exceedingly large and happy to make my expulsion his afternoon project. He blocked me with his hand. I shook my head. It was business as usual.

"He's coming in," said Elliot Lurie.

"It's a twenty-one club."

"I'll stay outside," I offered.

"Look, what can we do here," said Lurie. "He's a press guy and he wants to see the show."

"Tony!" The bouncer signaled for the club owner, and soon he was there. He had a wild head of hair. "He says he's a press guy."

Lurie explained that I was there to interview the band. He was a skilled negotiator. Many years later, Lurie would show up as a big-time head of music for the film company making my first movie as a director, *Say Anything*. . . . Life was like that. Some people returned, most disappeared, but right now all I could think was that I hated my baby face. Even on a day trip to Tijuana recently, the vendors had catcalled me on the street. "Hey, *poosy face*!"

Tony looked me up and down. I offered him a couple copies of the *Door*. He knew the paper. His club's events were listed in the paper. "You gonna mention the name of the club?" he asked me. "A lot?"

It was one of my dad's lessons of business. He called it Crowe's Law, and it went like this: *Be nice to people who are in a position to help you.*

"Absolutely," I said. "I'll mention your club *a lot*."

"All right," said Tony. "But you are *not* allowed to leave the dressing room. If you do, I'll have ya thrown out. This is a new club, they got their eyes on me, and I don't want to get busted."

"It's a deal," I said.

"Wait," said Lurie. "How's he going to hear the show?"

"Through the fucking door!" Tony was done with the negotiation. "With his ears. Against. The door."

Tony, Elliot Lurie, and the bouncer flanked me as I was led to a small room at the end of a hallway. It felt like a perp walk.

"I'll come back and get you," said Lurie. The door closed.

I went over my notes for Looking Glass and waited. I rewrote my questions with better penmanship. And I waited some more.

Suddenly the door flew open.

It was a man in a denim shirt with a familiar bushy mustache. "Look at this, Maury," he said. "We've got company."

Maury appeared next, a bantam-sized man with sprayed-on jeans and a guitar case. They both looked at me and my tape recorder. "Looks like we got an interview!"

Jim Croce, the opening act, had been mistakenly led to my prison room. He was engaging as hell and immediately introduced me to his friend and sidekick, Maury Muehleisen. They had an easy rhythm together, two guys who'd been to many cities and many small dressing rooms just like this one.

Croce invited me to begin the interview. I didn't have the heart to tell him I had no questions for him.

So I improvised. Soon, Jim Croce was telling stories. And they were good ones. He'd been a substitute teacher in Chicago, he said, and also a truck driver. His wife had once been his singing partner. They'd both had doubts about his increasingly pie-in-the-sky career. Finally, his last-chance third album, *You Don't Mess Around with Jim,* had spawned a surprise hit with the title song. The warning lights on his career were turning green. One of the things he'd always looked forward to, he said, were the interviews he could do with Maury. Oh, the stories they had. If only people cared.

"And here you are!" he said.

Jim Croce was engaging to everyone, even the overworked club waitress who came in for his drink orders and ended up sitting down on a bench and trading tales with Croce about the long work hours. She wrote down the drink orders from Jim and Maury and then looked at me.

"I'll bring you water," she said.

Another hour passed as they tuned their guitars and told more tales from the road. I talked a little about my own path into writing about music. Then something unexpected happened. The waitress brought in something that had been sent over by the local branch of Croce's record company. It was a thin yellow T-shirt with a rubbery image of Jim Croce's face on the front.

"Our first T-shirt!" he yelped.

We all applauded, and the waitress hustled back to work.

"Our first shirt," Maury repeated admiringly, even though his own face wasn't on the shirt. Croce immediately caught the disappointment in his sidekick's demeanor, and so did I. Awkwardness had entered the room with nowhere to go.

"You should have been on it too," said Croce.

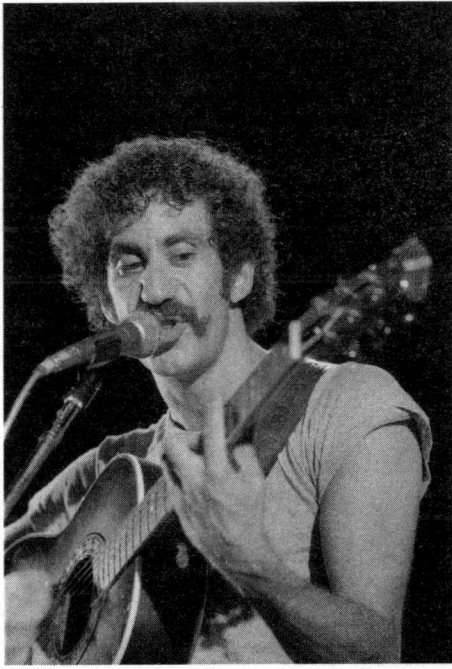

"Looks like we got an interview!" Jim Croce at Funky Quarters, San Diego, 1972.

Maury shrugged it off. "You know what," he said, "they wouldn't have made it if they didn't think the record was doing well. You know it's true!"

"Well, it sure is strange," Jim said, holding the T-shirt like it was poor Yorick's skull in *Hamlet*. "Staring at your own rubber face."

We all laughed. Croce stuffed the shirt in his guitar case. It wasn't just an interview anymore. We'd shared a real moment, all three of us.

Success was still fresh to them both, and the new single, "Operator," had officially made Croce more than a one-ish-hit wonder. It was starting to look like this music thing was more than just another stop in the life of a guy who'd maybe been headed back to driving a truck. I had the feeling watching them that this new notoriety was as exciting and weird as the strange rubbery shirt in his guitar case.

"We're breaking you out of prison," Jim Croce said as he and Maury headed for the stage to open the show. They pulled me into the shadows near the stage. I knew it was a bad idea. I watched as Croce took his personable *We're all equals here* dynamic into the spotlight. With Maury on a stool next to him, Croce weaved the songs and stories together into one big moving narrative. He played "You Don't Mess Around with Jim," the song I'd once made fun of in a review. Such is the power of human persuasion: now I not only warmed to the song, I liked it, along with another song of his about everlasting love, "Time in a Bottle." It was the moment when fandom takes hold. Suddenly I was rooting for Croce and Maury, for their lives, for their families, for their career. And somewhere in the middle of this reverie, I felt an iron hand clamp onto my shoulder. It was Tony, his eyes flashing with beastlike anger.

"The vice squad is in the house," he said. "Get back in your fucking room, you little prick!"

After the show, Croce's dressing room was filled with guests and new friends. Looking Glass were playing their big hit, "Brandy," but nobody left his dressing room. Especially me, for every imaginable reason. Croce wrote down the name of his motel on El Cajon Boulevard, the Aztec, and invited me to come visit the next afternoon so we could continue our adventure together. I vowed to skip school and meet them there.

"Wait," said Croce. "It's the summer. Why are you going to school?"

It was a question I had asked my mother many, many times. The idea was that I would have so many units, I could graduate early and take some time off before law school.

The next afternoon, I took a bus out to the motel on El Cajon Boulevard, near the college. Jim and Maury were by the pool with guitars. Jim was shirtless, soaking up the sun and still basking in the success of last night's show. We laughed about my dressing-room prison. I even saw the yellow T-shirt with Croce's rubbery face on it again. The waitress from the night before was wearing it as she said goodbye. Freshly showered, she was headed to work.

"Good luck," she cracked cheerfully. "Get yourself a fake ID. You almost lost us our liquor license last night."

We all laughed again, buddies from the night before. She disappeared around the corner with a wave.

"Oh God," Croce said quietly.

Maury strummed his guitar.

"What did I do?" Croce said.

We went to the hotel room to continue our interview from the night before. The conversation was more thoughtful. Soon Croce was talking about missing home. The other day, he said, someone had asked if he'd ever had an organic garden. The idea was ridiculous to him.

"I grew up in South Philly," he said. "I'd never even seen a *carrot* except for in a supermarket." He put his songwriter's touch on the story. "You can't grow carrots in concrete."

At one point he used the word "abomination" in casual conversation, then chastised himself for it. "I just used that word because I come back to the hotel room and there's no magazines, all that's there is . . . a Bible."

I asked him if he was religious.

"I'm not religious," he said, and laughed. "I'm quite *sacrilegious*."

Soon he was turning himself inside out. "I try to be as positive as I can be, try not to get ruffled too much. Only when I go home." He laughed ruefully. "You get home, you don't know where you are."

I asked him where he'd be in five years, if he thought he'd written a song that felt timeless to him. He said he'd written about eight songs that might qualify. The new ones were simpler, more lyrical. He was hopeful about the growth steps he was taking. I turned off the tape recorder. Something had passed between us over the last day and a half. We exchanged addresses and promised to keep in touch.

It was a little bit of a crossroads for me. We didn't discuss the indiscretion or the waitress who'd sashayed off with his first T-shirt, the one without Maury, but I'd clearly had a front-row seat to his moral quandary. It was an issue that would return again and again. What did I owe an audience of music fans like me? Did they need to meet the waitress too, or was the gift of a soul-searching personal interview enough? The best interviews allow you to appreciate the artist and the work in interesting new ways. I often thought about Jim and Maury and the carrots that don't grow in concrete. Sometimes the story isn't the one you came to write but the one that finds you instead.

I never did write that story about Looking Glass.

Never tell me the odds.

—ALICE CROWE/HAN SOLO

To pick up spending cash, rock journalists often took anonymous writing assignments from the record company publicity departments. A "bio," a two-page summary of an artist's career, was helpful when sent out to press outlets. A moonlighting rock writer could net a couple hundred dollars writing a bio for the record company. I often wrote for the in-house Warner Bros. Records publication *Circular*. When they needed an interview done with Gram Parsons, the reclusive former member of the Byrds and the Flying Burrito Brothers, I jumped at the chance. Parsons was putting out his first solo album, *GP*, with an all-star backing band. He wanted to talk about it.

Parsons was as influential as he was mysterious. His real name was Ingram Cecil Connor III. His reputation was shot through with famous associations, groundbreaking career moves, traces of old Southern money, and glorious decadence. He'd hung out with the Rolling Stones in France. One of their greatest songs, "Wild Horses," had been influenced by Parsons. He'd been a kind of one-man cheering section for the grand and not-previously-cool royalty of country music. In a world where the zeitgeist was hard rock, Parsons advocated for George Jones, Merle Haggard, and Porter Wagoner. And in no small part because of Gram, country rock had arrived as a genre of the future. There would not have been the Eagles without Parsons.

January 1973. The interview with Parsons would happen in the afternoon, at the Van Nuys ranch-style home of his road manager, Phil Kaufman. My notebook was full of too many questions as usual. I was a Byrds fan, and also a big fan of country rock. I had taken the bus to Los Angeles and grabbed a ride to the location with the photographer Kim Gottlieb and her husband, Jeff Walker, a Parsons fan and the editor of his own magazine, called *Music World*. Kaufman's rambling abode on Chandler Avenue was deep in the Los Angeles Valley, but it felt like the backcountry of Texas. We were all excited for this rare Parsons sighting.

"He's not up yet," barked Phil Kaufman. He was a short stick of dynamite in a large cowboy hat. "Let's get you a coffee."

Kaufman returned with an enormous mug and shoved it into my hand. It was more like a soup urn than a cup. My grandmother used to drink Sanka from a cup this size. It had a saying on it: "Only One Cup a Day."

Phil Kaufman's personal history read like a roller-coaster ride through the dark side of rock culture. He first arrived on the scene as Mick Jagger's chauffeur during the making of *Beggars Banquet*. Kaufman met Parsons through Keith Richards. They became lifestyle buddies and more. Kaufman talked his way into managing the Flying Burrito Brothers, though he had no experience in the job. He was just one of those guys who knew how to stir the drink and make sure no room ever got too boring.

Kaufman had also served some time at Terminal Island prison, where he made the acquaintance of Charles Manson. Manson's album *Lie: The Love and Terror Cult*, his failed bid for rock stardom, was produced by Kaufman when both were out of prison. Phil had a knack for charming difficult people. His outrageousness made famous people comfortable. A person like this could sometimes be found at the side of greatness, like a spiritual sidekick who feared nothing and nobody. Neil Young had a producer pal named David Briggs, and Dylan had his best friend and tour manager, Bobby Neuwirth. Gram had the Road Mangler himself—Phil Kaufman.

Kaufman herded us into his large living room filled with musical instruments and comfortable couches. A drum kit sat in the center of the room. Musicians were gathering. Parsons was in town to rehearse and prepare for a tour. Our interview was set to happen before the rehearsal. But Parsons was still asleep, and I wondered if time was getting tight. Kaufman waved away the issue.

"It's meant to happen and it's going to happen," he announced. Everything he said was punctuated with a wink or a laugh. "And look what we got!"

Gram Parsons slipped into the room wearing a floppy hat, a long-sleeve Harley-Davidson T-shirt, and a *Mona Lisa* smile. He sat on the sofa and rubbed his eyes. His jeans had a patch on the knee: "Apple Wine Is Fine." He had just woken up, and the whole room downshifted to a lower gear. The day that began with coffee now had the feeling of a mint julep. He arrived like a talented character actor enters a movie, with a secret behind his eyes. Phil introduced us.

"Hi, howareya."

Parsons spoke in a quiet Southern accent. His hands were smooth and soft. The more he woke up, the more he had the air of a well-educated, stony young prince. He spoke about country artists the way a planetary scientist discusses the cosmos. I knew immediately how he was able to talk the Byrds, a pop-rock band, into playing country music.

Parsons was excited about his new album. He'd recruited the key members of Elvis's top-flight touring band to back him on the album, he said, but couldn't afford them for his tour. Talking as he sank deeper and deeper into a fluffy sofa, he showed no nervousness about finally starting a solo career after energizing and leaving two high-profile bands. What he did show was sleepiness. I worried about that too-comfortable sofa.

I asked him about *Sweetheart of the Rodeo*, the seminal album by the Byrds. It was mired in legend and controversy. The album began as a concept by the band's leader, Roger McGuinn, who wanted to make a double album that spanned all genres of American music. Parsons took the wheel instead and advocated for a straight-up country album. The result was a game-changer, the birth of an entire genre. The combining of country and rock was a shotgun marriage between two warring factions. The traditional style of a Tammy Wynette didn't belong in the same universe as the Rolling Stones . . . but Parsons knew it could. And though some whispered behind his back that he was a dilettante, or a highbrow druggie capable of disappearing for weeks to party in France with the Rolling Stones, Parsons's experiment with *Sweetheart* created what is now known, fifty years later, as "country." During our interview, Parsons dismissed the album for the first time publicly. "McGuinn re-sang three of the songs and fucked it up," he told me.

After about an hour of conversation, he started to show some nervous energy. He told a story about a compelling woman he'd met, a singer he'd seen performing at Clyde's, a club in Washington, DC. Chris Hillman from the Byrds had told Parsons about her. Parsons was impressed and invited her to sing on *GP* the previous October. They hadn't spent much one-on-one time together, but she was flying in that day to audition for a spot on the tour. The closer it got to her arrival, the more animated Parsons became.

"Her name is Emmylou," he explained. "She makes *amazing* eye contact. Now, that's a gift. And Emmylou"—he liked saying her name—"she also has perfect pitch. And she knows how to sing the toughest duets in country music. I want her to sing on the tour. You'll meet her. She was a waitress, picking up tips and playing in clubs."

Kaufman invited Parsons to start the band rehearsal, but it was a slow-moving endeavor. Parsons tried out songs, fiddled with microphones, and kept asking Kaufman when Emmylou would arrive.

A shy and exceedingly quiet woman showed up an hour later. She'd just come from the airport, and Phil was doing his dance of excitement, making her feel important. She had dark folk singer hair and a stoic get-down-to-business expression, interrupted only by an Audrey Hepburn smile.

"This is Emmylou Harris," said Gram.

"Emmylou!" Kaufman shouted. "Grab a guitar and get to work!"

Soon they were holding guitars, facing each other in chairs. The chemistry was crackling. You can see it even now in the photos taken by Kim Gottlieb that day. I slipped a hand into my shoulder bag and pressed record. The run of songs was stellar. "White Line Fever," the Merle Haggard song, was first. Then came a heartfelt version of the Bobby Bare hit, "Streets of Baltimore." By the time Parsons called for a cover of "I'll Feel a Whole Lot Better," the old Byrds song, their connection had grown into a quiet bonfire. The last song was "Love Hurts," the Boudleaux Bryant hit first performed by the Everly Brothers. Parsons was smart to put down his guitar. The rehearsal was a master class in what Parsons wanted from his solo career, an immaculate sampling of authentic aching country. Still fresh from the airport, Emmylou had crossed every hurdle. The afternoon ended with a photo session on the porch of the home.

Gram Parsons's tour lurched into existence on rickety legs but gained strength as it went. Reviewers couldn't get enough of that singer from Maryland, Emmylou, who ignited Parsons with their duets. As I moved on to other stories, I couldn't shake that bonfire afternoon

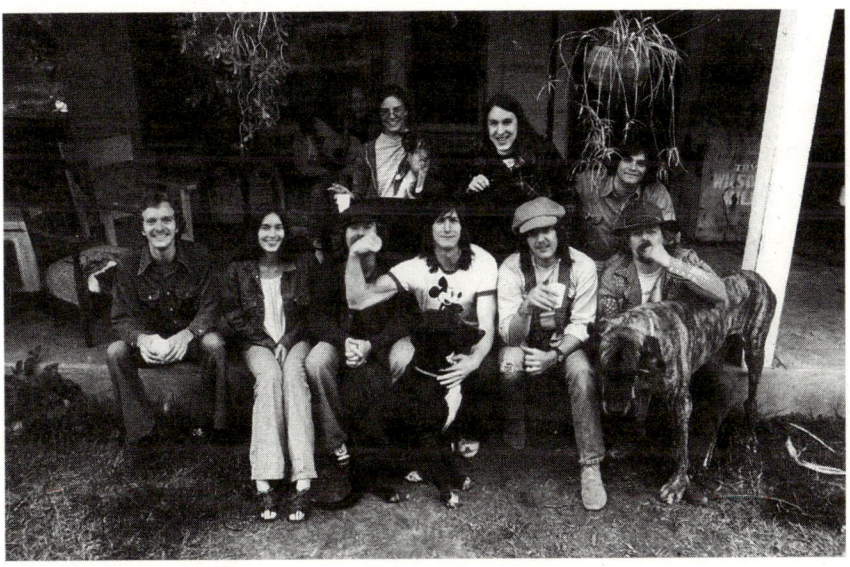

An afternoon to remember. Gram and Emmylou and Co., 1973.

of Parsons and Harris singing, face-to-face, finding their destiny and more, in real time.

His sleepy charisma stayed with me too. Parsons had a very particular sense of stony nobility. He was like a prince in a waking dream, and it wasn't until the next century that I would meet another artist with the same temperament. The singer-songwriter Ryan Adams felt like part of the same DNA chain. I felt a strong sense of déjà vu. It was like meeting Parsons again in the guise of a younger artist.

The depth of the romance between Emmylou and Gram, and what grew from that afternoon, is a tale that belonged to them. As with George and Tammy, or Porter and Dolly, or many of the country stars Parsons loved, there's more pleasure in the myth. I profiled her for *Rolling Stone* and visited a recording session for her second album, *Pieces of the Sky*. A few years back, we crossed paths at a Rufus Wainwright concert. She looked at me like I was a remnant of a life gone by. Though it was only one afternoon, she introduced me to a friend as "a kid who used to follow Gram and me around."

I wanted to pay a little tribute to that Van Nuys afternoon in a short

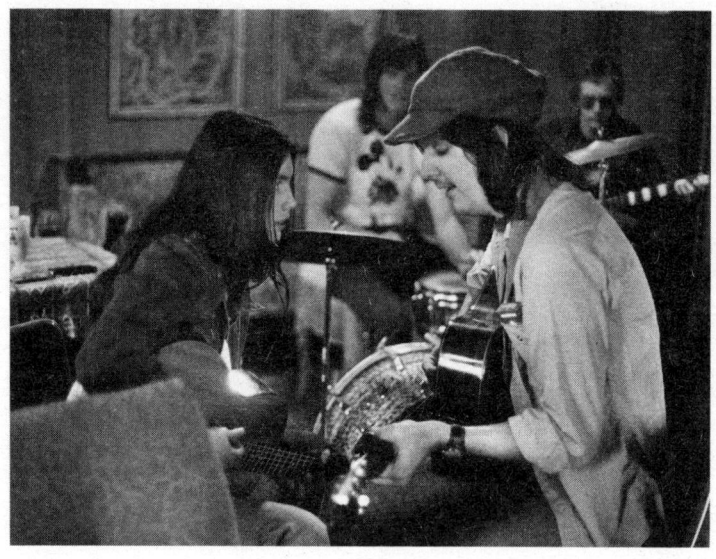

hotel room sequence in *Almost Famous*. The Seattle singer-songwriters Pete Droge and Elaine Summers are singing a song written in the style of Parsons and Harris. It's called "Small Town Blues." It's just a quick moment in the movie, but it's an Easter egg that still takes me back to that grand souvenir of that day when Gram and Emmylou faced each other, throwing off sparks, and there were only blue skies ahead. Maybe blue skies are always a myth.

But if I ever fell in love, I thought, I wanted to fall in love like *that*.

Turn every loss into a victory.

—ALICE CROWE

Thanks to being sentenced to summer school for so many years, I had enough credits to graduate high school at the end of my junior year. Faced with college, I knew 1973 would be the year I'd have to choose a career path. On one side was the great lawyer J. D. Atkinson, Kentucky hero and grandfather to my dad. His photo was framed near the front door. He sat at his desk, looking up from his legal work, with an expression that said, *Stop listening to Led Zeppelin and get serious.*

On the other side was the World's Greatest Rock Critic, the connoisseur of all that destroyed brain cells. My head was still with Atkinson; my heart was almost all Lester Bangs.

A-Able Answering Service was coming off a banner year. My dad had predicted the future, and the future was rewarding him with the success he'd sought after leaving the military to devote more time to his family.

One day something appeared in the local newspaper that caught his attention. A New York company had created a new contraption for the home market. It was a small, transistorized machine that was constructed to answer and take recorded messages from phone calls . . . *at home*. It was already causing a stir in the telephonic community.

A few months later, I was picking up cassettes at a Radio Shack and spotted the Phone-Mate Model 400. It was the first commercial residential telephone answering machine. I had started to miss calls myself, and I didn't want to make a big deal of asking for a spot on my dad's answering service exchange. I brought home the machine. I showed it to him, unsure how he might respond to me purchasing the machine hell-bent on putting him out of business. I had given comfort to the enemy.

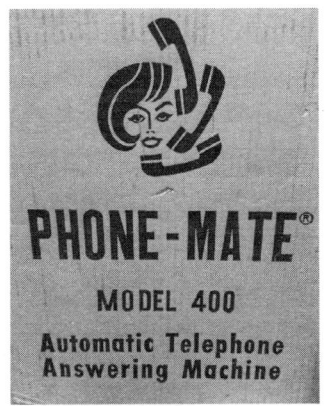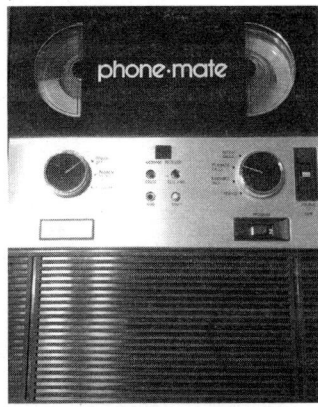

The Phone-Mate 400: the future arrives with little warning.

My father shrugged it off with an easygoing smile. He'd dabbled in hotel ownership, leaned into investment, and succeeded in real estate, but the Answering Service business was his pride and passion.

He explained that the brain reacted in a certain way to human speech. Studies had shown that even in small children, conversation calms the basic instinct of fight or flight. We both regarded the boxy Phone-Mate machine. He was unbowed and supremely confident.

"People don't like talking to a machine," my father said. "Nothing beats the sound of the human voice."

A positive mindset is essential to success.

—ALICE CROWE

By February of 1973, I'd ricocheted back to Los Angeles, staying at the home of Bobbi Cowan and Neal Preston. I liked visiting Columbia Records, down on Sunset. The record company was only a small part of the building that broadcast Channel 2 in Los Angeles. You'd walk past the live news sets, maybe brush past a game show host, and then finally find a corporate-looking office at the end of the hall. That was the publicity office for Columbia Records. The head publicist at Columbia was Michael Ochs, brother of Phil, the pioneering folk singer thought to have been the subject of Dylan's "Positively Fourth Street." It was common practice to grab as many promotional copies of the new albums as you could hold. I grabbed an armful that day, including the first album from a new singer-songwriter, Bruce Springsteen.

There was buzz around Springsteen, a young artist from New Jersey. His album, *Greetings from Asbury Park, NJ*, sported an elaborate postcard-style cover. He was already a favored child at his record company, signed by the elder statesman of talent acquisition, John Hammond. Hammond had a signature look, a buzz cut and a jazz hound's tweed jacket. He'd signed Bob Dylan and Leonard Cohen and many other heavyweights to the label. Like John Prine before him, Springsteen had also acquired that rare early title—"the new Dylan." It was often a kiss of death but Springsteen had his own spin on things; his music often had a carnival-like joy to match the blizzard of lyrics.

Columbia Records booked a media-only event to present Bruce Springsteen to the press. His Los Angeles debut was set for the Troubadour, the folk and blues club in West Hollywood. Springsteen was opening for another of the label's high-hopes signings, a group called Pan. Along with Springsteen's first album, Michael Ochs had given me a promotional postcard that was also an invitation to the event. I immediately said yes. "It's pronounced *steen*," he instructed me, "not *stein*."

Getting into the Troubadour was a hit-or-miss thing for me. There was a two-drink minimum inside the club. I didn't drink alcohol, but I loved their hot chocolate. Sometimes I was able to order two hot chocolates and then hide in the shadows. A sharp-eyed bouncer would often eject me, but I'd developed a protector in a waitress named Pam. She was tough and rebellious and enjoyed the game of hiding me. Pam later became famous for throwing a very drunk John Lennon out of the club during a performance by Ann Peebles.

"Do you know who I am?" Lennon demanded.

"Yeah," Pam countered. "You're the asshole with a Kotex on your head."

The Troubadour bar was adjacent to the club's performance area, and that woodsy room was *alive*, an Algonquin Round Table for local luminaries and wannabe artists. My first night there felt like a page out of Guy Peellaert's *Rock Dreams*. I recognized Phil Ochs himself, Michael's famous brother. Ochs was a lumbering presence with a cigar and a long brown leather jacket, a bull looking for a china shop. A few minutes later another luminary entered the room. He looked like he'd strolled right out of one of Annie Leibovitz's memorable photos for *Rolling Stone*.

"That's Brian Wilson," someone whispered. And there he was, the heart-wrenching genius who'd created my older sister's favorite songs. He was unshaven, wearing a bathrobe, and was holding a silver beer stein. He shuffled through the room like a monk observing his flock, and then he left.

There was a newer wave of regulars too. They were tall and lean, with perfectly faded Levi's. Along with the songs, they also had a *look*. Down the street from the Troubadour was a clothing store called Maxfield Bleu. Maxfield sold a specific style of collarless shirt, first worn by Jackson Browne, that became a kind of uniform among the younger singer-songwriter crowd. The personal songwriting movement had moved solidly into the mainstream thanks to the success of the Eagles and David Geffen's new record label, Asylum Records. The Troubadour bar was now *their* clubhouse.

On February 26, I safely glided past the bouncers and settled into my seat in the Troubadour bleachers. An earnest young man in a black leather jacket took the stage with self-effacing nerves or grace or both. Bruce Springsteen opened with an acoustic song, "Mary Queen of Arkansas." He was accompanied by a band member, Danny Federici, on accordion. Springsteen, the great curly-haired New Jersey hope of Columbia Records, began his Los Angeles debut.

The audience was not hushed. Glasses clinked. Clive Davis, the president of Columbia Records, had flown in for the occasion. He looked uneasy at the noise. Then Springsteen's amp malfunctioned. He had a lot of lyrics to remember. The songs were still new. He quietly battled for the crowd's attention.

"Spirit in the Night" was followed by "Lost in the Flood." By the time he'd finished "For You," the audience had fallen into rapt attention. The response was loud and appreciative, and they were still buzzing as the next band soldiered through their set. By the time the evening was over, an excited cluster of new fans were waiting to meet Springsteen. I stuck around too. The word was that Clive Davis was bringing Springsteen down to meet some of the press.

Peter Philbin, a reporter from the *Los Angeles Free Press*, where I'd recently scored an assignment to write about John Prine, was in the house too. His editor, Chris Van Ness, was outside in the bar area. Philbin excitedly buttonholed Van Ness to get a feature assignment on Springsteen. I watched as he loaded his microcassette recorder and waited for a chance to meet Springsteen. He couldn't help it. Philbin was a big guy with a roaring grin. It was the look of a besotted music lover who'd found a new artist to champion, a place to put your hopes and dreams. Springsteen would see that same hopeful expression on millions of faces as he looked out from thousands of stages, but that was all to come.

Davis finally appeared, walking young Bruce Springsteen into the eager gathering outside in the alley. Springsteen looked shy but earnest, like a slightly nervous out-of-towner. If there was major-league ambition hiding in that black leather jacket, I couldn't see it yet. Davis gestured to Springsteen—*Pull your hands out of your pockets, meet people.* As Bruce posed for a few photos, Davis looked on like a prom night father. Finally, it was Peter Philbin's time to meet Springsteen.

Philbin was in no mood to be stingy with his enthusiasm. He was also a sometime stutterer. I watched as he pumped Bruce's hand and aimed his microcassette recorder at Springsteen. Philbin excitedly began his interview.

"You've been said to be influenced by—" Philbin stopped for a moment. He was caught in a stutter. "By—by—"

"Bob Dylan," Springsteen offered.

Philbin shook his head. "By—"

"Elton John?"

Philbin shook his head again.

Springsteen was valiantly trying to help Philbin out of the holding pattern. One would become one of the foremost artists of the century, and the other one of his most significant supporters. Philbin would write memorably about the show. ("Never have I been more impressed with a debuting singer than I was with Bruce Springsteen on Monday night.") He would also soon follow Springsteen to New York, become friends with him, and dedicate much of his life to helping Bruce's career. As an executive at Columbia Records, Philbin would be the one to rally the label's enthusiasm when they were unsure about his third album, *Born to Run.* That was all to come as a small crowd now gathered, everyone quietly rooting for a breakthrough for Philbin and his interview with Bruce. And then there was daylight.

"Van Morrison," Philbin said.

"YES!" Springsteen shouted. "Van Morrison! Van fucking Morrison!"

"But in Bruce," added Clive Davis, "you have an *original*."

Suddenly everybody was celebrating this small but seismic moment. Springsteen's shyness receded. Philbin was a hero. The small alley grew even more celebratory. Springsteen had made a mark in a tough town for newcomers. It's on a night like this that music might spin your life around, give you new passion, point you in an unexpected direction. It was becoming more than a hobby for me, day by day.

Through Neal Preston, I'd met his business partner, the photographer Andrew Kent. Andy was friends with a guy named Doug Bleek. He was a Hollywood denizen who'd gone to Beverly Hills High and worked in odd jobs around the entertainment business. He was also known to have a collection of bootleg films like the Rolling Stones' *Cocksucker Blues*, underground recordings, bloopers, and more. His friend Phil Savenick was another collector and an archivist for television shows. One night Phil revealed that a secret movie project was filming nearby, in Bel-Air, at the home of the director Peter Bogdanovich. The filmmaker was Orson Welles, the legendary director of *Citizen Kane*. It was called *The Other Side of the Wind*. Phil said they were looking for extras for a party scene.

I never expected to graze the world of movies, but that night became a first glimpse of the filmmaking culture that hummed throughout Los Angeles. The house was an ornate mansion with Chinese lights strung across the backyard where the extras were gathered. We huddled there for hours, waiting to be filmed. Occasionally Bogdanovich would appear with Welles in the backyard. Bogdanovich, wearing an ascot and a worried look, was usually in serious discussion with Welles, who roamed happily with a cigar and seemed unconcerned with directing the movie.

"In the world of music, who would Orson Welles be?" I asked some of the other extras.

The conversation kept us occupied for most of the night. Who had created early masterpieces and then abandoned their original promise? The extras were mostly struggling actors but some were hard-core film enthusiasts who'd bluffed their way onto the set just to watch Orson Welles direct. They discussed Welles as a grand figure who had squandered his importance with lifestyle and ego and food. They all agreed that Brian Wilson was the best comparison to Welles. It broke my heart a little to think that Brian Wilson had already been written off so casually. Wilson, whose music had made my sister's heart sing. Wilson, whose melodies were so transporting and heavenly.

I silently pledged to never dismiss my heroes so easily. Just because you went to the Troubadour in a bathrobe didn't mean that you were finished. I think it was that night that I brewed a philosophy about fandom. If you were a *true* fan, you owed an artist loyalty. You owed an important artist belief. If you love John Lennon, you ride out *Pussy Cats*, knowing that around the corner can still be a "Beautiful Boy."

Somewhere around 1 a.m., we were all sent home from the backyard of Bogdanovich's mansion. Welles never finished the movie in his lifetime. He died about thirteen years later, leaving it unfinished until Bogdanovich stitched together a version in 2018. Our party scene had been cut, but that night still feels important. The renegade filmmakers of the seventies, like Bogdanovich and Hal Ashby, were using music brilliantly in their movies. They were becoming more and more like rock stars themselves. The old-time directors were fading away. Welles was already a ghost with a cigar, haunting his own movie set. The horse was galloping without a rider.

Phil had gone to Beverly Hills High in the same class as Richard Dreyfuss and already had a hundred Hollywood stories. Phil loved TV more than movies. He even had a motto—"TV is OK." He worked mostly as a television producer and cherished his encounters with TV legends. He once worked on a Bob Hope special and late one night, Hope, who was nocturnal, wandered out of the production office and onto the street. It was just after 2 a.m., and the nearby club Madame Wong's was emptying out after a punk-rock show. There was Bob Hope, then seventy, one of the most successful comedians and real estate tycoons in Los Angeles history, chatting with buzzed fans of the band Fear. Phil happily waded into the conversation.

"Mr. Hope," he said, "can I ask you a question?"

"Sure."

"What's sex like at your age?"

Hope took a professorial approach. "What's your name?" he asked. Phil told him.

"Phil," Hope asked, "do you like sex?"

Phil confirmed that he did.

"Do it now."

Half the staffers hate you.

—BEN FONG-TORRES

I graduated high school as a junior, three years early. I had enough units and chose over the summer not to take a lame-duck senior year. It wasn't like I had a friend group to share an unforgettable final year of high school with. I looked younger than everybody. The world was calling. My diploma came in the mail.

In June of 1973, *Rolling Stone* published an article I'd written about the band Yes. It was a full feature, several thousand words long. It was a big step forward, and I couldn't help but think that I'd come to write for *Rolling Stone* at the perfect time. The magazine first launched in the late sixties. The editors' favorite artists were mostly rooted in that time period, many of them from the Bay Area, like Van Morrison, the Jefferson Airplane, and the Grateful Dead. The regular staffers were sometimes dismissive of the newer hard-rock bands. I began collecting assignments on all the bands they listened to, like Deep Purple and Yes. One day Ben Fong-Torres called the house, and my sister happened to be there. She told Ben how old I was. Ben added a small author's note to my story that mentioned that I wrote for the San Diego *Door* and the *Los Angeles Times*. It ended with "Crowe is going on 16."

Ben chuckled when we next spoke. "Half the staffers hate you," he said.

I laughed weakly and tried to pick up a few more assignments. Summer was here and my mom had announced a new adventure. She had often peeled off from the family and flown solo. When I was seven, she'd decided to take a college course at a university in San Miguel de Allende, Mexico. I roomed with her and went to Catholic school, where I learned to drink jugo de siete, a street drink made of seven fruit juices, or the warm corn drink atole. Even as a kid, I knew my mom was on a blissful sojourn of educational discovery, trying to forget the ache of my undiagnosed sister back home.

I became obsessed with Jesus. Everywhere was another deeply empathetic portrait of Jesus, eyes upraised. I fell in love with one portrait in particular. Though I never would have known it at the time, Jesus looked like Eddie Vedder, complete with a bleeding heart. We moved to a different hostel or dorm several times and I took the large portrait with me under my arm through the busy streets and the chaotic traffic. The portrait is still here in my writing room, leaning against the wall, rescued from the garage, a reminder of an idyllic summer that was perfect until my accident-prone ways interrupted.

My mom and I were exiting a taxi in downtown Guadalajara and I had blithely opened the door on the traffic side. When an oncoming car sheared the door off, I nearly got killed twice, once by the car and the second time by the taxi driver. My mom intervened, and he was quickly vanquished. We escaped Mexico with a small fine.

That was then. This was July of 1973; she was going to take a course in women's lib at the University of San Francisco. We would live in a dorm room. This was an exciting break for me because *Rolling Stone* was in the Bay Area. I gathered assignments from all the usual places— *Creem, Zoo World*—and some record company work. Before long I had set up interviews with Jerry Garcia from the Grateful Dead, Van Morrison, and one of my favorites, the singer-keyboardist Lee Michaels. Michaels performed as a duo alongside a hulking mountain man of a drummer named Frosty.

"You should not meet Van Morrison," a fellow writer instructed me. "He's very cranky and he despises interviews."

He was wrong about Van Morrison on all three counts. Our interview was spirited and fun. Early in our conversation, Morrison explained that all of his records that were now regarded as his masterpieces had initially received unfounded critical reviews. I explained that I didn't review records, and we were fine.

My mom and I arrived at the dorm in mid-June, and the burnished wood walls of the student housing were shiny and impressive. The building was filled with women, not unlike the women staffers at the *Door*. They were all ages but mostly young. Everybody met in the main living room area, which was dominated by puffy chairs and a poster of Angela Davis.

My mother, the oldest of all the students, tangled with the younger women almost immediately. They wanted to watch regular TV and my mom was obsessed with the Watergate hearings. She won the argument, using me as a weapon. "He needs to see this. This is history!"

Soon they accepted her. I knew they would. My mom had a golden gift, and it was her ability to *listen* to people's problems and issues. They told her everything, and soon there was a line of women who needed to unburden themselves to her. She kept track of all their names, their exploits, and the intricate problems in their relationships. One of the younger women even fell a little in love with her and made a midnight visit to her room in a nightgown. My mom was candid.

"I'm straight," I overheard her saying, "and I think I would just disappoint you. I don't think I'm very good at sex!"

One afternoon I got a ride to the Grateful Dead's office for an interview with Jerry Garcia. Rock Scully, one of their managers, was well-known as one of the guys who hired the Hells Angels at Altamont, the disastrous festival that ended the so-called Summer of Love. Scully and the Grateful Dead had figured out the key to career longevity in the fickle business of rock. The Grateful Dead were not worried about pleasing record executives or critics. The fans were their lifeblood, and the band catered almost exclusively to the loyal network of Deadheads.

Garcia sat in a reclining seat in the wood-finished offices located in a San Rafael complex. I asked him about the hippie concept that music should be free and belong to the people. He was immediately gregarious and delightfully prickly.

"Fuck people's music, man," Garcia said, and laughed. "That kind of thing really *irks* me."

This was decades before Napster or Spotify, but Garcia could see it coming in the summer of 1973. The people's hippie, the guru of the Summer of Love, was already militant about not giving music away for free. "To get so you can play music," he continued, "you have to sacrifice a lot of what would have been your normal life. You know what I mean? For lack of a better phrase, you have to pay the dues to get so you can play music. It's not a thing you just *do*. If that were so, everybody'd be making their own music and there wouldn't be professional musicians. There'd be no need for them. For someone to deny the fact that you spent a certain amount of your life working on some sort of discipline and learning how to play . . . *that's* the rip-off. That's the state versus the individual. Anytime someone comes down on artists and claims their work on any level, I think that's pure bullshit. There's been too many great musicians who died poor. *People's music?* It just ain't so."

Scully wandered into the room, catching the tail end of Garcia's statement. "That's the confusion that's created a lot by the press," he said, "who identified the Dead with a sociological movement that happened in the Haight-Ashbury, right? So by the time the Grateful Dead got to New York for the first time, nobody would cover them as a music story. Instead, the band got treated as some artifact from the decadence of the West Coast culture . . . something from Babylon."

Garcia, then just thirty-one, agreed. "That's all gone now," he added with a wave of his hand. "They don't ask or talk about that much anymore. It's pretty clear now that what looked like it might have been some kind of counterculture is in reality just the plain old chaos of undifferentiated weirdness."

I was loving this summer.

A couple days later, Columbia Records sent a car to drive me to the Mill Valley studio home of Lee Michaels. He'd scored a top ten hit in

1971 with "Do You Know What I Mean," but I'd followed Michaels since seeing him in concert with my sister at her alma mater, College of the Desert. His stringy blond hair flying, Lee Michaels held sonic court from his Hammond B-3 organ while Frosty thundered from the drum kit alongside him. From a distance Frosty looked like a pile of molten lava in a tie-dye shirt. He often mixed his beats with bare-handed drumming, a style that later influenced John Bonham of Led Zeppelin.

As a support act on a concert bill, Lee Michaels often stole the show from the headliner. Sometimes he'd play a song called "The War" for over fifteen minutes. He didn't talk much onstage. It was hard to tell if Lee Michaels was a happy savant or just bored by the idea of casual speech.

Michaels's home in Mill Valley, north of San Francisco, was called Lee Michaels' Record Ranch. It was an enormously expensive, hand-crafted country home. He'd clearly benefited from the recent boom in the record business. Artists were lately being fought over like baseball prospects. Michaels, however, failed to follow up "Do You Know What I Mean" with another lunker-sized hit. The record company was getting antsy about their investment. Lee was also known to get sidetracked. In the late sixties, he indulged his appreciation for exotic cats. Before the food and waste issues overcame him, Michaels had seventeen tigers and cheetahs roaming his property.

On this day, an enormous truck with African rosewood paneling was parked outside Michaels's home. It was actually a recording studio. Michaels bought and outfitted it himself, he said, so he could back it up into the mountains, or anywhere, and make a record.

"You can mix your tapes and watch the ocean, or gaze out at a forest," he explained.

I was fascinated by his seeming lack of purpose. He was eager to show me around but quiet about his musical intentions. His long stringy hair fell over his striking blue eyes. He looked like a despotic prom king. He had stoner dignity. He didn't eat meat, eggs, milk, or the enemy—yogurt. By the time I left, with little quotable material, I realized that Lee Michaels actually had a canny sense of survival. He was following the orders of his record company to do the interview but had expertly followed his own orders to remain mysterious. This was one smart, despotic prom king.

In the years that followed, Michaels's musical career would wane. He suffered a severe neck injury that limited his performing, and in 1982 he retired from the music business. Michaels then got sidetracked again, this time with spectacular results. He took his mother's family recipe for a special buttery shrimp marinade and started a restaurant called Killer Shrimp. The franchise took hold and Michaels sold it for a cosmic payday in the early 2000s. Today, he does no interviews. Like few others from his generation, Lee Michaels escaped the house-always-wins era of working musicians in the '50s, '60s, and '70s. He played the record business at the top of the seller's market, continued to finance an idyllic life, and turned a random family recipe into an enormous shrimp fortune.

"Wait," he said as I was waiting for the car to come pick me up that summer day in 1973. "I want you to have something."

He disappeared and came back with a gallon-sized mason jar packed with freshly grown purple-and-green-flecked marijuana. Lee Michaels' Record Ranch clearly produced more than music. I could barely stuff the large jar in my bag. It smelled potent. Heading home, the driver rolled down the window to clear the air, constantly checking me out in the rearview mirror. I looked like a kid, but whatever was in my bag was world-class dope. As we drew closer, I dreaded my mother would smell it on me and that would be the end of my afternoon interview sojourns.

I couldn't find a trash bin to throw it away as I approached our dorm. By the time I entered the dining room, my mom was holding an encounter session with a group of her fellow feminists. She asked me how the interview went.

"Fascinating," I reported. "But he gave me this as I was leaving."

I withdrew Lee Michaels's mighty weed-packed mason jar. The other women in the room were silent, eyes glazed with desire.

My mother shrieked. "OH MY GOD," she cried. "He could have gotten you arrested! You could have been put in *jail*!" She grabbed the jar. The other women were still speechless. "We have to dispose of this!"

All eight of the women rose and moved to the jar, anxious to help.

"I know a place," one said. "No one will ever know!"

"We'll protect you," said another. "Let's split it up so no one gets caught with all that."

"Oh, thank God," said my mom, surrendering the jar. "It's so strong I can barely breathe!"

I have a feeling that jar lasted her friends most of the summer.

A week after the Lee Michaels visit, I collected an invitation from Ben Fong-Torres to visit the *Rolling Stone* offices. I took the bus from San Francisco State to the address I knew so well, from the many packages and letters I'd sent. The redbrick building housing *Rolling Stone* at 625 Third Street loomed ahead. The MJB Coffee building was just two doors down and the whole neighborhood smelled of strong coffee. Ben met me at the front door and walked me back through the desks that populated a large open space. There were a few cubicles and a lot of open desks. There was a boisterous mailroom guy named Banjo with long, long hair. And there were Tim Cahill, Paul Scanlon . . . bylines I knew well. At the back was Ben's office. Cynthia Bowman, his assistant, sat out front. She had short, stylish hair. *Rolling Stone*'s music coverage all flowed from Ben and Cynthia and their charmingly cluttered office.

It was a busy summer. I'd also scored a *Los Angeles Times* assignment from Robert Hilburn himself. I'd convinced him I could write a profile of Led Zeppelin. They were notoriously press-shy, but I'd become friendly with Danny Goldberg, their publicist and a former rock writer himself. Through Goldberg, I set up an interview with Jimmy Page that was scheduled to happen at the Continental Hyatt House (of course). The Zeppelin tour to support *Houses of the Holy* had begun.

Dancing Days

I couldn't help but have a crush on some of the college women. I may have graduated three years early, but my hormones were now catching up. Sometimes in LA, I'd meet someone just a year or two older. I had more women friends than men, but I'd noticed a trend. They told me all their secrets, but before long, the secrets were all about someone *else*, someone older, and often, somebody who didn't treat them very well.

"Someday you're going to be a wonderful boyfriend," said one.

Every day, I waited for *someday* to start. I was tired of being the mascot. I quietly hoped one of them would look past my clownish personality and just take me to the other side of the river. It never happened.

Meanwhile, Ben Fong-Torres was giving me more and more assignments. One day I flew to Portland to meet Lee Michaels on tour. There was a girl at the hotel whom I'd met with Neal Preston in Los Angeles. She lived in Portland and her name was Pennie Trumbull. Her nickname was Pennie Lane. She wasn't a groupie; she made that clear. She wasn't after a boyfriend. She was a Band-Aide. It was the music that drew her to shows and to meeting musicians. She had a school for Band-Aides. They were called the Flying Garter Girls.

Pennie and her Flying Garter Girls were well-known in the concert world of the Pacific Northwest. Pennie was also extremely personable. She knew the art of being a pal, and I can't imagine anyone who wouldn't have fallen under the spell of her friendship. A whiff of sadness was mixed with her infectious confidence. She insisted on sexual boundaries. She didn't believe in her girls exposing themselves to emotional turmoil or heartbreak by having intercourse.

"Only blow jobs," was her motto, "and that's it."

I sensed that they didn't get a lot of pushback on the motto. Pennie and the Garter Girls felt they were doing a service to the true fire they felt—their love of rock. I still hadn't seen much of the debauchery I'd read about in *Rolling Stone*. There had been a "Groupies" issue of the magazine, and I didn't detect much poetry in the women they'd featured. They were mostly spacy, bleary creatures who sometimes made plaster casts of rock stars' penises. The Garter Girls felt awake and alive.

On the afternoon before the Lee Michaels show in Seattle, I was in my hotel room when the phone rang.

"Whatcha doing?" Pennie asked.

I told her I was just hanging out, going over notes and getting ready for the show.

"What's your room number?"

Soon there was a knock on the door. It was Pennie and two of the Garter Girls.

"We're looking for a place to get ready," Pennie said.

"Come on in."

I retired to the other part of the room, surrounded by yellow legal tablets filled with questions for Lee Michaels and his new drummer, Keith Knudsen. The girls fanned out and took over the other bed and the bathroom. I'd never seen anyone inhabit a room and make it their own faster. Suddenly scarves were fluttering over the lamps. The lights were turned down. One of them already had the room service menu out. The TV was on. My workspace had turned into a nightclub, and it was still the afternoon.

"You don't have to leave," said Theresa with the long, ringleted hair. She invited me to stay exactly where I had been, on my own bed. Pennie was more interested in the menu. She was craving eggs Benedict, which she said was very hit-or-miss at this hotel. Annette was glued to the window, where she was sure she'd seen a glimpse of Simon Kirke from Bad Company, even though she knew they were still in Los Angeles.

After the show later that night, Lee, Keith Knudsen, and a bunch of Seattle regulars, including the Garter Girls, hung out in my room. *The Midnight Special* was on television. I had the growing feeling that I wasn't the world's best road host. People began to politely peel off, one by one. Lee Michaels disappeared discreetly, as did his drummer, and before long, it was just me and the remaining Garter Girls I was apparently now hosting as roommates.

One of them leaned over. "Wanna get seduced?"

It wasn't the most electrifying invitation ever. The interest level was far lower than what they'd displayed over the room service menu earlier. But room service was closed, and apparently, I was one step above sleep in terms of options.

Steely Dan was performing "Do It Again" on the television. Soon it was a crowded, chaotic room, and I think I was only partially on their minds while they were watching television and showing affection to each other. And sometimes to me as well. It was a blizzard of scarves, and I'll leave it at that.

Pennie herself left the room before participating in any of this, but she was clearly the ringleader who blessed their endeavor. She had exited with a trace of laughter and a little mystery. And I somehow captured the exact feeling a couple decades later in *Almost Famous*.

Otherworldly

S eptember 1973. Things were heating up. I kept a Day-Timer schedule book, covered in promotional stickers, and religiously kept daily
notes about upcoming concerts, phone calls, and potential interviews.
One of the myriad publicists I kept in touch with was Mike Hyland
from Capricorn Records. He was a cheerful young media whiz based
in Macon, Georgia. His job was largely pretty simple. Mike spent most
of his time saying no to journalists who wanted to interview the label's
prized attraction, the Allman Brothers Band.

6 Friday 187 · 178

BROTHERS AND SISTERS SHIPPED
LED ZEPPELIN IN CHICAGO
CALL LEE MICHAELS RE: INTERVIEW
TENTATIVE JIMMY PAGE 4:00 PM
CALL FROM DANNY GOLDBERG 12:00
JOE WALSH AT WINTERLAND
CALL PAT RE: WEEKEND
CALL MIKE HYLAND
CALL ROCK RE: GARCIA INTERVIEW

7 Saturday 188 · 177
) Moon's first quarter 08.26
Sun rises 03.52 Sun sets 20.18 · Moon rises 12.56 Moon sets 23.02

LED ZEPPELIN IN CHICAGO
JOE WALSH AT WINTERLAND
DAD COMES IN

The Allman Brothers Band was preparing to release a new album, *Brothers and Sisters*. They were still mourning the death of their leader, the brilliant guitarist Duane Allman. Duane was the elder of the two Allman brothers, and his shocking death was a devastating blow to the band, not to mention his sensitive younger brother, Gregg, their keyboardist and lead singer. (The band had also suffered the death of bassist Berry Oakley in a similar motorcycle accident.) The fact that the Brothers, as they called themselves, summoned the strength to stay together and find even greater success was the most compelling story in rock. But that story was not to be told, and especially not to *Rolling Stone*.

Shortly before Duane Allman's untimely death in 1971, *Rolling Stone* had sent one of their seasoned writers on the road to profile the band. Grover Lewis was known for double-fisted, after-hours profiles of icons like Paul Newman and Robert Mitchum. Lewis joined the band on the road, along with the photographer Annie Leibovitz. Lewis and Duane Allman did not get along. When the tour ended, Duane returned to Macon. Lewis went home to plunge his journalistic sword into the band, and especially Duane.

Lewis's story gleefully mocked the band and their Southern camaraderie, sometimes even phonetically *("You better get out yo' pen and pencil...")*. He leaned heavily into the raucous behavior and drug habits of the touring party. His purplish accounts of Duane's cocaine use—Allman called it "Vitamin C"—were lethal. The piece went to print. Two days later, Allman's motorcycle skidded into oncoming traffic in downtown Macon. The article ran, along with some of Leibovitz's iconic photography, the same week as Allman's death.

The band was horrified. The roadies were outraged. Lewis had done a healthy share of drugs himself, they said, but left it out of the story. The last thing the Allman Brothers Band wanted around them was another journalist, much less one from *Rolling Stone*. There was a blanket credo—no more interviews. As Mike Hyland told me, "The last two words this band will ever want spoken around them are *Rolling* and *Stone*." I'd written small stories about a number of the other bands on Capricorn Records, groups like Wet Willie and Captain Beyond. Hyland often needed promotional bios written quickly, and I'd come through many times. We had a good relationship. Still, I was surprised when Mike called one day with an interesting offer involving Dickey Betts, the lead guitarist from the Allman Brothers Band. Betts had been the band's not-so-secret weapon. When Duane died, Betts stepped up in every way.

Dickey Betts, now asking to be called Richard Betts, wanted to publicize his North American Indian Foundation. His longtime interest in Native American culture had grown since he'd met and married Sandy Wabegijig, also known as Sandy Blue Sky. (She'd inspired his hit song "Blue Sky," from their album *Eat a Peach*.) I collected a small assignment from *Rock* magazine for a phone interview with Betts. I also mentioned this to Ben Fong-Torres, who gave me an instant commitment for an article of any size if I was able to get an interview for *Rolling Stone*. We both knew it was doubtful, given the magazine's recent history with the band.

"Don't ask Richard about the Allman Brothers Band or the new album," Hyland instructed. "This is a specific thing, and he only wants to talk about the Native Americans."

Richard Betts's easygoing drawl reminded me of family members on my dad's Kentucky side. He spoke earnestly about the plight of the Native Americans, their battle against prejudice and stereotyping, and the importance of bringing greater mainstream understanding of their traditions. We spent about twenty minutes discussing the issues, backward and forward. Soon I ran out of questions, and he ran out of answers.

"Other than that, we're just working on the new album," he said. "I think it'll surprise you."

I held my tongue. Was he opening the window for a conversation about the Allman Brothers Band's new album? I climbed in the open window.

"How far along is it?"

Betts proceeded to give me some tidbits and cheerfully thanked me for the conversation. Mike Hyland called a few minutes after we hung up. "Dickey—I mean Richard—loved his talk with you," he said. "I may ask you to write a story about the new Allmans album for the new bio." The bio, as it was known, was the two-or-three-page promotional item that every record company sent out to the press along with a new record. Most rock journalists could make an easy seventy-five dollars writing a bio, and I had grown pretty good at it. (Lester Bangs used the blank side of promotional bios as stationery.)

I was still only sixteen. It never stopped being a thrill. Asking questions of my favorite artists, things I wanted to know as a fan, and getting the assignments to do just that. I'd been published in *Rolling Stone*. I still could barely believe it. Ben Fong-Torres had become a phone acquaintance. His interviews with artists like Marvin Gaye and David Crosby defined what it was to conduct a deep-tissue, sometimes even confessional long-form interview with an artist.

I had a good scorecard with Ben. He was increasingly happy with my coverage of the bands that I was interested in: bands like King Crimson, Deep Purple, Jethro Tull, and Black Sabbath. But I dreamed of getting bigger stories too.

"What if I were to get an interview with the Allman Brothers Band?" I asked Ben.

"They don't like us," he answered immediately. The Allmans had joined a short list of bands that feuded with the magazine. Led Zeppelin was another.

"I may be talking to them for their bio," I offered. "What if I were to get them to agree to a story for *Rolling Stone*?"

Ben was silent. "That would be a feature," he said. "Maybe a cover." He paused. "But they'll never do it after the Grover piece."

A cover story in *Rolling Stone* was beyond the realm of my imagination, but somehow, I had to try. Within a month, I'd interviewed Richard again and written the bio for *Brothers and Sisters*. His song "Ramblin'

Man" was the lead single and quickly became the song of the summer. Southern rock had become the genre du jour, and the world was more fascinated than ever with the very private, mystique-filled rebirth of the Allman Brothers Band.

"Guess what," said Mike Hyland. "Dickey loved the bio you wrote. You're approved to go on the road with the band for *Rolling Stone*. You'll talk to Dickey and the rest of the band. Not sure you'll get Gregg. We're sending you on the first leg of the tour."

Hyland explained that Dickey Betts had stuck up for me in an Allman Brothers Band meeting. Even Phil Walden, the band's manager and the head of Capricorn Records, agreed it was time to crack the ban on *Rolling Stone*. I asked if I could bring my best friend, Neal Preston, with me on the road to do the photographs.

"Sure, we like Neal."

I called Ben Fong-Torres and gave him the news. If he was overjoyed, I couldn't tell. Impressed? Maybe a little. Nervous? *Definitely.* He gave me five thousand words, then tiptoed into magical territory. "It might be a cover."

Only one problem. I had to talk my parents into letting me go on tour. Though it would only be for three days of shows up the California coast, our family negotiation went for hours. My mom had signed me up for some courses at City College in advance of law school. I agreed to getting homework in advance, nightly phone calls, and of course, "don't take drugs."

September 21, 1973. I first met up with the Allman Brothers Band in San Diego on the afternoon before their show at the Sports Arena. The band's road manager, Willie Perkins, introduced me to the roadies and a few band members. Perkins was a polite man of few words who always had one hand clamped to a mysterious silver briefcase. He told no secrets. Duane's death was clearly still fresh. Emotional guardrails were firmly in place. I decided to interview the roadies and work my way up.

I spoke with the band's tour manager, Twiggs Lyndon. Next was Red Dog, the Brothers' head roadie. Red Dog was a big personality, well-known in roadie circles as a hardworking ambassador for the band. I interviewed him in a backstage room as we listened to his mixtape of favorites like Bob Dylan's "I Want You" and Jackson Browne's "Redneck Friend."

"You have to enjoy every aspect of this trip," he told me. "Have a ball. When we have a party, we have an *Allman Brothers Band* party. Everybody boogies. There's no better sight in the world. It's family, man."

Red Dog had been an early member of the Allman Brothers family in Macon, Georgia. "In the beginning, we were on mushrooms for weeks," he recounted. "One time Gregg—I don't even know if Gregory is aware of it—he did something, and I was upset. I was angry, man. I was just going to pack my bag and split. Somehow or another, Duane was hip that something was wrong. We were up at Rose Hill Cemetery. We were very high, and he said, 'What's bugging you?' I told him something was wrong. We got to rapping and lay down on the ground and he said, 'Just look up,' and there were these trees. 'Just look up, see those treetops, those branches? They've all grown together. You see how hard the wind is blowing? The tree doesn't come apart.' That stuck with me ever since."

We sat quietly for a moment; the memory made him emotional. We listened to Luther Ingram's "(If Loving You Is Wrong) I Don't Want to Be Right."

I felt like I was on the edge of the biggest story, the biggest emotional *journey*, of my life. Stretched out ahead was the spooky, soulful, mysterious tale of the band's rebirth. Soon I was so comfortable I even asked Red Dog about the rumor that the Allman Brothers Band family, that loyal group of loved ones, had held a séance with Duane's body before burying him. He didn't deny it. "Hell," he confided, "they say a lot of stuff about us. But none of it comes close to the truth. I'll help you get the truth into that tape recorder of yours."

There's always a hidden hero in every journalistic adventure. For every writer who lands a good story, there's a good Samaritan, or publicist, or family member, who helps them get there. Sometimes all you have to do is listen. Red Dog would go on to clear a path for me, all the way to Gregg Allman himself.

Years later, Red Dog told me it wasn't that big of a deal, he just "showed me where to look." After the band's experience with Grover Lewis, they had plenty of reason to be cautious. Lewis had a literary pedigree. After palling around with profile subjects like Robert Mitchum and Lee Majors, taking shots at an earnest band from Macon, Georgia, must have felt like low-hanging fruit. Red Dog told me how the bad blood started.

Annie Leibovitz asked the band to pose together brandishing their communal band tattoos—a small Allman Brothers Band mushroom they'd inked on their ankles. Lewis was standing nearby. After a few snaps, Betts had had enough. He pulled down his pant leg and said it felt silly.

"No sillier than getting a tattoo in the first place," said Lewis.

"One more crack like that," Duane snapped, "and I'm gonna knock your block off."

Lewis's hit piece on the Allmans was one of his last articles to be published. The word around *Rolling Stone* was that he acquired a case of writer's block so crippling he couldn't enter the same room as a typewriter. The more the roadies talked about Lewis and how he hoodwinked them into embarrassing themselves, the more I resolved to write the definitive story they could all be proud of.

Gregg Allman hadn't officially agreed to be interviewed for the story. I watched him flash through the backstage of the Sports Arena. *The same path as Elvis!* His flaxen hair and crisp white suit stood out in the sea of denim. At his side was his new fiancée, Janice Blair, in a dark velvet jacket and toothpick pants. Together they looked like Allman Brothers Band royalty. They traveled in their own bubble.

Dickey—I mean *Richard*—Betts was instantly obliging when we finally met in person. Plans were made to interview him the next day in Los Angeles on the balcony of his room at the Continental Hyatt House. His trust in me stamped my passport, and he promised to put in a good word for me with Gregg Allman, who hadn't talked with a journalist since the death of his brother. I met Allman briefly outside the band's dressing room. He nodded politely but distantly when I told him I was looking forward to a chance to "talk," meaning interview him.

That night, I watched the band from the stage of the Sports Arena. I still have the note I wrote to myself on a small, folded piece of paper. The note read: "Otherworldly." To describe an Allman Brothers Band show as anything else, at that time in their career, would have been dishonest. *Otherworldly.* The Brothers had done the unimaginable. They weren't playing without Duane; they were playing *for* him. Six feet away from Gregg Allman at his Hammond B-3 organ, watching him summon a howling version of "Whipping Post," I could almost feel the wind pushing against those intertwined branches at Rose Hill Cemetery. *Otherworldly.* I could almost hear Duane's voice too, looking up at those trees and telling Red Dog in a soft psilocybin whisper, "The tree doesn't come apart."

Neal Preston felt it too. Photographing the show from the stage pit, he caught my eye. On all our adventures, there was an unspoken com-

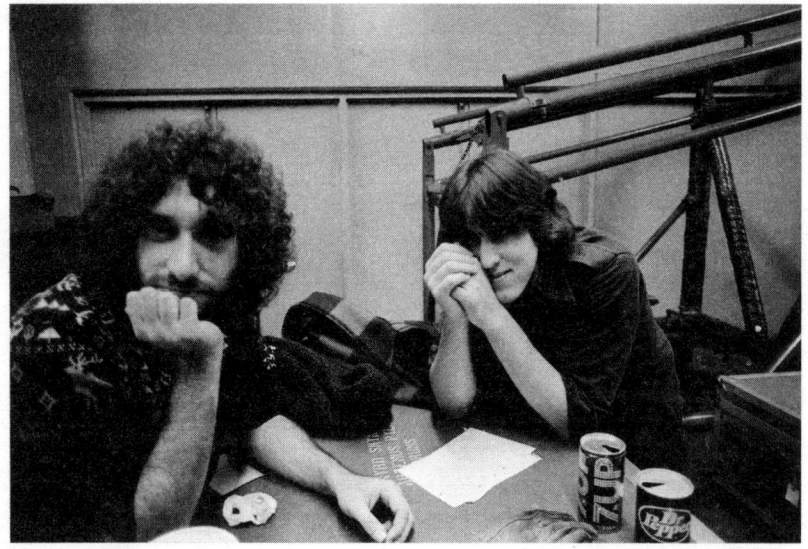

Team City: Neal Preston and me, backstage with camera bags and notepads.

munication between us. We were living in the moment, but we were also storing all of these one-of-a-kind memories for later, when we'd bring them out and polish them like cat's-eye marbles, sitting across from each other on twin beds. We called it "the Recap." We'd sit cross-legged on our beds, surrounded with the booty from the day. Film cans, photos, cassettes, notes, and memories of the people we'd met.

There was already a *feeling* about this tour. Spirits were being summoned right before us, in real time. I couldn't wait to write about it. America's most compelling band was performing a hypnotic three-hour concert every night. It was a master class in the blues, often hitting dizzying heights of improvisation, all while outrunning the ghosts of the past. The band's unspoken motto sounded a lot like my own family motto, the one my mom had once taped to my bedroom wall. A version is usually miscredited to Winston Churchill, but with those four *never*s, it feels like it belongs to her all the way.

Never, never, never, never give up.

—ALICE CROWE

E very man on the Allman Brothers tour was addressed with the same term of endearment: "brother." The whole adventure operated on camaraderie. I'd previously only done my interviews in hotel rooms or on the phone. Those days were over. The story was everywhere. I was constantly darting into bathrooms to take notes. Sometimes I'd walk in on one or two roadies or hangers-on dipping into their stash of cocaine. Sometimes it was offered. I shrugged pleasantly. No judgment. We were on the road now. *Everybody boogies; everybody gets off.* Soon I was calling everyone "brother" too. I still do.

The next day I interviewed Dickey Betts again on the porch of his room at the Continental Hyatt House. He was unguarded and trusting. The conversation flowed easily. Betts reiterated his offer to put in a good word with Gregg Allman, who floated distantly through the hallways as if stepping on clouds, usually with Janice Blair. Jackson Browne had shown up backstage at the Los Angeles Forum, and Gregg was animated as he hugged him.

Browne had been an early friend to Gregg and Duane Allman when they first hit Los Angeles in the late sixties, living out of the Mikado Hotel, a run-down place near the Hollywood Bowl. The Allman Joys, as they were then called, became the Allman Brothers Band. Gregg was joyful seeing Browne again. He was particularly rapturous about his song "These Days." I had written about Jackson Browne's friends the

Eagles, and Browne also made a point of telling Gregg I was a true music fan. I was grateful. I was trying to build a chain link of trust When the time came, I knew I would have to ask Gregg Allman some hard questions.

The Los Angeles show was a spine-tingler. It was their first time at the venue without Duane, though you'd have been hard-pressed to say he wasn't in the room. Every long spiraling jam felt like a séance. After the show the band and crew returned to the Continental Hyatt House. The Brothers liked to pick an after-party room where band and family could drift in and out. Guitars were always present. Red Dog gave me a seat of honor on a couch with drummer Butch Trucks and pianist Chuck Leavell. Gregg Allman materialized, picked up a guitar, and began jamming on a communal version of "Come On in My Kitchen." I picked up the unattended guitar leaning next to me. I knew a few rudimentary chords, not many, but I strummed along. Allman briefly turned and acknowledged me with a curiously amused look. *We were jamming.* I was starting to feel accepted by them, maybe too accepted. I next felt the guitar lifting ever so gently out of my hands, upward and over my head. It was Red Dog, removing the guitar as if a heavenly creature other than himself had decreed it, and passing it to someone who could really play. It wasn't the last time a roadie would show me the guardrails.

Sunday afternoon in Phoenix, two days later, and the Allman Brothers Band were staying at a motel near their gig at Sun Devil Stadium. Nudged by Mike Hyland, the publicist back in Macon, Gregg agreed to our interview. Neal and I were killing time in the coffee shop, waiting for word that Gregg was ready to talk. We saw someone wandering though the motel courtyard. It was Tamarind Brown, a girl we'd sometimes seen and chatted with backstage at shows in San Diego. She was the daughter of a reverend, stylish and well-appointed. When sometimes introduced to Neal and me by a musician passing through town, she'd pretend to meet us for the first time.

Now she was crestfallen and smeared with tears. She'd traveled from San Diego with one of the other bands playing at the Arizona stadium.

They'd tried to sell her to the Allmans' road crew for a case of Heineken. We tried to cheer her up, but she couldn't stop crying. She needed a place to stay. I'll never forget her sad face when Neal asked her if her father knew where she was.

"No," she said. "He's probably preaching today."

I went back over my questions as we waited in the coffee shop. Overhead, "You Don't Mess Around with Jim" by Jim Croce played. I shuffled through some fond memories of dodging the vice squad with Jim and Maury back in San Diego. Soon another Jim Croce song was playing. Then another. I started to get a bad feeling. Then came another Croce song, "Operator," and finally a somber-voiced DJ confirmed my worst fears. Croce and Maury had both died in a plane crash in Tennessee. They weren't distant celebrities to me. We'd shared secrets and I felt the wallop of their unlived lives. The news hit me hard. And then, a few minutes later, another news report mentioned that Gram Parsons had overdosed in Joshua Tree, California. His body had been found partially burned. In custody was his road manager, the Road Mangler, Phil Kaufman, who'd hijacked Parsons's body and tried to cremate it— supposedly in accordance with Parsons's wishes.

In an instant, everything felt temporary.

Death had touched my family only a few years earlier, but this felt different. The news found an empty spot way down deep inside me and renewed feelings that I'd been running from. I couldn't stop thinking about all that we didn't know that day in San Diego, sitting by the pool. I wondered what it might have been like if a man from the future had taken a seat on the lounge chair beside us and told Croce those songs would roam the earth much longer than he would. And I wondered about Maury and his skinny jeans, and the T-shirt that didn't feature him, walking off on the waitress. Why were the waitress and I the two who lived? Where was the T-shirt? These thoughts would always lead back to Cathy.

"Let's try Gregg's room again," said Neal.

Gregg was ready to talk. He was staying in a bungalow that opened into the pool area, a courtyard with a pool table. Shirtless, wearing small denim shorts, Allman was shooting pool when I sidled up to him and asked if he wanted to talk now. Neal Preston was there and took a casual photo of that very moment when Gregg finally agreed. We all disappeared into his motel room. It was dark, with one semi-curtained window. He stayed shirtless on the bed, holding an acoustic guitar as a kind of shield.

I watched Gregg's fingers fumbling with a nearly empty pack of cigarettes. The air conditioner hummed. His thin, wiry body seemed to carry the weight of the world. I couldn't tell if he was shy or careful. I decided on shy. He had a faraway look, staring at the air conditioner. I turned on my tape recorder, and he snapped back to attention with my first question. I asked about Jackson Browne.

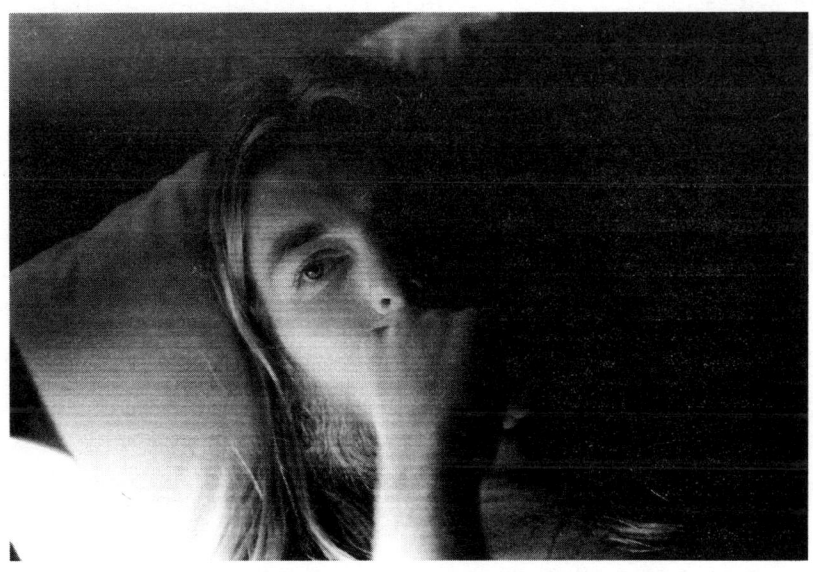

The Arizona motel room/*Rolling Stone* interview, September 1973.

Gregg's reticence melted as he talked about Jackson with a kind of rapture. He spoke warmly about their early scuffling days in Los Angeles when they were both starving musicians holed up at the Mikado. And Allman was almost religious about Browne's songwriting, particularly the song "These Days," written when Jackson was a world-weary teenager. It was one of my favorite songs too, and Allman said that he planned to cut the song for his own upcoming solo album.

He dialed the front desk and asked for more cigarettes in a gravelly voice.

Kids were shouting and yelling as they cannonballed into the pool outside, but it was stark and moody in Gregg's room. Neal quietly snapped shot after shot of Allman in the evocative lighting.

Allman pulled out a small vial and took two quick sniffs. He offered some to me, and I was quick to turn it down. He nodded and said something along the lines of "smart kid." It wasn't the first time I'd heard that. Everybody, it seemed, had a stash. Turning it down, I was usually met with some kind of grateful comment that meant, essentially, *Excellent, more for me*.

Gregg then offered Neal Preston the vial. Neal was still a functioning stoner then. I could never tell if he was high unless it was late at night and he'd smoked way too much pot. His eyes would become hooded, and we called it "Hooded Pre." Hooded Pre meant sleep was near. This afternoon in Phoenix, Neal took two quick blasts and then gave the vial back to Allman. He'd looked at the white substance and registered that it was also flecked with brown, the first indication that all was not just cocaine in the vial. It was a speedball, meaning cocaine and heroin, a homemade hybrid if you liked your roller-coaster ride mixed with sparkly ups and dark, twisty downs.

Neal later admitted to becoming nauseous. I couldn't tell. I continued my interview for another hour, and Gregg warmed to the conversation. At a certain point, as he veered into the tough areas of the recent deaths in the band, including that of his own brother, he hugged the guitar, and it calmed him. He took the opportunity to play a couple songs too, Jackson Browne's "These Days" and his own "Come and Go Blues." It was a thrill. Gregg Allman at his intimate best, his haunting voice filling

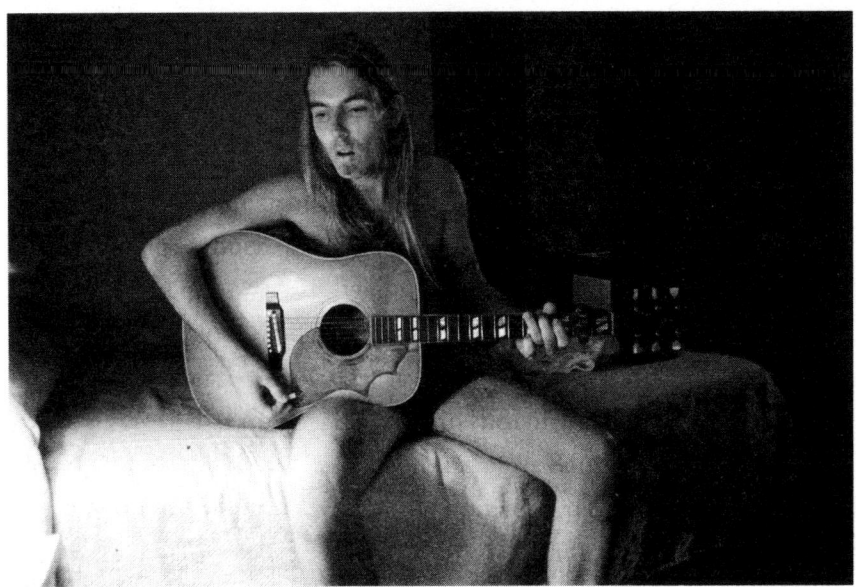

Motel room serenade/Gregg plays "These Days," September 1973.

the motel room with a single guitar backing. I checked several times to make sure the tape recorder was recording.

The conversation wound through the difficult past and inched into territory I knew I would need for the story. Gregg Allman, then only twenty-five, had been hiding out a lot. In his band. In his head. In his music. In drugs. There was so much on his shoulders that it seemed a miracle he was able to appear so functional much of the time. The guitar was his shield. Making it a part of the conversation changed the environment in the room from a *Rolling Stone* interview to a kind of personal hootenanny. It was a brilliant move, for both of us. And I knew I would treasure that recording of him singing those songs forever.

Relaxation was always the key to a good interview. Interviewing Humble Pie for *Creem* the previous year, I'd started my questions with guitarist Steve Marriott before their San Diego show. His answers were quick and workmanlike. We finished the interview just after the show.

Marriott was drenched in sweat, a towel around his neck. A fat hash-and-tobacco cigarette was in one hand and a green Heineken was in the other. He offered me the hash joint; I declined but showed no judgment. He was colorful and irreverent. All the quotes came from the second session.

I didn't know much about cocaine until this tour. Suddenly it was popping up everywhere, under code names like "blowzine," "Bolivian marching powder," and "krell." For the roadies, it was energy in a bottle. In Gregg Allman's case, you don't sing like that unless the blues are a part of you. I didn't judge him either. But I have to be honest here. Every time Gregg pulled out that little vial of coke, with the spoon attached to the lid, I couldn't shake the image of my teacher-mother popping up just over his shoulder. *You're killing brain cells!*

Most of our conversation that Arizona afternoon dealt with the early days of the Allman Joys, when Duane first took his angelic-looking baby brother under his wing. Suddenly Gregg seemed years younger, laughing about his brother sneaking him into Jacksonville, Florida, bars with fake IDs "so that little blond kid could sing the blues." He laughed. "Man, I was barely sixteen. Can you believe it?"

I laughed along with him. I was glad he didn't ask my own age. I was sixteen too, at that very moment.

The Allman Joys broke up and became the Hourglass. The Hourglass traveled to Los Angeles to make it. "We stayed first at the Mikado Motel," he said, "then at the Cahuenga down by the Hollywood Bowl. A real garbage motel, and all of us in one room. The manager caught us and we moved down to an even worse joint on Lash Lane. This place had no name at all. I got up the first morning we lived there, thinking I'd go swimming. As I'm walking down the hall, there was this door open. I happened to look in and there's this cat lying on the floor, covered up with a blanket. Cop standing there. The cat had left a note and downed ninety-five Seconals. It was the first dead person I'd ever seen."

We were just starting to drift into the big issues: the death of his own brother, Betts's increased role in the band, and his own clear loneliness. He'd mentioned that loneliness in passing, and now I was ready to dig into those areas he'd never discussed in public. There was no story without it, and the air was crackling with the stories he was ready to tell.

It was then that Gregg reached for the brake. There was a show to do that night. We made an agreement to talk more in the next city. I raced back to my room, thrilled with the material I'd gotten, especially the recording of him playing solo in the room. There's always that terrifying moment before you're sure that you didn't fuck something up with the recording. Racing home from a good interview and discovering you've recorded two hours of silence. The journalist's nightmare. I pressed play. Sure enough, it was all there.

I called Ben Fong-Torres in San Francisco and reported that the first interview with Gregg was in the can, and that it was emotionally revealing. There would be another session, but the floodgates had opened. Ben made it official. The Allman Brothers Band was going to be a cover story.

Word spread through the crew that Allman had enjoyed our interview. The other members all contributed interviews of their own. Chuck Leavell, the band's keyboard player and newest member, was warm and revealing. So were Butch Trucks and Jaimoe, the band's two powerhouse drummers. Everybody missed Duane with an almost unspeakable ache. Everybody dug deep and told secrets. I had a paper bag filled with the priceless interview recordings. I'd even carefully knocked out the tabs in each cassette, so they could not be mistakenly recorded over and lost.

Plans were made to finish the final interview with Gregg after the show in San Francisco. It was the last night when I'd be with them. We were all staying at the Miyako Hotel, a popular hotel for rock bands, located in Pacific Heights. The next day the Brothers would travel to Hawaii for a tour-ending show and I would fly home and write the story. There was a quick deadline; it was a hot story for the magazine. I tried not to think about how I was going to distill the mountain of material I'd gathered as I stood on the Winterland stage and listened to Bill Graham individually introduce each member by instrument and name, finally ending, in his dramatic Bill Graham cadence, with "From Macon, Georgia. Please welcome. The great great. Allman. Brothers. *Band.*"

The band was on fire. The pain and the release of their last three years were on full display. I felt emotional, and I decided that it was the best concert I'd ever seen. By the time the Allman Brothers Band left the stage after "Trouble No More," you'd have been hard-pressed to find anyone in that concert hall who wouldn't call them the best American band on any stage, anywhere, at that moment in 1973.

"Call the room in an hour," Gregg told me as he swept out of the backstage area and into a long black car, with Janice on his arm.

An hour later, the door to suite 101 opened and Gregg Allman beckoned Neal and me inside. The Japanese-themed motel featured paper-thin sliding doors and rice-paper lampshades. Gregg slumped onto the sofa and lit a cigarette. I took a seat in one of the two empty chairs. The room was a little cold. Jan was sitting against the headboard, behind the sheer curtain that surrounded the nearby bed. Neal took some haunting photos of Gregg looking at me, ready to talk. Years later, one of the photos would become the cover of Allman's autobiography, *My Cross to Bear.*

Sensing our oncoming personal conversation, Neal slipped out of the room. Whether it was the cool evening, or the low light in the hotel room, or Gregg speaking to an audience that included his fiancée, it's hard to know. But Allman let down all his defenses. He spoke freely about his deceased brother and the pressure of the last few years.

"The real question," he said, "is not why we're so popular. I try not to think about that too much. The question is what made the Allman Brothers keep on going. I've had guys come up to me and say, 'Man, it just doesn't seem like losing those two fine cats affected you people at all.' Why? Because I still have my wits about me? Because I can still play? Well, that's the key right there. We'd all have turned into fucking vegetables if we hadn't been able to get out there and play. *That's* when the success was, Jack. Success was being able to keep your brain inside your head."

Any journalist will tell you. Sometimes you hear something so quotable that you can see the words in print in real time, right before your eyes. The room changes when deep truths are being spoken, when raw honesty is in the air. I couldn't wait for the recap with Neal. I knew I had my story. Everything after that was everything I'd ever hoped for. It was no longer an interview. It was Gregg Allman's confession, an unburdening. Our talk went until the early hours, when the world was quiet, the Pacific Heights traffic outside was silent, and the only sound was his quiet voice and an ice machine in the hallway. I went back to my room and sat down on the bed.

"You're not going to believe it," I told Neal.

At 2 a.m. the phone rang. Neal answered. He listened for a minute and then hung up. He looked shaken.

"Gregg wants you to come to his room." Neal paused. "He wants you to bring all the tapes. And he wants you to bring some identification."

I was overcome with a feeling of fear and shock. I didn't know what I'd done wrong, but some kind of reckoning was coming. I started to shake.

"You're coming with me," I said.

Neal agreed.

I held the paper sack full of tapes. I wasn't sure if they'd be listened to or destroyed. *What did I say or do?* I decided to keep one, the tape of the Arizona motel interview, the one where he'd played "These Days." I couldn't give that one up. I brought my wallet. I had no driver's license, but I'd just gotten a California ID. In my head, I saw the death of the dream—to be taken seriously, to work for *Rolling Stone*, to earn a cover story. What kind of fool had I been? Was it a joke? We rode the elevator in silence. I was still shaking.

Janice Blair answered the door. She had a funereal expression, with a hint of embarrassment. She led me to the living room where we'd talked ninety minutes earlier, back when the world was different. Gregg sat in a chair. His long flaxen hair was now flat to his head, dark with sweat. He seemed more sleek, more elegant, but his eyes were nowhere near this room. *Otherworldly.* He was a ghostlike version of himself. Gone was the shy, careful guy from Arizona. The room was thick with dread, like I'd stepped into *Rosemary's Baby.* Gregg looked and me and nodded his head for what seemed like a full minute. *The swishing shapes of the anadromous fish moving beneath the surface.*

He was angry and taunting. The tone in his voice was one of a bitter man, relishing retribution against not just me but everybody who had ever tried to rip him off or slight him with prejudice. I felt silly and naïve. I just wanted out of there, to go home to my room, to my records. To my family. To the law school across the street, where I could be like my great-grandfather and protect other people from the kind of evil that was right before me.

"Are those the tapes?" He pointed to the paper bag in my hand.

"Yes."

He seemed almost mocking. I could see Janice behind the translucent bedroom drapes, her legs pulled up to her chest, listening with quiet dread. She could see me shivering. Gregg was looking at me with betrayal daggers in his eyes. It was like a scene from a bad crime show, one where the snitch has been caught—*me*—and the next scene would begin with me in a body bag.

"Who are you?" Gregg asked.

I was shaking again. "You know who I am."

"Let me see your ID."

I handed over my ID. He examined it.

"Sixteen years old?"

I nodded.

"Sixteen?" He shook his head. "Sixteen! *You're underage.* How do I know you aren't with the FBI? You've been talking to everybody." He had a singsong, schoolyard tone. *"Asking questions. Taking notes with your eyes. Making tapes. I could have you arrested."* My mind raced.

When did I cross the line? Was it asking Red Dog about the séance rumor? "You're gonna give me all the tapes right now," Gregg demanded.

I was shocked and humiliated but increasingly irritated at his sadistic singsong taunts. It reminded me of the kid from junior high, Tom Tobin, the one with the Clark Kent glasses who mercilessly ridiculed me for my lack of pubic hair. I snapped.

"Tell me this," I countered. "You told me Duane snuck you into clubs when you were underage, just to get experience. You were sixteen. Well so am I. How is it any different? How am I breaking the law?"

For a moment he was silent. Then he began to laugh. What happened next scared the shit out of me.

"See that chair next to you?" he said. "See that chair?" I saw that his pupils were pinpricks. "My brother is sitting *right there*, right now, and he's laughing at you."

I was shaking again. "I'm not from the FBI," I said.

"You could have had us all busted," he said. "Give me the tapes."

I handed him the brown paper bag filled with all my precious tapes, except for the one I couldn't surrender. He was adamant about writing a strange semilegal on Miyako Hotel stationery. "Let it be known to all that the contents of this package are solely owned, and are the property of Mr. Gregory LeNoir Allman, and cannot in any way be legally copied or reproduced for any use except by same." He informed me that he was going to give the tapes to his mother in Florida for safekeeping.

"Sixteen," he kept muttering, like I'd tricked him.

I tried not to cry and succeeded. I tried not to continue shaking and failed. He called his bodyguard to come and cosign the agreement. It was now early morning, and nothing was making sense. All I knew was that the dream was over. There were no magic shoes. I was a guppy, impressionable and unformed. Everything bad that anybody had ever said about me—all of it was true. Clearly, life was filled with deep, dark, hideous caverns and everything before this had been a joke.

Tom Tobin types ruled the world. *Where are your pubes, little cunt?!*
Where are they?!

Riding the elevator back to the room, I knew *Rolling Stone* would
find out and I would never work again. If I told them everything that
had happened, I'd have to write it. And just like that, I'd be Grover
Lewis, but *worse*. Another takedown story about the Allman Brothers
Band, my favorite band, in *Rolling Stone*, my favorite magazine.

The sun was coming up. Back in our room, Neal vowed to fly to
Honolulu to rescue the tapes. I knew it was too late. The tapes would
end up in a trash can, or Gregg's mother's house, or worse. Talk about
a recap. Neal and I discussed what happened and we picked through
our theories. I'd dug too deeply, asked too many questions. And perhaps
Gregg had gotten high, gotten paranoid, and thought about me walking
out the door with tapes full of everybody's secrets, including his own
painful confessions of grief. Or maybe he'd thought about the fact that
I hadn't done any of the offered drugs. *Wait! He's a cop!*

I just wanted to go home. I zombied my way through the San Francisco airport to the gate for the flight back to San Diego. I collapsed into
a plastic chair. I was still in shock, watching tourists walking by with
loaves of San Francisco bread. Kids were shrieking and flights were
being announced. I heard none of it. I was in a daze. I had one tape and
no record of any of the conversations I'd had. I thought backward in my
mind. *If only I hadn't used up all my cassettes, I could have given him blank
tapes!* Who was I kidding. It was all over. The warm bath of self-ridicule
was starting to feel comfortable. The darkness was calling. Not only did
my musical hero steal my tapes, and my future . . . he summoned his
dead brother! The world's finest slide guitarist! *To laugh at me!* Soon
everybody would be laughing.

"Cameron?"

It was a girl's voice, chipper and curious. I turned and saw a strange
apparition in a red-and-pink uniform topped with a tall pillbox hat. It
wasn't a hallucination. It was my sister, in between flights.

"Cindy?"

"What are you doing here?"

I told her the whole awful story. She listened with watery brown eyes. She did her best to soothe me but had another flight to catch.

"It's not your fault," she said. She found someone to trade for her next flight, and we sat in the skinny airport chairs. She offered me a sister's true love and stroked my hair in silence. Finally, she had to fly away. "It's heartbreaking," she said, "but remember this. None of this is your fault. You never had a chance to be a kid. Now you will. You're free to be exactly who you want to be, you don't have to please Mom or Dad or *anybody* anymore. You're free!"

Arriving home, I kept up a brave front with my parents. I *had* gotten the story no one else had gotten. The full story of the Allmans, from beginning to present. All of it! I didn't mention the rest. I had only one tape. Barely any proof of the entire disastrous adventure. I avoided calling Ben Fong-Torres and slipped down to my bedroom to sleep. My lack of real celebration sent a loud signal to my parents. Later my dad knocked softly on my door.

"What doing?" he said. He liked leaving the extra words out of the phrase "what are you doing."

"Nothing," I said. "Just tired."

He sat on the corner of my bed. "Shut up and deal," he said.

It was another of his favorite phrases, always said with good humor and a twinkle. *Shut up and deal* meant *Talk to me*. I didn't realize until years later that it was the last line in what would become my favorite movie, Billy Wilder's *The Apartment*. For me it was still just a dad joke. I told him everything, and he told me I didn't have to prove anything to him.

"Sometimes," he said, "people are no damn good."

My plan to be a lawyer was always meant to be a tribute to him, to the Kentucky side of our family. Now I would be able to give Jimmy Crowe that gift. It was my thank-you to him for leaving the military, for trading his medals for a life with us in the desert, and for having a third kid. Fuck Gregg Allman. My dad was who I wanted to please.

The next morning, I sat down with my mom at the table where we ate her mostly inedible meals. My dad was now at work, "sitting on a house." I still hadn't answered the ringing telephone downstairs that was probably *Rolling Stone*. I was alone with my mom. She'd once called me Candide. Candide was the hero of Voltaire's story of a young man battered by life's misfortunes while blithely believing in a kind of bulletproof optimism. That wasn't me anymore. Doom was just around the corner, on the other end of the ringing telephone in my bedroom. I knew the days of optimism were over. Candide was dead. So was my older sister, whom I still knew so little about.

"What did the psychologists say Cathy's problem was?" I asked my mom bluntly.

"I can't talk about it," answered the mother of Candide, evenly and with finality.

"Did you find her, or did Dad?"

She shook her head. The verboten subject was now at the top of my mind. I'd been ten years old on that July day when her body disappeared from our lives, but Cathy's presence was never far. Lately I'd become obsessed with something that had come to me when I last visited her ashes, tucked into the wall of the mausoleum courtyard in Riverside. The gate to the courtyard was almost always locked, but I could see her engraved crypt if I hiked around the back. Often, I paid my respects by tossing a flower through the breeze-blocks. I realized that I still thought of her from the perspective of a ten-year-old. To a ten-year-old, Cathy was a full-grown adult. These days, I told my mom, I saw things with more perspective. Cathy was still a teenager when she died.

"Don't do this to me," my mom said.

Later that night, I made a phone call. It was about one in the morning, Birmingham, Michigan, time. He was still up, of course. I could hear the scratchy sound of the Raspberries in the background. Who listened to the sunny pop of the Raspberries at one in the morning? Only the world's greatest rock critic. He was probably writing one of those coffee-stained masterpieces on the back of a record company bio. I told him what had happened.

"You made friends with them," said Lester Bangs. He sighed loudly and coughed. "That was your mistake. They make you feel cool, and I met you. You are not cool." He pronounced it with playground derision—*kewl*. He chalked it all up to the pursuit of idol worship, and he thought that I just might have saved my own life by blowing the story. Getting in bed with the corporate pursuits of *Rolling Stone* was one of the first mistakes we'd both made, he said. Again, he used the word *we*, which he had to know was a gift I didn't deserve. I wasn't in his league, or his universe, and it was clearly an epic belly flop. He considered it a badge of honor. He left me with a battle cry and a laugh in the middle of the night. "We're from fucking San Diego," he said. "We're uncool!"

Two days later, I still hadn't checked in with *Rolling Stone*. I'd reported the incident to Mike Hyland, who now feared for his own job. I was over at Sandy and Sharie's house—two kids my own age who often held nonstop parties at their condo—when the phone rang. Sharie handed the phone to me. *How did anybody know I'm here?* Someone important had called our home phone. My mom assumed I was with my friend Chuck and gave them Chuck's number. Chuck's mom told the caller we were at Sharie's. I was wary about who it was and why they'd worked so hard to find me.

"Hello?"

"Hello, Cameron?" It was a chipper, feel-good Southern voice. "This is Phil Walden of Capricorn Records." I'd never spoken to him before. He was the big honcho, the manager of the Allman Brothers Band, the head of their record company, the manager of the late Otis Redding, and a close friend of Jann Wenner, the editor and publisher of *Rolling Stone*. There was nothing good that was going to come from this phone call. This was the part where I got blamed for everything.

"Hey, Cameron, guess what?" Phil said. "Ol' Gregg's been working awful hard, and he called me up today and said, 'Phil, I got this bag of tapes, and *I don't know how I got 'em.*' So he's gonna return them to you. Should I put them in the mail or what?"

I stammered that "Ol' Gregg" could give the bag to Neal, who was still in Hawaii. I wasn't sure where this was all going.

"Great!" He mentioned nothing more of the incident. "Write yourself a good story and you call me if you need anything else. Are they a hell of a band or what?"

I hung up and immediately called Neal in his Honolulu hotel room. "I got the tapes from Willie Perkins," he said. "I also got the group shot we needed." He paused. "The show was *incredible.*"

Sitting on the stairs, I knew I had my career back. In the next room, neighborhood kids were drinking Kahlúa-and-cream drinks and listening to records. Life had delivered me a story with a twist, but it was too dangerous to ever write about. Maybe later. The tapes arrived via FedEx the next day. It was my brown bag, all the tapes intact, with Mama Allman's address written on the sack. I set the tapes down and before I began transcribing them, I ran to the top of the hill in our condo complex and looked across the bay to the Sports Arena. I believed in it all again. The music, my family, the magic shoes. The circus hadn't spit me out after all.

I turned the story in. I was slightly late with it, and Ben received it with muted enthusiasm. It was go-go-go, barely enough time to make publication. Ben vectored the piece into the hands of associate editor Tim Cahill to help sharpen the lede. Cahill was good-natured about taking it on, but I could tell the lack of sophistication in some of my writing irked him. He helped me sculpt the enigmatic and spooky first paragraph that set the tone for the entire story. If my work made him cranky, his contribution certainly made me better.

My first *Rolling Stone* cover story is well remembered by the community of Allman Brothers Band fans. I'm proud of that. It's the first

intimate account of the band's history and rebirth after Duane. I held
the issue in my hands a good long time before I could even open it. I'd
kept the nightmarish episode with Gregg to myself and didn't tell Ben
Fong-Torres until much later. Not long after the issue hit the stands, I
received a *Brothers and Sisters* postcard from Red Dog. It read:

Cameron

No matter how hard the Rain May Fall
No matter how dark the clouds May be
Remember We All Must Climb The Wall

Love,
Red Dog

I often wondered about Gregg's recollection of our nightmarish San
Francisco encounter and his own strange rendezvous with the empty
chair.

One day in early 1992, Neal Preston was sent to photograph Gregg
for *People* magazine. In between snaps, Allman asked what ever happened to Neal's sidekick, the writer for *Rolling Stone*. Neal said that I'd
become a writer-director. Gregg smiled and said he wanted to call me
up and, well, maybe apologize or something.

"We really put that kid through the wringer," he said. They tried to
call me a couple times. My phone was busy. Gregg and I didn't connect
again until much later, when we'd both lived a lot more life.

A fictional version of the stolen-tapes story became a large part of
Almost Famous. The incident was also recounted in Allman's autobiography, *My Cross to Bear*, as a "hazing the rookie" prank that he'd cooked
up with Dickey Betts. In his telling, they returned the tapes just as I was
catching a cab to go home. Rock autobiographies are like that. A complex or morally ambiguous incident can become a benign chestnut,
mostly untrue. He'd heard that the movie was at least partially based on

the 1973 tour they'd invited me along on and he feared a skewering. Instead, in his 2012 book, Gregg wrote that the movie was "ingenious" in capturing the spirit of that 1973 tour. He'd wished he'd been able to watch *Almost Famous* with his brother, Duane, who he was sure had seen it from his "big seat."

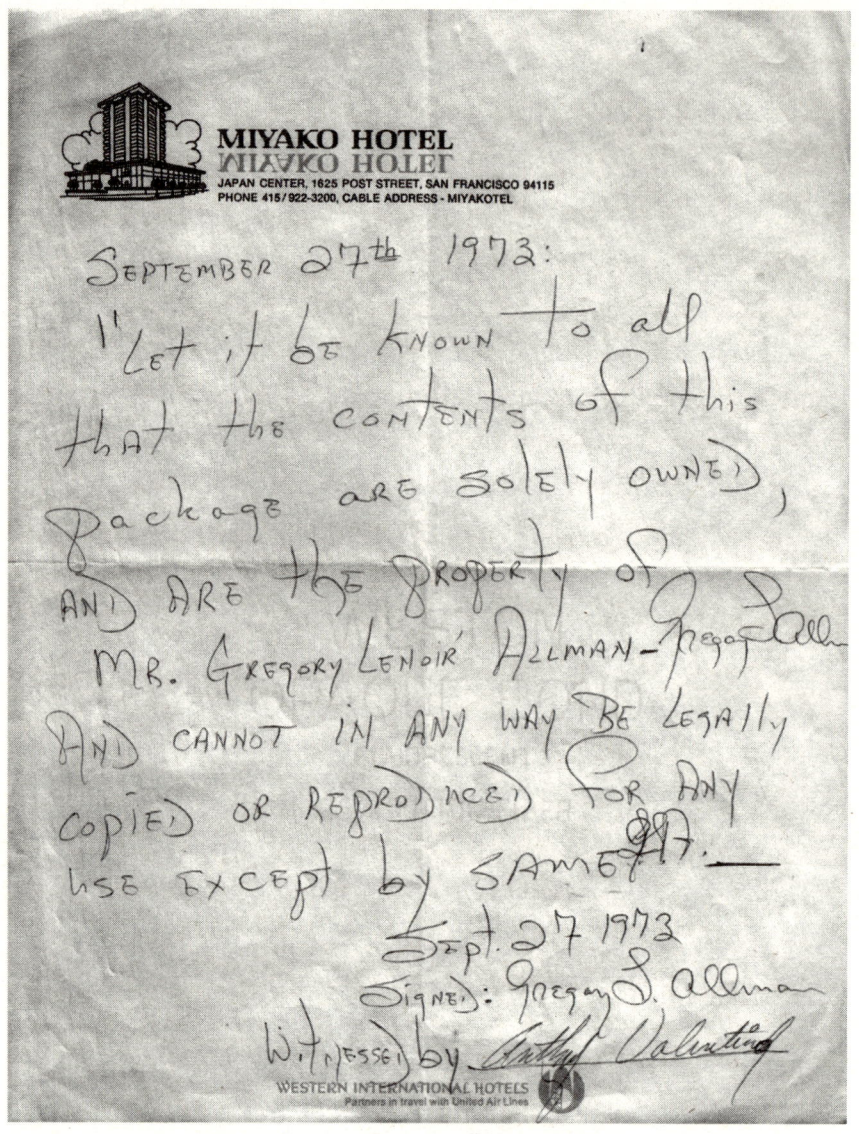

Gregg's spooky late-night document.

Don't Call Me Again

I was staying at Neal and Bobbi's apartment in Beverly Hills, on Oakhurst Drive. Their friend Maureen Donaldson lived down the hall. Maureen was a new arrival from the UK with a sparkly personality and a groovy lifestyle. She was quietly taking the town by storm, writing for *Teen Beat* and working as a stringer for Rona Barrett, Hollywood's premier gossip columnist. Rona was famous for her television reports,

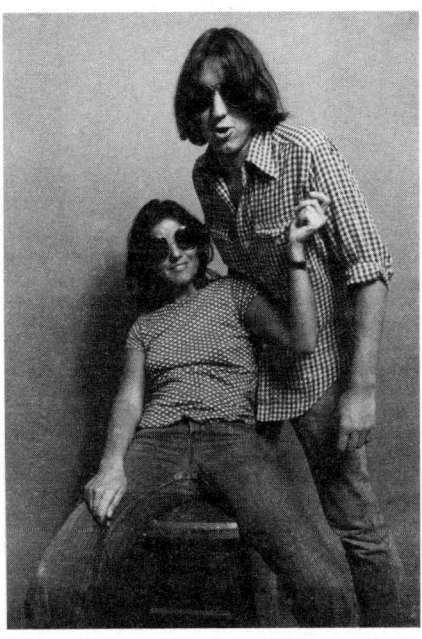

With Maureen
Donaldson, 1973.

where she faced the camera at a very careful three-quarter angle and confided the secrets of Hollywood. Maureen was her secret weapon. She was a modern, fashion-forward young journalist, the kind you normally see in a late-sixties movie about swinging London. She was elegant, energetic with a touch of bubbly, with the eyes of an astute blackbird.

Maureen was at the beginning of a secret relationship with a much older film legend she'd met earlier that summer. He had a full head of silver hair and wore thick black-rimmed glasses. He was a very big star, perhaps even the king of Hollywood for a good long while, but he was now retired, dining out with his friends, going to Dodgers games, catching up with his fellow stars of the now-fading golden era. He'd broken up with his wife and taken a shine to this lively young journalist.

Yes, Maureen was dating Cary Grant.

Maureen was like a cross between Sally Field in *The Flying Nun* and Emma Peel from *The Avengers*. She was a good friend of Neal and Bobbi's and would bounce over unannounced. Their master bedroom, at the back of the apartment, was essentially a large comfortable bed and an oversized TV. You could spend days lost in that room. Maureen would often arrive, plop onto the bed, and download her daily adventures. It was still the early days of her relationship with Cary Grant, and he'd been taking her around, introducing her to all his friends. With Neal and me, Maureen could let down her guard, lighting up a thinly rolled joint, stained with her peach-colored lip gloss. Then she'd dress up and act twenty years older on her date with Cary Grant. Her life was a grand romantic comedy. She was Audrey Hepburn, living her own version of *Roman Holiday*. And her costar wasn't even Gregory Peck. It was the guy whose fingerprints were probably on the script first. Cary fucking Grant.

Once I looked over her shoulder as Maureen paged through her address book. There in delicate writing were her lists of names, addresses, and phone numbers, some of them for the extremely famous friends of Cary. To a prank phone call aficionado like me, this was manna from heaven.

"I dare you to let me call Cary Grant," I asked her one afternoon.

She gave me a look. "What are you going to do?"

"You'll see."

Her eyes narrowed. She was considering it.

"I won't get you in trouble," I promised.

"What if he traces the call?" she said, this being decades before the advent of caller ID.

"He won't trace the call."

She opened the phone book to CG. "This is his private line," she said. "Don't get me in trouble."

I dialed. After three rings, Cary Grant picked up the phone.

"Hello," said Cary Grant, in the way only Cary Grant says hello.

I took on the persona of a drunken drug dealer/street character. "What's going on, man?"

"Well, not much exactly," Cary Grant answered crisply, without judgment.

"Whatchu doing, man? You need anything, need anything at all?" Now I pretended I was talking to somebody else in the room. "Stop it! Put down that gun!"

"Well, that would be a shame," said Cary Grant. "If that gun went off."

"Man, that's my friend Tommy. He's waving his gun around."

"Well, that can't be good," Cary Grant commented. "What else can I do for you?"

In less than a minute, Cary Grant had disabled my prank with delicious good humor. He was ready for more, but I panicked.

"Take care, man," I sputtered. "I'm gonna go get high with Tommy."

"And you tell Tommy hello from me," said Cary Grant.

I hung up. Neal and Maureen cackled with laughter. Cary Grant had vanquished me without even breaking a sweat.

"See how fun he is?" said Maureen.

"Fucking Cary Grant!"

"Yeah," she deadpanned. "I am."

I was ready for more. "Who else can we call?"

We looked through her phone book, and I picked Lucille Ball.

I dialed, hungry for more horseplay with major celebrities.

"Hel-lo," answered Lucille Ball in a husky whiskey voice. I knew instantly it was her.

"Yes," I said, thinking quickly. "This is Mr. Fontaine from the Beverly Hills Hotel." I winked to Neal and Maureen. I knew this character was good. "We seem to have found a purse of some kind, and it apparently belongs to you."

"Don't call me again, you ASSHOLE." The sixty-two-year-old genius of television comedy then jackhammered the phone down with incredible force.

"She's tough," said Maureen, grinning. "I should have warned you."

"I loved Lucy," I said, "but she did *not* love me."

Three years later, Maureen and Cary broke up. It ended well for both, and she remained extremely admiring of their time together. I was always impressed that even on the other end of a prank call, Cary Grant knew the room and knew how to join the party. As for Lucille Ball, all I can tell you is that Martin Scorsese missed a real opportunity when she died. Let it be known. I've never heard anybody both weaponize and *savor* the word *asshole* with such authentic force since my very brief chat with Lucy.

Sweet Home Atlanta

The Allman Brothers Band cover story was published in the December 7, 1973, issue of *Rolling Stone*. The magazine was on the newsstands a week earlier, just in time for another road trip for Neal Preston. Neal and I were both stone-cold freaks for the Who. Pete Townshend was a hero of mine, and not just for the emotional spectacle of his bravura guitar playing-and-smashing onstage. Townshend was a brainiac, the rare individual who thinks with both his heart and his mind, and the genius of his music was the war between the two.

He was also the best rock journalist. Townshend's confessional cover story on the Who, and his own newly found faith in the Indian spiritual leader Meher Baba, was something I'd read a hundred times. There was grace and conviction in how he wrote about rock. Add to that this important fact: there was nothing quite like a Who concert. It was a fast-moving current of anger and tension and release. I'd had a close call at their 1971 appearance at the San Diego Sports Arena. Just before the band took the stage, the lights dimmed and I left my cheaper bleacher seat and slipped onto the main floor. Nobody stopped me and I blended into the crowd.

Suddenly I was swept up in a surge of Who fans, and the human wave crushed me into the barricade. I was pressed against the stage. Eight feet away, with the crowd pushing behind me, the Who appeared in a shower of bright white light. Drummer Keith Moon came tumbling onto the stage. John Entwistle strapped on his bass and thumped out a few notes. Singer Roger Daltrey raced to center stage, microphone in hand, whipping the cord, pacing in a circle. Then came Pete Townshend in a silver jumpsuit, wearing a crown, guitar hanging from his neck. He spread his arms and announced to the Sports Arena crowd:

"Hello, San Diego, what a pleasure to be here in your trash can!"

They were almost the last words I would ever hear. The band tore into "I Can't Explain" at earsplitting volume. The crowd pressed further, and I was flattened against the barricade. Something was going to break, me or the barricade. Miraculously, I was then sucked beneath the throng of fans and spit out to the side, happy to be alive. Townshend had often said that rock, real rock, was about life-and-death passion. More than ever, I knew what he meant.

The Who released an ambitious new double album, *Quadrophenia*, a few months in advance of the 1973 tour. It was a dense, personal masterpiece and a more-than-worthy successor to *Tommy*, the rock opera that elevated them into the highest ranks of rock-era artists. *Quadrophenia* was also a further exploration in Townshend's use of synthesizers and tape loops. It was a complex piece of music.

The Who were great when they were angry, and the word was, as they headed for America, that they were *very* pissed off. The Who were but four players, and *Quadrophenia* was proving a challenge to perform live. There had been rumors of onstage fistfights and tussles with their stage mixer, Bobby Pridden. The entire endeavor was swaying on rickety legs. And sometimes, on rickety legs is exactly how you want to see the Who.

Several of us press types were flown to Atlanta for the beginning of the North American tour. The opening act for the tour was Lynyrd Skynyrd, a new band from Jacksonville, Florida. They'd been signed by Al Kooper, a talented writer-producer who had many credits, from writing the pop hit "This Diamond Ring" for Gary Lewis & the Playboys to playing in the Blues Project and forming Blood, Sweat and

Tears. Kooper was a kind of Zelig of rock. He even played keyboards on Bob Dylan's "Like a Rolling Stone."

Kooper saw Lynyrd Skynyrd play at the Atlanta nightclub Funochio's and immediately signed them to his label, Sounds of the South. He'd also hooked them up with one of the most important managers in rock. Peter Rudge and his company Sir Productions also managed the Who and the Rolling Stones.

The band was a tight-knit unit with three lead guitarists and a memorable front man in lead vocalist and songwriter Ronnie Van Zant. Skynyrd was part of the growing community of Southern-rock outfits like the Allman Brothers Band. I'd listened to their album (*Pronounced 'Lĕh-'nérd 'Skin-'nérd*) and was already addicted to their song "Simple Man." They were also riding the growing success of a radio hit that showed off their three-guitar attack. The song was called "Free Bird," and as we stood listening to their sound check, the song already felt like a classic.

Opening for the Who was a prestigious honor. It was also one of the more thankless tasks in rock. The battlefield is littered with the bodies of bands who had to face the Who's bloodthirsty fans. The last artist I'd seen open a Who show was a friendly, energetic gospel-rock singer named Mylon LeFevre. I've never seen anybody work so hard for so little. He began with a generous, bighearted welcome to the crowd. Twenty minutes later, he nearly left the stage in tears.

Neal Preston and I gathered backstage at the sold-out Atlanta arena, the Omni, while the clock ticked down to showtime. I was impressed with Mary Beth Medley, Peter Rudge's management partner. Mary Beth looked after Lynyrd Skynyrd. Rudge was in and out of the Who's dressing room, consumed with preshow jitters over *Quadrophenia*. Mary Beth was in her early twenties but had a skill set that matched the powerhouse that was Rudge. She'd been a college promoter while attending Stony Brook University and moved easily in the world of musicians. I watched her warmly tend to each member of Skynyrd so they didn't feel ignored in favor of the much bigger band.

Mary Beth mentioned that Ronnie Van Zant wanted to meet me. She led me to a small locker room tucked into the far recesses of the Omni. The room smelled like Vicks VapoRub and sweat. Jack Daniel's bottles, potato chips, and slabs of wilted cheese were spread out on a massage table. Van Zant sat quietly in a soccer player's cubicle waiting for showtime.

He was a tough-looking guy with straw-colored hair and tree-trunk arms. Though he looked like he could deck you with a single punch, Van Zant was exceedingly polite, with a soft and friendly lilt to his voice. He was the leader of this wild and woolly bunch. While the other members were burning their showtime nerves with rambunctious shouting and bouncing off the locker room walls, Van Zant was wisely conserving his energy.

He'd read the *Rolling Stone* cover story on the Allman Brothers Band. An early copy of the article was floating around, and Van Zant had read every word. Apparently, it was required reading among the Southern bands. He was curious and surprised by Gregg Allman's vulnerability in the interview. Lynyrd Skynyrd had been turned down by Capricorn Records, the Allman Brothers' label. He mentioned that Gregg had always been a little chilly to him; he didn't really know why.

"We don't play their kind of music," Van Zant said, leaning back against pieces of sports equipment. "We play a lot of English blues, like the Rolling Stones and Free." He was rapturous talking about Free's lead singer, Paul Rodgers. "Man, do I love that band."

Van Zant was an inspired storyteller. It was a gift that was evident in his songwriting. He was also the father figure of an extremely volatile band. We made plans to get together soon and do an interview for a piece on Lynyrd Skynyrd. It was the beginning of a friendship that stretched past his own life and throughout mine. There were no throwaway moments around Van Zant and Skynyrd. Life around the band was either dangerous or compelling or memorably funny, and often all three at once.

Ten minutes before showtime, the locker room grew serious. A hint of crowd noise wafted in with the hum of the air conditioner. Van Zant had something to say to each member, hands on their shoulders. He was soothing and challenging. As a bandleader, he had a quality I'd seen in Glenn Frey. He'd read his rock history. He knew what it would take to go all the way. He knew how to fire up a small room of jittery musicians with an us-against-the-world spirit.

As distracted Who fans drifted into their seats, Lynyrd Skynyrd opened with "I Ain't the One." There was a hard, well-rehearsed edge to the songs. With each Skynyrd song, the applause built. "Simple Man" was followed by "Tuesday's Gone" and "Gimme Three Steps." The band left the stage. The Who's audience, one of the toughest in rock, gave the band a rare gift. They demanded an encore.

The encore was "Free Bird." Van Zant roamed the stage barefoot, driving each of the three guitarists to play even more relentlessly. The song built to its soon-to-be-famous giddy peak. The song was still new; most were hearing it for the first time. Understatement: it would not be their last.

Peter Rudge wandered backstage in a big fur coat, looking stunned. "Nobody gets an encore opening for the Who," he said. "I've never seen this before."

Exhausted and happy, Lynyrd Skynyrd headed straight for the liquor and the local luminaries. The backstage was flooded with hangers-on, DJs, visiting press, and all kinds of regional human pageantry, but Van Zant remained in the dressing room. Reflective and happy, he was clearly savoring the band's knockout victory. Meanwhile, the stage was being turned over to the Who. The preshow music was now Jimmy Reed's "Bright Lights, Big City."

There was backstage drama over the underrehearsed new material. Townshend exited the band's dressing room in a zip-up shirt and white pants. Head down, he was pacing in small circles. Daltrey next emerged from the band's dressing room, saying hello to a few friends, bouncing with nervous energy. Fans on the side seats with a view to the backstage area began to cheer. The cheering spread. John Entwistle, the bassist, sauntered into position, near the others. They waited for Keith Moon, who had disappeared to backstage parts unknown. Then Moon appeared, corralled by a roadie, his dark eyes flashing with a trademark brew of menace and glee.

The Omni lights went dark. The crowd detonated. Very loud amps were switched on. This was always my favorite part of any concert. The very beginning.

"Ladies and gentlemen, the Who."

They took to the stage and blasted through a quick three-punch opening of "I Can't Explain," "Summertime Blues," and Entwistle's "My Wife." It was efficient and thrilling, but to the studied Who fan, the band wasn't the same cocky group who tended to explode right out of the box and let it be known they didn't give a fuck. Tonight they seemed preoccupied and burdened, especially Pete Townshend.

After "Boris the Spider," Townshend told the audience that *Quadrophenia* was still new and to be prepared for any shaky music cues. The show would gather steam, then falter and surge again with the new material. (Keith Moon's vocal on "Bell Boy" was an audience favorite.) Finally the band surrendered to their catalog of stage favorites, from "Won't Get Fooled Again" to "Magic Bus," and the evening ended on a raucous high.

After the show a small collection of friends and family, including Al Kooper, waited to say hello to the Who. The band's tall and officious road manager stood outside their dressing room, guarding the door like a security guard protecting the *Mona Lisa*.

"The band's just having a chat," he said. "Let's give them a minute."

He quietly waited. Inside the room was the sound of yelling, followed by metal chairs crashing against a wall, followed by more yelling. Then a long beat of silence.

"The boys will see you now," he said. He swung the door open. The band pleasantly greeted their visitors, though their sound mixer, Bobby Pridden, looked like he'd just lost a street fight.

Townshend was wearing a towel around his neck. He still looked preoccupied. I complimented his sonic bravery in adding the complex *Quadrophenia* material to the usual elemental explosion of a Who show.

"It was rubbish," he said.

"I thought the new stuff was—"

He waved the idea away. Keeping all the tape loops straight had given him a headache. Elsewhere, amid a still-overturned piece of furniture or two, the others discussed the show with rapturous locals. Every other sentence from the band members began or ended with "fucking hell." They were everything I wanted them to be. Candid, upset, explosive, and . . . oddly friendly. Townshend had created the stakes for the band long ago. The Who weren't a casual band. This music was live-or-die. He'd personally thrown the counterculture activist Abbie Hoffman off the stage at Woodstock for interrupting their show.

Decades later, that anger and the energy would still be present in his music. Townshend openly struggled with the purpose and promise of rock. It was more than just sonic wallpaper. There are few greater spokesmen for the passion and power of music, and the importance of creative authenticity. He was also one of the few artists who would confide in the press. On any given day, Townshend was the best interview in rock. His interviews were X-rays into his process, rock therapy in real time.

I was constantly amazed at how many *people* lived in the United States. Every city had phone books full of people, strangers, friends I'd never make. And in every city was at least a pocket of people like me, who loved music and craved the feeling of what happened in those arenas. I never was a jock, but following music was my sport, and it was always fun to find people with the same craving for this wildfire that was building everywhere, all these great bands, and most of them only a few months away from visiting your hometown.

Giddy with appreciation for everything that was happening, I struck up a conversation with a local radio rep, a young woman with long feathered earrings. Somehow, I had the confidence that had eluded me in school, when I could have used it. We both loved the Who. We were talking about the first time we'd seen the band. I was pleasantly telling the story about my near–death by asphyxiation and about how the show ended with a transcendent "Naked Eye." We were interrupted by the keyboard player from Lynyrd Skynyrd, Billy Powell. He was wearing a dark velvet coat and had a plastic cup in his hand. It was full, and clearly wasn't his first full cup of the night.

"What the fuck are you doing, man?" he said. "Who are you?"

I had met him earlier, when he was sober.

"You making some moves, man?"

I didn't know what to say. I had no moves, nor did I know how to make them. But a part of me was thrilled to even be considered some kind of moves-making guy. Powell took a step closer, and his drink sloshed in his hand. "I'm talkin' to ya," he said.

There was a look on his face I'd seen before. It's the look of someone with adrenaline moving up his arm, just before it becomes a punch.

"No, man," I said, "I was just—"

"*Billy*," said the woman with the feathered earrings. "We're just talking."

His jaw was set. I truly thought that he was about to hit me. The lopsided charade was interrupted by Ronnie Van Zant.

"That's about it!" he said to Powell. He'd cut through the small crowd around us. I hadn't even noticed him in the vicinity. He walked Billy out of the area, pausing to shoot me a shrug. For a few months, that was the last I saw of Ronnie Van Zant.

That night I also felt a spark in meeting Mary Beth Medley. She lived in New York, but we stayed in touch over the next weeks. Our conversations about music soon turned to conversations about ourselves. She was four years older than me, a hardworking music lover, strong and funny. Before long it was obvious that we were a match. Later she asked me about my previous girlfriends. What were they like? It was a hard question to answer. She was my first girlfriend. We moved in together a couple years later and one day we crossed the Rubicon of every music loving couple: we combined our record collections

But that was all around the corner on that fall night in Atlanta. When Neal Preston and I recapped the evening later, we decided on an obvious truth. The only thing that was almost as good as a Who concert was what *happened* at a Who concert.

Raw Power

Dechember 1973. Lester Bangs was coming to town. He let me know he'd be near my house, conducting a radio interview at the progressive station KPRI. Bangs's pal Larry Yurdin was the host. Yurdin was a broadcasting visionary, often credited as the rebellious originator of free-form radio. It was sure to be a meeting of the titans.

Located on the downtown corner of Ninth and Ash, KPRI's broadcast booth was visible from the sidewalk picture window. The station's DJs often drew open the curtains so passersby could groove on the real-time experience of watching them pull records and work the turntables. A small speaker piped the music onto the street corner. I arrived early, and Lester was already on the air, playing Iggy Pop's "I Wanna Be Your Dog."

Bangs lumbered around the radio studio, grabbing records from the cabinets, hurling album jackets around like Frisbees and offering his critiques on the artists that the station played religiously.

I was glued to the window. It felt like I was watching a live art installation entitled *Lester Bangs*. If he noticed me, I couldn't tell.

"Try not to scratch the records," Yurdin suggested mildly as Bangs pulled the vinyl from the album jacket for Jethro Tull's *Aqualung*. "They belong to the station."

Bangs promptly flung the vinyl across the room. "Why don't you play some real music, like Lou Reed?"

An assistant DJ exited for a cigarette break, and I asked if I could come inside. He propped the door open and during a break, I introduced myself to Lester. He was a big galumphing guy with a red Guess Who shirt under a black leather jacket. He had sweet eyes, like a kind neighborhood pooch, and a starter beer belly. Lester pumped my hand vigorously and treated me like an equal, a fellow veteran in the rock journalism game. Of course, I was a bat boy and he was the Willie Mays of the genre.

After his appearance on KPRI was over, he suggested we get a coffee. We walked out onto my street, into *my neighborhood*. He didn't have much time, he said, he had to catch the bus back to El Cajon.

He was twenty pounds away from being handsome, I thought, with half-combed hair and a hunched arm-swinging way of walking. On the page, his writing presence could be powerfully sharp and almost scary-brilliant. I was surprised how friendly he was in person, always slinging opinions like a dart player who didn't care if the darts ever hit the dartboard.

I pointed out a diner nearby. It was the very place where I would sometimes write. Kismet! He ordered a sandwich instead of coffee. A sandwich meant a greater time commitment. I kept a close watch for when I might bore him. I did impressions of the British musicians I'd interviewed. He listened and smirked. Finally, he leaned forward and gave me advice.

"Don't make friends with the rock stars," he said. "They'll ruin you. The publicists will ruin you. You gotta remember. They're all trying to use us to play up the glory of rock stars, and it will kill rock and everything we love about it." I nodded and began to make notes. He didn't stop me. "I'm telling ya, it's gonna get ugly. They're gonna buy you drinks. You're gonna meet girls. They're gonna fly you places for free, offer drugs. It'll seem like fun, but these people are not your friends. These are people who want you to write sanctimonious stories about the genius of rock stars. And they will ruin rock and roll and strangle everything we love about it, right?"

He said "we." I nodded like I deserved it. A few minutes later we were walking back to his bus stop.

"Soon," he continued, "it'll just be an industry of . . . of *cool*." The word dripped with sarcasm. For the first time, I was thrilled it had never been used in connection with me. "I mean, you're coming along at a very dangerous time. Real music, music that you can call your own, barely exists anymore. It's over."

"At least I'm here for that," I said.

He smirked again, this time appreciatively. "And beware *Rolling Stone*," he added. "Jann Wenner is a self-serving ass-kissing heap of guano. That magazine will change your stories and rewrite you and turn your work into *swill*. Watch out. You should make your reputation on being honest and *unmerciful*."

He stopped at the street corner. "I'm going to go back to El Cajon, see my mom, and then find my ex-girlfriend so she can break up with me again."

I didn't want to wear out my welcome, so I left him there, waiting for the bus to El Cajon. For years, I'd continue to see him standing on that corner, in his black leather jacket and Guess Who T-shirt, even when he wasn't.

"Call me anytime," he said, "I stay up late."

We gotta get you a woman.

—TODD RUNDGREN

Todd Rundgren quickly became one of my favorite artists. His angst-soaked, heartfelt songs like "Hope I'm Around" and "A Dream Goes On Forever" spoke to me. Here was a guy without chiseled Mick Jagger features. He had a long face and a kind of El Greco expression. He wasn't a typical good-looking Joe and he wasn't a surfer with perfect sideburns like Stephen Stills. He didn't look like so many

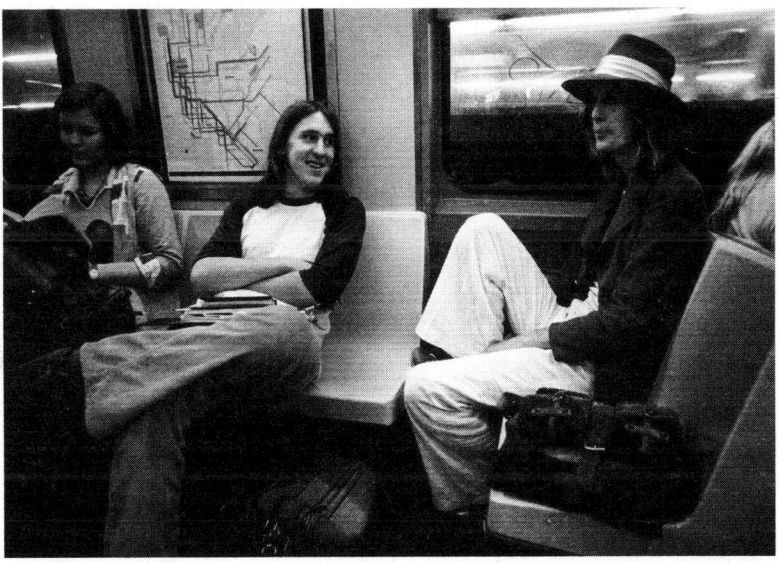

First time on the New York subway, with Todd Rundgren, New York City, 1973.

of my schoolmates who got all the girls. I couldn't put my finger on it
until I realized . . . he looked like *me*.

His girlfriend was achingly beautiful. Bebe Buell was her name, and
she had the fairest skin I'd ever seen. She clung proudly to Todd's arm,
giving awkward guys like me a distant hope. She spoke of Todd like he
was a mystic, a poet, and a genius for the ages. I pretty much agreed.
Rundgren seemed to bask in the adoration. He had a history of strik-
ingly beautiful girlfriends, which seemed at odds with his earliest songs
about pain and rejection and yearning.

It was Rundgren's "We Gotta Get You a Woman" that hit me hard
as a teenager. It felt like a personal anthem, a heartsick piece of pop perfection, about a kid who needed a girlfriend. I had begged for a *Rolling
Stone* assignment to interview Rundgren in Greenwich Village, where
he'd moved from his hometown of Philadelphia. Neal Preston was the
photographer, and I was able to get us two plane tickets and a single
hotel room at the Barbizon-Plaza. It was my first visit to New York
City. Neal and I landed on a sizzling summer night in June 1974 and
launched right into the heart of the music scene. The city was soggy with
heat and humidity. We went straight to the Bottom Line nightclub for
a performance by the English folk troupe Steeleye Span and ran into an
editor for *Circus* magazine, whom I'd only met on the phone. He was
drunk and friendly until I kidded him about leaving my name off a
recent story I'd written about the Yes keyboardist Rick Wakeman. He
instantly turned nasty. He signaled a bouncer to have me thrown out of
the club for being underage. This was nothing new for me. Wherever
alcohol was served, I was on borrowed time.

Neal and I made a late-night visit to Max's Kansas City, the legendary
restaurant and club, where I met a fellow rock writer, Laurel Delp. She
was moonlighting as a waitress. We knew each other's writing, and she
seemed more bookwormish than the other servers slicing through the
crowd in their black micro-mini skirts. Laurel made me feel like part of
the tribe, those who toiled late into the night for their free promotional
albums. She set down a cup of dried chickpeas that could shatter your

teeth and cautioned that we shouldn't eat them, but it was okay to toss one or two to get someone's attention. We'd just missed a performance by Bruce Springsteen at Max's upstairs, she said, but all was not lost.

"You want to meet Lou?" she asked. No last name was necessary. My heart skipped a beat. Could it be true? This was like someone offering to introduce you to Babe Ruth on your first trip to Yankee Stadium.

She walked me to the back room, where Lou Reed was sitting alone, cradling a drink. He wasn't wearing his usual sunglasses. I stood; he sat. I was struck by how much, up close, he looked like the comedian Jerry Lewis. Laurel gave me a nice introduction, informing him that I'd just had a cover story on Jackson Browne published in *Rolling Stone*. Browne had shared a colorful anecdote about Reed in the story.

"I read it," Lou said sharply. Whatever you'd call the opposite of impressed, that was his tone.

"He's kind of a boy wonder," Laurel offered helpfully.

Reed made a small hissing sound. Laurel laughed warmly—*Oh, that Lou*—and this being my first night in New York, I somehow took it as an invitation for camaraderie. I shared that Jackson Browne had name-checked one of Reed's friends, the Andy Warhol actor Rene Ricard, and had done a colorful imitation. Did Reed have the same memory? Lou Reed looked at Laurel painfully, as in *Take the performing monkey away*.

By early morning, Neal and I were on a corner outside a Nathan's hot dog stand in Greenwich Village. The nightlife was explosive with personalities, street performers, beggars, loonies. Somewhere a boom box was playing the Stylistics' "People Make the World Go Round." Neal and I were too buzzed to leave the circus and call it a night. We ate hot dogs with thick casings and briny sauerkraut. Soon a homeless street prophet with bloodred eyes cornered us for a ten-minute screed about the coming end of the world.

"The Arabs got the oil, *right?*" He continued the mantra with different emphasis. "*The Arabs* . . . got the oil. Right?" Again, we agreed. "Now, *Sadat!* He knows where the *action* is. They want to *take him out*." He drew closer. "And *Kissing . . . Kissing . . .*" It took him three tries to get the name out. "*Kissinger* is gonna go over there and *hook things up*." He drew even closer. "But it's gonna go *boom*. BOOM!" He paused. "BOOM!" He had a small crowd around him now. "Because the Arabs got the oil. *Right?*"

Looking back, he wasn't far off from predicting the global course of the next fifty years. We didn't know that then. Or did we? Rarely has a month or two ever gone by when Neal and I haven't just paused, apropos of nothing, and said, "The Arabs got the oil. *Right?*"

We thanked him, and he demanded to be paid. We only had a few dollars left, and it was less than he felt he deserved, so our street-corner Nostradamus lumbered off into the night, looking for another audience to whom he could declare the end of the world. I'd been chased by bouncers, gotten a lethal dismissal from Lou Reed, and been informed of the apocalypse. In other words, it was the best first night in New York City imaginable.

We went to Todd's home on Horatio Street the next morning. Rundgren was a dry wit, a great interview, and I enjoyed his goofy relationship with Bebe, as well as their dog Furburger. I only glimpsed tension

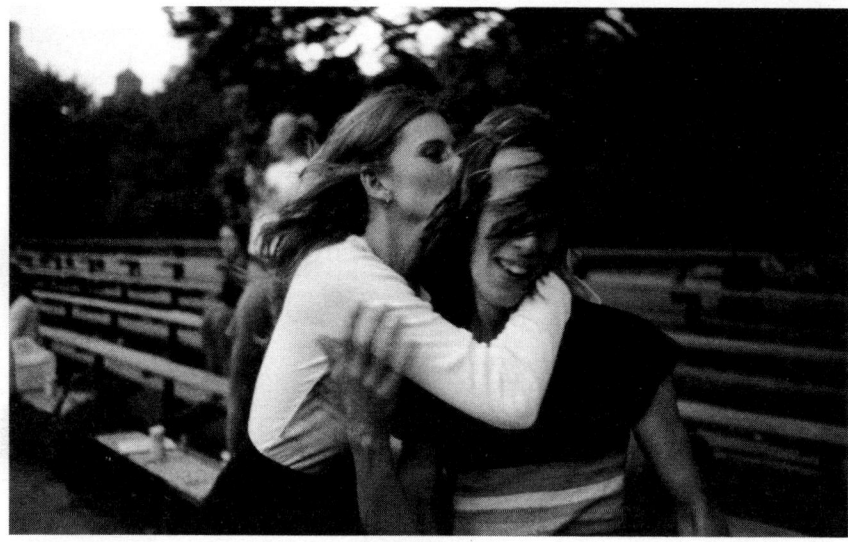

Todd and Bebe: Pop romance in Central Park, 1973.

briefly, but definitively, when I joined them at a radio interview where the DJ mentioned one of Todd's earlier songs, "Marlene," and Bebe exited in a snit. (Marlene, an early girlfriend, was a taboo mention. Good to know, since "Marlene" was another one of my favorite Rundgren songs.)

Todd and Bebe Buell were the twin toasts of New York, both dressed in the glam style of post–Ziggy Stardust. Max's Kansas City was their living room. They collected people as they went. The phone rang constantly at their home, and it was often a songwriter named Leonard Cohen. Bebe wasn't sure exactly what Cohen wanted. "I just think he likes being around me," she said. She seemed to know everybody in New York and was filled with gossip and party possibilities with all kinds of other stars. By the time I had to return to San Diego, the three of us felt like close friends.

I took a cab back to Friars Village from the airport. I felt more cosmopolitan, of course, battle-tested by New York and ready for more. In the living room was a meeting of the San Diego Liberation Committee, the feminist organization filled with several of my mother's favorite counselees. The meeting had drifted away from their political agenda and into a group therapy session featuring Gloria, a woman who often kept my mom on the phone until late at night, working through her romantic woes.

My mom was a world-class listener. She sat among her guests tonight, carefully tracking all the conversational detail, no matter how small, and holding forth from the treasured rocking chair that had once belonged to her father. My dad was tending to the answering services in the desert, and Cindy had already moved to Los Angeles. I went down to my room and began transcribing my Todd Rundgren interviews.

Soon there was a furtive knock. It was Gloria. "Can I talk with you?"

She wore a tie-dye shirt, like a Grateful Dead fan. My record collection lived in the crates on either side of my small room. There wasn't much room to sit. Waterbeds had been perfected, so I'd gotten one that year. Gloria sat on the white rim surrounding the undulating blue mattress. I was holding a pen, in the middle of correcting the transcription.

"I wanted to talk with you about your parents," said Gloria. "If you've noticed anything different about them, I can tell you why."

"I haven't really noticed anything different," I said.

"Your parents are going through a crisis," she said. "They may split up, and they may not. But I would be very kind to them if I were you."

She told me there had been a lawsuit involving a birdlike woman I'd once met at my dad's answering service, Tamara. I'd heard her name a bit. She was a supervising partner in the business and was engaged to another one of my father's business friends. She and my father had tumbled into a brief affair the year before. Tamara had returned to her previous partner and now they both were trying to blackmail my father into selling them a stake in his answering service business. My father refused, and Terah had called my mother to tell her about the affair.

While I had been in New York, Gloria said, my father and mother had gone to court to challenge Tamara. My mother testified on my father's behalf. But the previous few months had been spent deciding if they'd stay together. My mother, last month when I thought she was attending a seminar in Riverside, had gone to Mexico to look up an old paramour. It hadn't gone well, and she'd returned.

It was one of those moments when the aperture of your life widens. I hadn't sensed a thing. Tamara had seemed like a blank page when I met her, a small woman at a desk, just this side of invisible. My parents had been pleasant and typical in their behavior around me. But darkness had been swirling, just one floor above. *Beware of the dark shapes of the anadromous fish.*

She told me that my mother was thinking about leaving the family to live in a commune in Tennessee. It was called the Farm. It was then America's largest commune, a sustainable operation set on fifteen hundred acres in Summertown, Tennessee. My mother? Living in a hippie *commune?* Reminding all of the pot smokers that they were killing their brain cells while digging carrots and picking apples? *I don't think so.*

"How's my dad?"

"Fighting to keep his family," Gloria said.

I looked down. When I looked up again, Gloria was crying small tears. I felt curious. It was *my* family. I was the one who deserved to cry.

"Life is such a trip," she said.

Suddenly I wanted to comfort her. My head was full of images of my mother, chasing some guy in Mexico. My father, who always supported my mother in all her escapades, falling into an embarrassing affair with someone who didn't love him like we did? All I felt was compassion. All I could think was, *It's all true. All the complexities and fallibility and mistakes and heartbreak that live in the music I love, the stuff I thought lived in other people's homes, it lives in our home. It lives upstairs. It'll probably live in me too.*

"Life is a trip," I repeated.

She patted the spot next to her. She looked at me with a sad, sweet smile. I sat next to her on the corner of my waterbed. "Let's just hold each other," she said.

I was still grasping a pen in my hand. I felt lost. My world had turned topsy-turvy. As we adjusted ourselves to perhaps hug each other, I tumbled backward. I stabbed my waterbed with the pen, puncturing the rubber mattress. I raced to get the important waterbed repair pack they give you when you buy a waterbed. I frantically tried to patch the leak while Gloria, my intimate stranger, dabbed her eyes with a Kleenex.

"I only told you," she said, "because your mother wanted you to know."

I never saw Gloria again that year, or for many years. In that one night, my life split into BG and AG. Before Gloria told me about my parents' near breakup. After Gloria spilled the beans and I almost exploded the waterbed. My mom and dad never broke up, and when I told my dad I knew about Terah, we were sitting on a park bench. He looked embarrassed but hugged me. We held hands. We never spoke about it again.

When I told my mother that I knew about her trip to Mexico, her dalliance with an old flame, the lawsuit, and the turbulent near breakup they'd kept from my sister and me, she turned to me with a whiplash stare.

"Who told you?" she demanded.

I didn't answer. She looked at me, as if practicing ESP.

"It was Gloria," she said. I now knew her game. She "read minds" with the information she already knew.

"She told me you wanted me to know."

"Gloria told me the key to keeping a man is oral sex," my mom said. "I'm just not good at oral sex."

"I *do not* want to have this conversation with you."

"I agree," she said. "And Gloria talks too much."

"I agree."

"Plus, she had a crush on you."

"Really?"

"Gloria," my mom said, "had a crush on everyone."

Physical Graffiti

There was always something slightly forbidden about Led Zeppelin. For me, it was the X factor that gave them mystery and allure. They were darker than the other bands and they had a command of mystique. You didn't see a slew of interviews with them; you barely saw any at all. Their first album had been a sonic explosion, an announcement made from the first track, right off the bat, "Good Times Bad Times." Hard rock was their calling card, but it was their acoustic stuff that made them legendary. "Stairway to Heaven," of course, had both. It was the English folk tradition beneath the bombast that I craved.

They famously hated *Rolling Stone*. The rumor was that Jimmy Page and Jann Wenner had tangled over a girl in London. The magazine trashed their first album. There was no way I'd be able to land an interview unless I had an assignment they couldn't turn down. I called Robert Hilburn from the *Los Angeles Times*, who instructed me to write a pitch letter to the entertainment editor, Charles Champlin. Champlin, a well-known reviewer and interviewer, said yes. Sure enough, I was included on a short list with a handful of journalists granted interviews with guitarist Jimmy Page and singer Robert Plant.

The interviews took place at the Continental Hyatt House, on the seventh floor. As I was ushered into Page's suite, he was listening to Bob Marley and the Wailers on a portable record player. I knew instantly that Led Zeppelin were the band I wanted them to be. Page craved music and provided his own soundtrack for our interview. We shared a lot of the same favorites. He loved Neil Young and Joe Walsh, whom I'd written about. He was particularly enamored with Joni Mitchell. The acoustic side of Led Zeppelin, he said, is what gave the band its richness.

The story was published in the *Los Angeles Times*. It was a kind of maiden voyage into the mainstream for the band, and two years later, as they were about to release their album *Physical Graffiti*, I collected a handful of assignments and was invited on the road with them by Danny Goldberg, the band's publicist and an executive at the label they'd started, Swan Song. Neal Preston, who'd impressed the band with his photography, joined the tour with me.

They flew on a plane that was dubbed the Starship because it was outfitted for rock stars. The plane allowed the band to lessen the grind of touring. They could hub out of a city for a week, flying off to play shows and then returning to their hotel every night.

The 1975 tour began with rehearsals and a quick debut show in Minneapolis, after which they flew to Chicago to officially kick off their most consequential American jaunt. Early cover mock-ups for *Physical Graffiti*, the new album, were arriving for the band's approval. The two-record set was chock-full of new material destined for much fan worship, but few had even heard a note. I had an early cassette and listened with headphones, lugging my boom box on the cold streets of Chicago. Wet slushy snow was on the ground. For a Zeppelin fan who grew up in the desert, trust me, this was a heavenly way to first hear *Physical Graffiti*.

At sound check, Zeppelin played one of the new tracks with an ominous hypnotic beat, "Kashmir." It was sure to be a new crowd favorite. There would even be a single from the new album, one of the few the group released—this one was called "Trampled Under Foot." The Rolling Stones may have been touring the same year, but Zeppelin was selling out more shows without even the benefit of advertising. To be a Zeppelin fan was to be part of a private club. The music was like a joint passed between friends. They had quietly become the biggest band in the world.

Danny Goldberg knew there was a big story here. It was time to declare Led Zeppelin's might in the marketplace. We discussed Goldberg's secret plan to parlay my access into a *Rolling Stone* cover on the band. My head was swimming with all the giddy possibilities.

The opening show in Chicago was plagued by a small problem. Page had injured his little finger and wasn't fully able to perform one of their signature songs, "Dazed and Confused," a tour de force that featured his trademark moment of playing part of the solo with a violin bow. The song was dark and inviting, even mystical, and on any given night it could sometimes last a half hour or more. It was the emotional peak of many a Led Zeppelin show. Though "Dazed," as the band called it, wasn't on the set list for their debut show of the tour, the night was still a great success. The new songs, like "Ten Years Gone" and "In My Time of Dying," had landed powerfully with the audience.

After the show, the roadies would slip terry cloth robes around the band members and hustle them back to the hotel, in this case the Ritz-Carlton. I loved the nightly image of them fresh from the stage, in hooded robes, herded into limos by Richard Cole, their piratelike tour manager, like a mother hen. They were the undisputed kings of hard rock, huge and almost monolithic in their mystique, but in truth they were a gang of four with a small circle of roadies and a lean team led by their large and imposing manager, Peter Grant, a former wrestler. Up close, Led Zeppelin was yet another us-against-the-world-style operation.

Lisa Robinson, writing for *Hit Parader*, was the only other journalist invited on the tour. Lisa and I got along well and often stood onstage watching the shows together. The bands all loved her. She was the queen of dish. She began every sentence with "Darling . . ." and wrote her notes exclusively on pink Beverly Hills Hotel notepads, stolen from the bedsides of the hotel. I was still covering the tour for *Playboy* and other publications, and couldn't even tell Lisa about the secret mission to somehow talk the band into a *Rolling Stone* cover.

The key to getting Zeppelin on the cover of *Rolling Stone* was always going to be Jimmy Page. Page was the only member of the group who staunchly refused to talk for the magazine in any form. I would interview the other members first, and if Page still refused, Robert Plant would be on the cover by himself. Surely that prospect would lure Page into the idea of a group shot. Or maybe he would scuttle the whole endeavor. That was possible too, perhaps probable.

Back in San Francisco, Ben Fong-Torres approved of the idea and cheered me on with daily phone calls asking for progress reports. I was already nearing the end of the time I'd told my parents I would be away from home, and I was dodging most of my commitments at San Diego City College, where I was taking some classes. I had managed to talk my City College journalism teacher into counting my road trip with Zeppelin as a class credit.

After their shows, the band would return to the Ambassador Hotel and regroup to go out clubbing in Chicago. Because it was known they were in town, and fans were on the prowl, Richard Cole often slipped them into a gay bar just around the corner. It was a tradition that continued for much of the tour. Fans combing the streets looking for the band never realized they could find Jimmy Page and Robert Plant dancing together, unbothered, to a song by Gloria Gaynor or the Average White Band. I was always darting into bathrooms, making notes on little pieces of paper, often to the soundtrack of cocaine-sniffing patrons and sometimes sex on the other side of the stall door.

The glamorous life never quite found me. I was picked up at the gay bar by a woman named Dale. She was a single mother and a schoolteacher on her day off. She invited me to her apartment, and I watched her pay the babysitter. Her daughter went to sleep. We drank a Heineken or two and she told me about her ex-husband. Finally, we attempted sex on her sofa. We never finished. She blamed her IUD; it was hurting her. Later I realized it was the fault of my own amateur lovemaking skills. The evening that had begun with Led Zeppelin opening with a blistering live "Rock and Roll" ended with a sloshy walk back to the hotel and a wave to Dale in the window.

There was something about that cold winter. Bob Dylan's *Blood on the Tracks* had also just been released. The songs were running through my head. I doubt Dale would even remember me, but when I hear "Shelter from the Storm," I still see her early-morning face in that window, and I hear the crunch of snow. That's the power of music, and that's the poetry of the road. But oh, was I an amateur. I never went out clubbing after that. I went back to my room and transcribed my notes from the show, trying to read the words I'd scribbled in the dark.

The next day was the interview with Robert Plant. Plant is a music aficionado whose taste rivaled any rock critic or DJ. He can geek out over a Jefferson Airplane record from twenty years earlier, or play you a spectacularly obscure piece of world music you'll never forget. Most every great band has a member like Plant—a built-in scholar of the group's history and musical roots. He's the kind of front man who'll pick up a fan T-shirt thrown onto the stage and proudly wear it the next day. Combined with Page, it's an unstoppable duo. Our chat about Zeppelin was frank and funny, perfect for a *Rolling Stone* cover story. Shutting off my cassette recorder, I was sure it was all going to work.

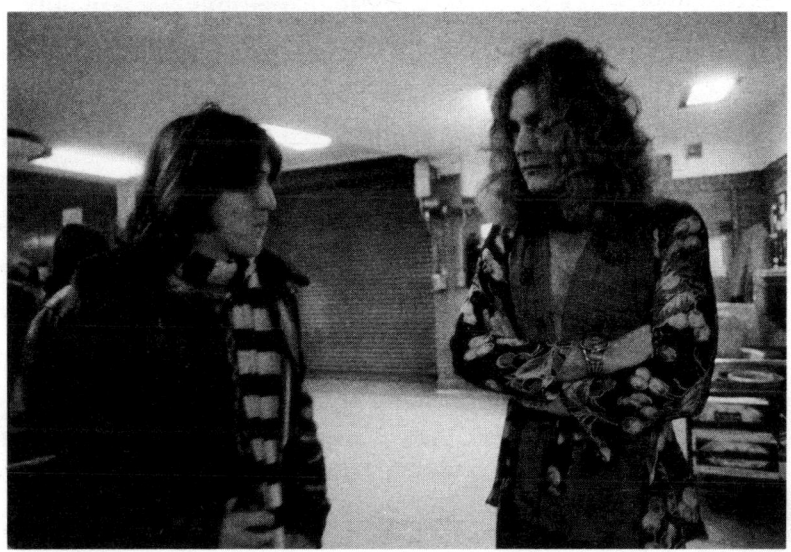

Backstage with Robert Plant at Chicago Stadium, 1975.

Try imagining a place that is always safe and warm . . .

—BOB DYLAN

I n New York, the nightly routine continued. Led Zeppelin and company would meet in the Oyster Bar at the Plaza Hotel around five o'clock. Richard Cole would divide us into cars that would take us to LaGuardia, and then we'd pile onto the Starship. I had already interviewed all the members of the band for a possible *Rolling Stone* piece, and the days were ticking by. My eyes had become bloodshot from the lack of sleep and resolution. The decision was down to Jimmy Page and whether he would allow the material to be used for a *Rolling Stone* cover.

The shows began to roll by. In Indianapolis, he was friendly but distant. Each show was topping the previous one as the band found their footing with the new material. Audiences only needed one listen to appreciate "Ten Years Gone" and, of course, "Kashmir" as they heard future band classics for the first time. The effect was dark and addictive. Sometimes an entire Led Zeppelin audience seemed to become drugged by their vibe. By Greensboro, Page had started to ignore me. By the next night, he began to look right through me. He was now aware that everyone but him had spoken to me for a potential *Rolling Stone* piece. Time was running out on all fronts. Back home, my parents were beyond flummoxed by the delays. I had been on the road with Led Zeppelin for over ten days.

Somewhere over Kansas, I took my shot and approached Jimmy Page directly.

"Why should I?" he countered instantly. Jimmy Page was not only the band's founder, he was the foremost authority on how the band should sound and be presented. Mystique and respect were not just words to him, they were essentials. "When I needed the magazine, they gave us a terrible review." He repeated a few of the adjectives from the scalding review written by John Mendelsohn. "Now they need me, and I don't need them. Why should I? For Jann Wenner? Never."

"I'm not Jann Wenner," I continued. "I believe in the band. Let me tell the whole story for the fans."

"All this time," he interrupted, shaking his head, "you were interviewing everybody for *Rolling Stone*."

I was losing this battle. I had interviewed everybody for other publications but had been saving some of the best stuff for a comprehensive *Rolling Stone* piece. The more I explained the plan, the more I looked like a traitor to him. But he was still listening, so I kept talking. And

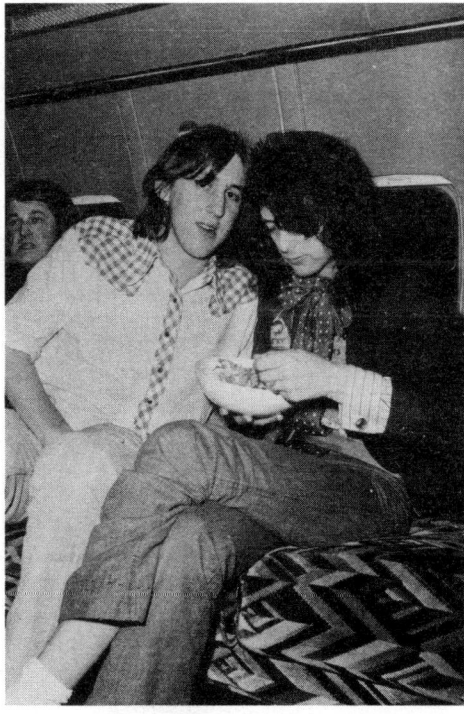

On the Starship pleading the case with Jimmy Page, 1975.

when he made himself some cereal, I followed him as he sat down and kept talking.

"This is your chance to speak directly to the fans, and I will not let the magazine touch a word. I mean, I can promise you that. I really can." A small voice was now telling me, *You are making less and less sense*. I foolishly kept talking. If I kept talking, he couldn't say no. "And as far as the bad reviews go, all I can tell you is that if I bought records according to what *Rolling Stone* gave good reviews to, I'd have the worst record collection of anybody I know."

This Jimmy Page liked. He laughed sharply, appreciatively.

"Well if Joe Walsh trusts you," he said, "then I should too." I wasn't sure I was hearing correctly. "We'll do the interview in New York," he said. He turned away and I caught a glimpse of mischief. I wasn't sure if I had gained an almost unthinkable victory or was about to become the butt of an elaborate joke. "But I'm going to do this for *you*, not Jann Wenner."

The interview was planned for later that night, back in New York. I rode the elevator up to Page's room, tape recorder in hand. He opened the door, wearing his stage clothes, loose black satin trousers and a black cowboy shirt of the same material. He looked like a rumpled schoolboy as he led me into the rambling three-room suite that seemed built for a Fellini film. Suitcases were spread open on the floor. Sitting in the middle of the main room was a film projector. "Kenneth Anger's coming by to show me his film," he said, "but let's start."

Page suggested we first listen to one of my cassettes. It was a rare interview with Joni Mitchell, one of his favorite artists. The recording was a wonderful conversation with Mitchell's friend the Toronto journalist Malka Marom. We were interrupted by the arrival of Anger, who'd brought the latest cut of *Lucifer Rising*. He'd asked Page to provide the film score. This would be the first time Page watched the film with his music attached. I sat next to Anger, the well-known occultist and author of *Hollywood Babylon*, as he projected his movie against the wall of Page's hotel suite. I was now officially a long way from taking communion at Catholic school or lugging a portrait of Jesus around Guadalajara

Anger held himself with rigid self-regard, sneaking looks at Page, who gave him a few notes. The film was supremely boring, but Page's guitar work was spiky and moody in all the best ways. After Anger left, we returned to the Joni Mitchell tape. Page was taken with her soft Canadian speaking voice. He found it as compelling as her singing.

We listened until two in the morning and then began the interview for *Rolling Stone*. Gone was all of Page's animosity for the magazine, and for Wenner. He spilled forth details about his childhood—never shared before—and about how he felt about Plant and the tour and the band and himself. He told me that he'd never felt that he'd live past thirty. But here he was, two years past his imagined expiration date, alive and thoughtful and lonely in New York City. He mused about traveling back to Los Angeles the next day, for a night, to see a girl he missed. He ended the conversation memorably and poetically, telling me, "I'm just looking for an angel with a broken wing . . ." When the powerful conversation was over, he asked if he could borrow the Joni Mitchell tape.

I never saw the Joni Mitchell tape again.

The Plaza was buzzing on a frosty winter afternoon a few days later. The Guess Who were playing on the stereo. My best friend, Neal Preston, was preparing the cover shoot. It was a scene from the apocalypse— Led Zeppelin posing for the cover of *Rolling Stone*.

The Who's Keith Moon showed up out of nowhere. Joe Walsh showed up too, along with his manager, my friend Irving Azoff, cheerleaders all. The mood was perfect save for one small issue. Page was late. Soon the tardiness took its toll. Bonham had someplace to go. John Paul Jones was pacing the room. Keith Moon left. Robert Plant was listening to music and grooving, but time was running out.

Finally Page appeared, brandishing a prankish smile. He had an idea for the cover photo. In his arms was a bushel of black roses. I couldn't tell if they were painted or had been grown that way. It was New York after all; anything was possible. As the band gathered by a window, Neal began popping photos off. The flash pulsed with the music. Page stood at the center with the same smile, staring down the barrel of the lens, holding the roses with a defiant, delicious expression that could only be described as . . . never bet against Led Zeppelin.

Neal fired off at least two hundred shots. Champagne bottles opened. The once unthinkable was actually happening. Led Zeppelin were posing for the cover of *Rolling Stone*. Watching it in real time, I felt that the moment Neal was capturing might be a candidate for the best *Rolling Stone* cover *ever*.

The next night was February 3, the band's opening night at Madison Square Garden. Page dramatically tossed aside the protective cast he'd kept around his disabled little finger and performed a forty-five-minute version of "Dazed and Confused." The next morning, as I prepared to fly back to San Diego with bloodshot eyes, I heard the bad news.

Neal's flash malfunctioned. It was a once-in-a-career fuckup. The light source was a millisecond behind the camera, and none of the shots were usable. Everything was pitch-black, save for a single heartbreaking slide. Ghostly and faintly visible was half of one shot. It was just enough to glimpse what we already knew. The famous Led Zeppelin Black Roses cover would have been a *Rolling Stone* cover for the ages. Neal was traumatized. He's *still* traumatized. The magazine quickly pivoted to a composite of Neal's live shots, hastily hand-tinted so we'd make the deadline.

The article was rushed into print. There was a rumor that they'd even decided to give me a gift awarded to few writers for the magazine: they were going to credit me with a byline on the cover. It was a surreal thought that sailed far beyond my wildest dreams. I was just happy the article felt top-notch. I'd even asked Plant a version of the question one of my Zeppelin-averse editors had urged me to ask, essentially, *Why do you write such hippie-dippie lyrics?* Plant was happy to answer the question with gusto. They'd never been so communicative about their music and process.

Cynthia Bowman, Ben's assistant, promised to send me an early copy of the magazine as soon as the first run came in from the printer. I knew

I would get it on the next Saturday afternoon. I was so anxious by Saturday morning that I took my friend Chuck, the young maintenance man from our condo complex, up on his offer to go fishing in the San Diego harbor. The issue would be there when I returned.

Not long into the fishing trip, I asked Chuck why he and his friends were giggling so much. They confessed that they'd all taken acid—they'd spiked the open cans of Budweiser. I looked at the beer in my hand, the one they'd offered me, and realized they'd dosed me too. I'd never taken LSD and was terrified of what it might do to me. A few hours later, I knew. I was curled up on a beanbag in the corner in Chuck's friend Alex's house, shivering as his snake ate a mouse. Someone put on a George Carlin comedy record. It scared me. I prayed I'd come down enough to leave, grab the issue of *Rolling Stone* from my mailbox, and get past the juggernaut that was my parents in the living room.

Finally I felt sane enough to go home. There in the mailbox was a manila envelope from *Rolling Stone*. I tucked it under my arm and tried to move stealthily past my mom and dad, who were indeed in the living room.

"Son," my dad said. "Could we talk to you about something?"

I looked at their faces. It was all too much. The *Rolling Stone* in the envelope. Their probing eyes. It was all about to spin away from me.

"We're worried about your sister," my dad said. "What can we do better?"

Somehow, I was able to put together a heroic speech about Cindy. How she was steadfast and true to her own ideals. She was destined for greatness. She was her own person. Just love her. Don't worry.

"You're going to make a good lawyer," my mother said.

Once in my room, I ripped open the envelope and saw a very early copy of the magazine with Neal's cover and my byline—not the cover shot they'd wanted, but the fans would never know. I put on *Physical Graffiti* as I reread the story. It was a Led Zeppelin interview for the fans. For those who doubted it would ever happen, there it was. The people's band telling their story directly to the readers, in *Rolling Stone*.

I sat holding the issue with both hands, hoping it wouldn't disappear. When I woke up eight hours later, it was still there.

The issue would be one of *Rolling Stone*'s biggest ever. A couple of weeks later, a box from Ben Fong-Torres arrived. It was filled with letters to the magazine. Zeppelin fans had written from all parts of the globe. The letters were overwhelmingly filled with fantasies, questions, stories, and thank-yous for the interview. *Rolling Stone* had finally placed a bet on Led Zeppelin, late as they were, and the response had been a whole *whole* lotta love.

Jann Wants to See You

"Jann wants to see you," Ben Fong-Torres said. His normally jaunty phone voice was grave. "Can you fly up tomorrow?"

A meeting with Jann Wenner was the final perk of success at the magazine. An audience with the man who had only been spoken about or seen as a bustling and charismatic presence around the office, disappearing into his office to take a call from *Mick* or even *John and Yoko*. Or the one who stood among the reporters to announce that they'd landed a piece by Howard Kohn and David Weir that broke the inside story of the kidnapped heiress Patty Hearst.

Part of me worried that Lester Bangs might be right, that if I spent too much time around Jann, I'd be too close to the flame. I'd get burned like the others, or worse, become part of the establishment that would squash the rebellious spirit that made rock what it was. I was happy to function as the Kid, the new nickname I'd acquired. The guy who flew up from San Diego and wrote all those stories about the bands that nobody knew about in the main office. They were the Van Morrison–Bob Dylan crowd. I was Jethro Tull and Deep Purple and the Eagles. I was the mascot to the cool women staffers and copy editors in the tie-dye shirts.

But an audience with Jann Wenner. The mind raced with the possibilities. Would he make me a contributing editor? Or maybe tell me about the mysterious woman he'd sparred with Jimmy Page over back in

England? All this raced through my head as I flew in the overcrowded pink and orange PSA jet from San Diego to San Francisco. I still didn't drive, so getting to and from the airport was always a negotiation. I was forever trying to find a cool answer to the uncool issue, *When are you going to get a driver's license?*

Meeting Jann was sure to be sensational. He'd been famously characterized in the pages of the magazine and elsewhere—charismatic, charming, tough, loyal, mercurial. I was ready for anything. Ben picked me up at the airport and I'm positive he could see my beaming face a mile away. I popped into his car and immediately felt the gravity in his voice. Gone was Ben's usual late-night DJ hipster panache.

"It's not a good day for Jann," he warned. "Ralph Gleason died."

Gleason was the music critic for the *San Francisco Chronicle*. He had a face like a Rembrandt painting, usually with a pipe and an expression of settled judgment. He was one of the first established journalists to spot talents like Lenny Bruce, Bob Dylan, and Jann himself. The fifty-eight-year-old Gleason had functioned not only as an investor in *Rolling Stone* but as a father figure and mentor to Wenner. I offered to return home, but Ben insisted I come to the office. Wenner still wanted to talk to me.

Ben led me to Wenner's corner office, and there was Jann, looking nothing like the energetic and youthful dynamo of his photos. On that day he was the oldest-looking young man I'd ever seen, a solitary presence at his round wooden table, slumped before a three-quarter-full bottle of vodka. It was early afternoon. An Annie Leibovitz portrait of John Lennon hung over his shoulder.

"Hiya," he said. We shook hands and I could see that he'd been crying. "I wanted to talk with you a bit, but I'm about to go home." For a few minutes, Wenner spoke of the enormous loss he felt, losing Ralph, feeling so alone, still referring to Gleason in the present tense.

"Listen," he finally said. "You missed the story." My heart sank. "I mean you clearly love Led Zeppelin, but what was your purpose here?"

I stammered something about wanting to accomplish what was once unthinkable. A cover story on the band who hated the magazine the most. Like me, there were many fans who wanted to read about them in *Rolling Stone*.

"But you didn't write about what you saw, what you felt." He rubbed his face. It was still red with tears. "You wrote what *they* wanted you to write, not what *you* wanted to write. What did *you* see? What did *you* feel? What did you want to say about them? Because this article could have been dictated by the band. What would a *real writer* have written?"

The words *real writer* slammed me in the chest. What was the opposite of a real writer? I didn't even want to think about it. Would a *fake writer* have fought like I did to get Jimmy Page to agree to the interview? I was too wounded by Jann's almost tearful criticism to consider a comeback until much later. Would a *real publisher* have rejected the article? No, he didn't. He ran it, and it was already a big seller. But here he was, on a very dark day, trying to give me some guidance. He could have easily canceled the meeting.

Wenner gathered his things and prepared to leave the office. I was surprised when he asked me to meet him at his house before I went back to San Diego. An hour later, I was sitting in his living room. Jane Wenner, his dark-haired wife, listened to him from the kitchen, taking concerned calls in the background. He'd brought the vodka bottle from home with him, and it was now almost empty. He was smoking cigarettes one after another.

"If you want to be a *real* writer," he continued, "you've got to read real writing. Sometimes you have to suffer to get it right."

He disappeared into a back room. Of course I suffered. I was suffering *now*.

Jann returned with a copy of Joan Didion's *Slouching Towards Bethlehem*. "Joan Didion," he announced. He put the book on the table before me. It was well thumbed. This was the Wenner who started *Rolling Stone* and pushed that whole coffee-scented office full of writers to their best work. Now he was goading me to do the same. "Read this book," he said. "The whole book. It's going to inspire you. Take my copy. Return it when you're done. The best writing—the best music—is personal, and it takes a stand. *Did you take a stand?* You should also seek out her Doors piece, her portrait of Jim Morrison. It's the best profile of the band ever written, and she's already nailed it before Morrison even enters the room."

I still haven't returned the book. Today it's dog-eared and propped against the wall near my cluttered writing desk, wedged between *The Life-Changing Magic of Tidying Up*, which I still have to read, and a book my mom slipped me a few years ago, *The Bright Light of Death*. (She pressed it into my hands, along with a three-ring binder of instructions. "In case I die while staying at your house," she explained pleasantly. "But don't worry, I'm healthy.") Joan Didion's *Slouching Towards Bethlehem* became my reminder of that day when a little part of me died. But another part of me sprouted wings. A lasting gift of inspiration from Jann, given on his own worst day. Several years ago, I sent the copy to Didion's friend Shelley Wanger and asked her to ask Didion to sign it, which she did. She wrote her name in a clean single line above the title, the way a student signs a textbook.

How I Learned About Sex

In the fall of 1975, I received a surprise phone call from *Rolling Stone* writer-editor Tim Cahill. I was happy to hear from him. Cahill sounded playful, not at all the put-upon soul who'd helped me whip the Allman Brothers Band article into shape. He told me that the magazine was doing a theme issue about men. Muhammad Ali would be on the cover. If I wanted to write about my own life, not just about music, this might be a good opportunity. I immediately agreed.

"The subject," Cahill told me, "is how you learned about sex."

I was thrilled. It was clearly a vote of confidence from the magazine. I also wanted to impress Cahill, who'd driven me to add a whiff of mystery and poetry to the Allman Brothers story. I could feel myself standing straighter. Nothing wrong with a little bravado. I felt like one of those writer's photos in *Playboy*. A guy with a pipe and the knowing look of an intellectual. Sure, let's write about sex.

By nightfall, dread had arrived.

Tens of crumpled pages later, I had nothing. I had nothing but humiliating sexual near-misses to write about. Why did I want to write something so embarrassing? My first foray into autobiographical writing was as disastrous as the romantic encounters I'd been asked to document. I was learning that to be clever, you first had to be sophisticated. I was neither. Trying to write the article was like being lost in a room full of fun house mirrors, and I was a clown in every last one.

The deadline was Friday morning. I had to put something in the mail. By late Thursday night I was still under the covers of my bed, thinking about the excuses I could give Tim Cahill the next morning. I decided on a kitchen accident. Something that made typing impossible. No, it had to be better. Bronchitis. Or better yet, *pneumonia*. What the hell, *Rolling Stone* was in San Francisco, they'd never know the real truth. The real truth was that my entire sense of confidence had been based on my writing about music. The last thing I wanted to write about were my checkered experiences with sex.

I crawled out of my bed and decided the only path was to just put words on a page. Something. Anything. They'd reject the piece, of course, but at least I wouldn't have chickened out. I typed out eight embarrassing pages. There was freedom in knowing how amateurish and confessional it was. No one would ever read it beyond an editor or two.

I wrote about how I learned about sex from my mom in a laundromat. Her explanation was so clinical that I thought intercourse was a medical act to be performed in a doctor's office. I wrote about my doomed forays into dating, about being pale in a San Diego school where tanned surfers were king. I wrote about how I'd invited my secret surfer-girl crush, Karen Wilson, to see Fleetwood Mac and Savoy Brown at the San Diego Community Concourse. She said yes, and I knew I would impress her because I was going to interview Fleetwood Mac backstage before the show. We attended the show together, and she sat nearby while I talked with Mick Fleetwood, John McVie, Christine McVie, and then-guitarist Bob Welch.

Halfway through the interview, a tall and rugged blond Fleetwood Mac roadie entered the dressing room. He asked the extraneous hangers-on to leave, giving the band their necessary privacy. His eyes met with Karen's. "Let me get you a better pass," he offered. "Come with me."

I didn't see Karen again until Spanish class the next Monday. She thanked me for a great night—with someone else.

Two days later, I picked up my bedroom phone to hear someone laughing. "Cameron, it's Cahill."

"I'm sorry."

"Sorry?!" He was still laughing. "This is the best thing you've ever written. By *far*."

"It's embarrassing."

"Exactly! And that's the best part!" He was adamant. "It's just disaster after disaster. *We loved it!*"

I was mortified. "I don't even know what I wrote."

"This is good stuff," Cahill announced. "The embarrassing stuff is always the best stuff. We're going to publish it, and we already commissioned a very embarrassing caricature of you nude. You're gonna love it!"

He was still laughing when he hung up.

It was a day of discovery. I'd discovered that the once-stern Tim Cahill had a wonderful laugh. I'd also discovered my writing voice. The personal tone of that embarrassing article is now my favorite kind of writing. In fact, it's the tone of this book.

The Mirror

"Woody loves you," Russ Shaw was saying.

I was headed home after three days on the road for a *Rolling Stone* story on David Crosby and Graham Nash. I'd spotted Russ in the Indianapolis airport. It was hard to miss him among the Midwestern travelers. He was wearing a waist-length rancher's coat with a plume-like feathered collar. The Irish guitarist Rory Gallagher was trudging at his side in a worn-out Pendleton shirt. Russ was an important figure in the annals of '70s rock. I think about him often. He's one of those characters, unknown to most but consequential in many of the biggest musical events of the era.

Russ Shaw worked for Warner Bros. Records, the artist-friendly label with many prestigious acts, from Rod Stewart to Bonnie Raitt and Frank Sinatra. He was the colorful head of artist relations, which meant he was equal parts publicist, confidant, fashion peacock, comedian, and troubleshooter. When a difficult star had a problem with somebody or something at the label, Russ could solve it with one wine-soaked meal. Or he might even show up with a singular article of clothing, such as a white suit on a hanger, that ended up being the unasked-for perfect touch for the artist's tour wardrobe.

"Ron Wood is putting out a solo album," Russ confided as we stood in the airport. Everything he said sounded like a secret curated just for you. "You *must* talk with him. We'll be in Los Angeles next week. Get an assignment!"

It was September 1974 and the beginning of a lengthy adventure, one that would have never happened without Russ. Our meeting at the airport began a series of events and a journalistic coup I never could have imagined on that day in Indiana.

Some stories take a long time. It was the year before the Led Zeppelin cover story had landed, and this would be a rendezvous with yet another artist who was wildly averse to interviews. Ron Wood was a key figure in what happened next.

Russ had been tasked with launching Ron Wood's first solo album, *I've Got My Own Album to Do*. I'd interviewed Wood back when he was still in the Faces, the guitarist sidekick to Rod Stewart. The one thing you needed to know about the man everybody called Woody was that he made friends easily. Ron Wood could meet you on the twelfth floor of an elevator ride, and by the time you hit the lobby, your name was on the list for the show, you were friends for life, and chances were you'd name your first child Woody. He was also a human caricature of himself. The dark black rooster hair. The perennial look of pleasant surprise, the cigarette hanging from his lower lip, the festive drink in his grip.

A few weeks later, Russ ushered me into Woody's fancy room at the Beverly Wilshire hotel. I'd taken the bus from downtown San Diego, and Russ had even booked a small room for me.

"Cameroon, my boy," Woody shouted. Woody looked like he'd been up for a couple of days, but his wardrobe was sparkling. Hawaiian shirt and tight black pants. Somehow the cigarette never fell from his lower lip. "Have you ever had a Pimm's Cup?"

Woody proceeded to fix me a Pimm's No. 6 Cup, his favorite. He poured a healthy glug of the vodka-based drink into a ginger ale mixer and presented the refreshing cocktail with a sliced cucumber. "The cucumber," he confided, "is *essential*." I sipped at the concoction very carefully, and for the next two hours, Woody filled two cassettes with secrets, laughs, and tales about how he talked his famous friends into performing on his solo album.

Spending time in Woody's hotel room at the Beverly Wilshire was like watching a parade of rock's biggest stars. Everybody checked in with Woody, looking for a party or a chance to kibbitz or possibly stay up for days with him. Wood pointed to a pile of clothes and some shoes in the corner. "That was Jimmy McCulloch," he said, referencing the guitarist from Thunderclap Newman and, later, Wings. "We had a great time last night. Don't know where he went."

His phone was always ringing, from George Harrison to "Keef" himself. I never once heard him say, "Don't come by, I'm busy." Soon we retired to a back room to listen to music. Woody had a bag of cassettes, and bubbling with enthusiasm, he played a bootleg of a performance by his original band, the Jeff Beck Group, from Detroit's Grande Ballroom in 1969. I stashed my own cassette recorder in my orange shoulder bag, and I left it running as we listened.

He listened with his eyes closed. When the music slipped into a state of reckless abandon, his eyes popped open wide, mouth agape, as if he were in disbelief that *his own band* was this good. With his trademark rooster hair and arched eyebrows, he looked like one of his own doodled caricatures of himself.

We were listening to "All Shook Up." Jeff Beck's unhinged solos blasted out of the dirty recording. There was a buzz at the front door. Russ answered the door and a moment later found Woody to announce his latest surprise visitor.

"It's David," he said. "He heard you were in the hotel."

Woody jumped to his feet, and a moment later, David Bowie bounced into the room. He had a shock of red hair and moved jauntily, as if hanging from the strings of a marionette. He was dressed in a light green suit, his mouth open in a silent scream of delight, and his smile seemed to stretch all the way around his translucently pale face. I was struck by his laughter and his theatricality. He looked almost animated, someone's cartoon creation. They hugged ferociously. All of Woody's hugs were ferocious.

"I'm in town playing the Universal Amphitheatre," announced Bowie.

I was immediately stricken with fear. Though my tape recorder was hidden, I would soon be outed as a journalist, the enemy. Bowie was managed by a famously anti-press manager, Tony Defries, who had been known to physically eject journalists who even entered the vicinity of his client. He was single-minded about controlling Bowie's image. Mystique was everything. No one had interviewed Bowie in any depth in years. He was the unicorn, the most sought-after subject to every cassette-slinging rock writer like me. I dreaded how Woody might introduce me. The word *interview* or even *writer* would be disastrous.

"This is my friend Cameron," he said. "We're listening to the fucking Jeff Beck Group at the Grande Ballroom."

Whew. Bowie swooned and joined us. He sat down on the corner of the bed next to Woody and begged to listen. Soon we were all sharing delight and rapture at the shitty recording of a great band at their peak. I'd made it through the early danger zone on the wings of fandom. I was included. Soon, Woody produced another bootleg. It was a famous British bit of contraband, unknown to me, a drunken routine recorded after-hours by Peter Cook and Dudley Moore called "What's The Worst Job You've Ever Had."

They both repeated the boozy punch line that drove them wild with laughter: "Plucking lobsters from Jayne Mansfield's bum!"

Woody and Bowie went on to act out the entire recording, word for word. After an hour Bowie sighed and announced that he had to leave for his sound check across town. Before he left, he grabbed Woody's knee.

"I'm having a party in my room after the show," he said. "It'll start around midnight. Can you both come?"

"Yeah!" said Woody. I'm not sure that Ron Wood ever answered no to a party invitation, whether he was able to come or not. "We'll be there."

"I'll give my man Stuart your names," said Bowie. "It's room three eighteen."

I called home to San Diego and told my mom I'd be home a few days later. The usual speeches followed. *You're making managers rich. Don't take drugs. Why did I let you leave home so young?* Because I was still technically writing about Ron Wood, and this being the halcyon days of record company extravagance, Russ Shaw picked up the tab for two more nights.

Stuart the bodyguard answered the door at room 318. He'd been given our names and invited us inside. The room was still fairly empty. Bowie was spinning records on the stereo against the far window. I loved what he was playing. It was the best of Philadelphia soul—the Spinners, the Stylistics, the O'Jays. I knew all the songs. The Spinners were one of my favorites. The silky depth and sugar highs of Thom Bell's writing spoke to me in a serious way. It was Philly happy/sad.

Meanwhile, I always had one eye peeled for Tony Defries. I knew him from photos; he was a girthy man with a vulgarian look. He was nowhere to be seen at the midnight party. There were others. Bowie's assistant Corinne Schwab was never far from the artist, but other than Schwab there was no real retinue around him. Glenn Hughes from Deep Purple was there. Hughes, one of the great white soul singers, was someone I'd previously championed in *Rolling Stone*. Deep Purple were a band that *Rolling Stone* had devoted little attention to. (Their guitarist-leader Ritchie Blackmore had memorably thrown a steak across a restaurant during our interview. It was a reader favorite.) I'd accompanied Purple to the California Jam festival, where Bowie had noticed Hughes's soul-stirring vocals. He too had bonded with Bowie over a deep love of R & B and soul. At the party, Hughes promised not to out me as a journalist, and I had another link in the chain of complicity.

Singer Claudia Lennear was also there. Lennear was famous from Joe Cocker's *Mad Dogs and Englishmen*, and from singing backup vocals with the Rolling Stones. I'd ridden the elevator with her earlier. When she realized we were going to the same party, she casually shared that a radio station had been installed in her tooth.

Also in Bowie's suite was Freddie Sessler, a roly-poly middle-aged man with a comb-over and a heavy Israeli accent. Sessler spent a lot of time darting into the bathroom with some of the guests. I was told he lived in upstate New York. He'd made his fortune, someone whispered to me, in the pencil business. I loved pencils. I still do. So I made a note to talk to Sessler about what exactly went into the business of pencils.

Bowie moved among all his party guests, always the perfect host, offering an aside, a quiet joke, his mouth open so wide it looked like it had taken up half his face. And there was Woody too, Pimm's in hand, who managed to make everybody feel like a friend for life. It all made for a warm, fun atmosphere, with a soul soundtrack that had already informed his not-yet-released album *Young Americans*.

"What do you want to listen to?" Bowie asked me. He was standing next to his record player. He still had his stage makeup on from the show he'd performed earlier that night.

"The Spinners," I said immediately.

"Do you like the new one?"

"Thom Bell," I said, "can do no wrong."

We called out song titles to each other.

"'Ain't No Price on Happiness,'" Bowie said.

"'Love Don't Love Nobody,'" I suggested.

"'He'll Never Love You Like I Do,'" Bowie countered instantly. He knew Thom Bell's work and why it was good.

Soon Bowie was telling me about the album he'd been recording in Philadelphia at the very same studio as the Spinners, Sigma Sound, and he fished out a cassette. "Do you want to hear something?"

He slipped in the cassette and played an early rough version of a song he'd recorded with sumptuous, almost spooky backup singing by then-unknown Luther Vandross, "Somebody Up There Likes Me." It was surprisingly emotional, dark and addictive, a world away from the rock and roll boundaries he'd exploded just a few years earlier. This new

Bowie music was like a Philly soul dream. It was thrilling to hear and he seemed thrilled to play it for me. I asked him to play it again.

"What's the worst job you've ever had?" he asked in the Peter Cook–and–Dudley Moore voice.

"Plucking lobsters from Jayne Mansfield's bum!"

We laughed and listened to the song again.

Leaving that night, Stuart said, "David wants you and Woody to come back tomorrow night."

And so, we did. The atmosphere was similar, and so was the soul soundtrack. There was also cocaine. I didn't do it. I also didn't judge it. A guest or two would dart into the corner, or the bathroom, and emerge energized and jagged. The more I declined to share in somebody else's cocaine, the more popular I became. (As long as they were sure I wasn't a narc.)

The cocaine seemed to come mostly from Freddie Sessler, who doled out hits from a small glass bottle. His spoon looked like it was filled with tiny diamonds. He was said to be close with Keith Richards. Both nights he said he was leaving in the morning to go back east, back to work in the pencil business. Both nights he returned to the party. Clearly the pencil business was one in which he could make his own hours.

"So, Freddie," I asked him as Bowie played a Delfonics track in the next room, "what's the pencil business like? I mean, what goes into the manufacturing of pencils?"

He gave me a look of confusion and suspicion. Then he asked me why I wanted to know.

"I like pencils."

He seemed annoyed. "They're pencils. I don't know what to tell you. They're made of wood. You put the lead inside. They're pencils."

Soon he left to visit another bathroom. I would later see Freddie around many other artists, at many other events. I later learned a lot about him. He loathed the word *dealer*. He was a rich superfan who never charged for the high-quality cocaine he brought to the parties and the backstages of the '70s rock world. He was also a Holocaust survivor who was said to have made an early fortune by inventing the Perma Weave hairpiece. Sessler later developed a source for highly sought-after Merck cocaine, along with quaaludes and premium-quality psychedelics, which he supplied gratis to all his favorite bands. In his day Sessler was a memorable man with many friends. When he died in 2000, Keith Richards was one of the few to show up at his memorial. He was never in the pencil business.

As we left that second night, Woody asked me in the hallway, "Do you want to interview him?"

"Bowie doesn't do interviews," I said. "His manager forbids them. If David knew I was anybody other than just your friend . . ."

"His manager isn't here," Woody said with a wink. He said almost everything with a wink. "He likes you. I'll get you that interview."

I laughed and didn't take him seriously. We agreed to meet at Bowie's suite for the after-show party the next night, but this time Woody wasn't there. Woody had returned to England. Glenn Hughes was there, so I felt okay about sticking around. So was Claudia Lennear, who petted my arm like I was a puppy before continuing her rounds. We'd formed an odd little family, the nightly Bowie party regulars, but after a while I decided to leave. It was then that Bowie took me aside.

"Look," he confided. "I'm going back to New York, and I'm going to fire my manager. I don't fly, so I'll be taking the train. I'll call you when I get back to LA. We'll do an interview. Give me your phone number."

I gave him my number and knew instinctively he'd never call. This was how you behaved as a friend of Woody's. You never said no. I appreciated Bowie's good manners, the odd menagerie at his parties, and our bonding over the happy/sad majesty of Thom Bell songs like "People Make the World Go Round" and "La La Means I Love You."

Eight days later, the phone rang in my teenage San Diego bedroom. The voice was distant; the sound of the train created an echo on the line. "Is that Cameron?" Bowie told me he'd done exactly what he'd planned to do. He'd left New York, left his manager, and boarded the train to Los Angeles alone. He'd be arriving to stay at Glenn Hughes's house that Sunday night. Later he'd be joined by his trusted assistant Corinne Schwab and a childhood friend and photographer, Geoff MacCormack, also known as Warren Peace. He gave me an address in Beverly Hills. He was insistent about only one thing: "Don't tell anybody."

It wasn't always easy to keep the secret. Bowie was still the most sought-after interview subject in the world of rock journalism. I mentioned it to no one, not even Ben Fong-Torres.

Within a day or two, I met him at Glenn's place in Beverly Hills. Later he moved to the home of his manager, Michael Lippman, and after that a nondescript yellow home on the corner of Coldwater Canyon Drive. I felt like I was in on a big secret or part of a witness protection program bent. When I encountered him again in a back bedroom, Bowie was at first turned away in the half-light of a window. When he looked over to greet me, the light checkered across his face. Surely, he knew the effect. Bowie, it seemed, never threw away a chance for a striking introduction.

He was immediately chatty, talking about Ron Wood, his exodus from New York, the separation from Tony Defries, the newness of the road ahead, and James Dean, the angsty actor from *Rebel Without a Cause*. He was immersed in Dean, whom he called a beautiful hustler. He imitated Dean's swagger. I wondered if he was preparing for a movie or a character to play. Soon I would find out both were true.

Geoff MacCormack was also in the house. MacCormack was playing "Lost in the Flood," from the first Springsteen album, in the other room. I asked if I could turn on my tape recorder. Bowie nodded. In another room, an unanswered phone rang. Bowie asked me what I read and what I wanted to be as a writer. I told him I wanted to tell stories. He clocked my desire with a smile and scooted forward.

"You can ask me whatever you want," he said. "Hold up a mirror and show me what you see."

For the next eighteen months, I did exactly that. It felt like even more than a journalist's dream. It was an artistic challenge from David Bowie.

All of This Will Be Forgotten

"All of this will be forgotten," David Bowie announced. He was cheerfully gripping the wheel of a yellow VW bug on La Brea Avenue. It was seven in the morning and he was talking about the Eagles. Kraftwerk, the mesmerizing techno-whiz band from Germany, was what he preferred. It was Patti Smith, who was doing something interesting in New York. He loved Joni Mitchell but especially championed the young artist from New Jersey, Bruce Springsteen, whose music he'd recently covered while recording in Philadelphia. Springsteen had even hitchhiked from New Jersey to visit the session.

We'd just come from Cherokee Studios on Fairfax Avenue, a dingy part of Hollywood. Bowie had been helping record demos for Iggy Pop, an early influence who was now on the emotional and chemical edge of self-destruction. I'd been tucked into a back wall while Iggy struggled through a new song, powered by a female bass player, Jean Millington, from the pioneering all-girl group Fanny. The results had been slim to nothing. We drove mostly in silence. I was drowsy but had the feeling Bowie was just getting started on another day of creative zest. He had projects. He was thinking about writing his autobiography. He had a meeting scheduled with director Nicolas Roeg, who was interested in him for an upcoming film. He was toying with a new persona, a man of rigor and purpose. He told me the title of the autobiography he wanted to write, *The Return of the Thin White Duke*. I never stopped asking him questions, and he never seemed to mind.

"LA is my favorite museum," he announced another morning, again sitting behind the wheel of the yellow VW, which belonged to his manager's wife, Nancy.

What others saw as a mundane row of fast-food joints and faded shopping plazas, Bowie saw as a kind of art installation. It inspired him. He was always collecting information, bits of songs or thoughts. None of the morning workforce sitting in traffic around him seemed to notice. The ghostly-pale man with the electric red hair and blue cap was David Bowie. He'd been up all night jamming, crafting, creating, and recording a new song in real time—"TVC 15."

He was seeking newness in his music. He was seeking a stripped-down new life and an equally sleek new persona. Still in an open marriage to Angie Bowie, with a four-year-old son, he would arrive somewhere with lots of suitcases and little human baggage, just his loyal sparrowlike assistant Corinne Schwab. He was seeking, period. The problem was none of it could last. Particularly on a diet of milk, red peppers, and cocaine.

He'd left a message to call his house. "I'm at Cherokee tonight. Come and visit."

When I showed up at Cherokee Studios, producer Harry Maslin was behind the board. He nodded to the studio room. *He's in there.* Bowie's roots in theater were always present. Even the first moments of a casual meeting were an impact opportunity not to be squandered. If you were expecting a random image—say, Bowie tinkering with an amp or making coffee—you'd be wrong. I found him in the back corner, kneeling just behind a sound baffle, holding a twelve-string guitar. His reddish-blond hair was tucked into a blue cap. He was bathed in the smoke of his Gitane cigarette, and when he heard my voice, he turned perfectly into the beam of the red light above his head.

"It's you," he said.

It was what Billy Wilder once called *flesh impact*. Wilder was talking about Marilyn Monroe, but he could have been talking about David

Bowie. In life, as in cinema, their presence went beyond spectacle and emotion. It was something you *felt*.

Soon he was recording "Wild Is the Wind," a world-weary ballad most famously recorded by Nina Simone. He lifted an acoustic guitar and strummed out a rhythm part, kneeling now, directly under that yellow light. The effect was typically cinematic for Bowie, a marriage of sight and sound. Many a control room would be buzzing with meaningless chatter, technical conversation, or just plain small talk. Not here. It was silent here. He stopped playing.

"What month is it?" Bowie asked.

"September," said Corinne.

"Day?"

"The twenty-fifth. Early twenty-sixth."

"No wonder," he said immediately. He consulted a black notebook. "It's a great day for ideas but not good for carrying them out."

"Don't let that sway you," said Corinne.

"No no." He looked concerned. "I want to get this right. This song has a good European feel. Should be a good bridge to that sort of thing. Whatever's next. Yeah, fuck it, I'm ready."

His hat cocked over his carrot-colored hair, a blond streak at the center, for a moment he looked like young Frank Sinatra dipped in red and yellow ink. A minute later, he had moved into the darkness and was dancing and clapping quietly to a playback of "TVC 15." ("It's a song about a holographic television," he confided. "The only piece of fiction on the album.") My note from the night, on a scribbled scrap of paper: "Snapshots. David Bowie lives his life as a series of perfectly staged snapshots."

The *Station to Station* sessions were as focused as his interview monologues had been wild and careening. He knew exactly what he wanted to hear and how to ask for it. He often built the songs in real time, on gusts of adrenaline and other substances, dancing as he shaped the beats. I slipped my hand into my orange bag and pressed record while he cut "Golden Years," watching from the back of the control room. He whipped through a new song, still unreleased today, called "Shady." For "TVC 15," he'd arranged pillars of colored lights and danced through the columns as he recorded the song.

Back at home, Bowie was also reading several books, studying numerology, boning up on the occult, studying fascism for a possible movie role, exploring Kirlian photography, painting, and beginning an autobiography. He scrawled symbols on the curtains, wrestled with his own bouts of paranoia, and was dabbling in keeping jars of his own urine. All of this while carrying on erudite conversations with me about life, art, and lately even the secret life of James Dean. Sitting cross-legged on the bed he rarely slept in, he often waited for a new topic the way a star basketball player waits to be thrown the ball. As many questions as I could summon, he was ready.

Few knew he was even in town. I didn't have a driver's license. He often drove me back to Neal Preston's house in the yellow VW. No one ever recognized him, even in full regalia with bright-red-and-yellow hair. He said he was thinking about a career in the movies, but continued writing songs throughout. He kept me in the room while he polished and recorded *Station to Station*. He rarely stayed still, ate very infrequently, and was getting thinner and thinner.

Soon Bowie had moved again, to a nondescript Beverly Hills home that his wife, Angie, had found on North Doheny Drive. Angie Bowie seemed to have several residences around the world. To say their marriage was open would be too restrictive. When Angie and David Bowie were together, with son Zowie (and a nanny) in tow, their life became a '70s rock star sitcom. Angie had a sharp tongue, a half-English accent, and a hand-on-her-hip personality. Looking in the refrigerator, she'd launch wisecracks on the lack of food, except for extra-rich whole milk cartons. ("Oh joy! More milk for Daddy!") As Zowie charged around the house, Bowie seemed immensely charmed by his "normal" little family, the Dagwood to Angie's Blondie.

I wondered if it was a glimpse of the quiet soul who lived within Bowie. I liked to think it was a peek at David Jones, the young man from

Brixton, South London, the son of a teacher, who traded in a different life to become David Bowie. Without Angie's entertaining presence, however, Bowie could sometimes slip into the manic behavior of a man playing Whac-A-Mole with a plethora of demons.

He was always happy to see me, anxious to share the latest adventures. I took his invitation to "hold up a mirror" seriously. I wanted this to be a complete portrait of this roller-coaster time in his life. Over the months, I became acclimated to the normality within his insulated lifestyle. He was easy to be around and forever obliging. Oh, sometimes there might be a hexagon drawn on the curtains in his bedroom or a bottle of urine on the windowsill. He might cheerfully take me to the edge of the indoor swimming pool adjacent to his bedroom.

"The only problem with this house," he said, "is that Satan lives in that swimming pool." It was as if he were pointing out a pesky problem with termites. "I've seen him!"

Why me? I wondered. What was it that made him call from his train trip to announce his arrival in Los Angeles, when only Glenn Hughes and a handful of others knew and were sworn to secrecy? What convinced him to take me—*a journalist!*—along for the ride? There was a clue in one of my early visits to the Doheny home.

He was sitting cross-legged on the bed he rarely slept in. A satanic symbol was written in crayon, or maybe ashes, on the window shade. His friend Geoff MacCormack was talking about his intense fandom for Bruce Springsteen. Bowie made a comment about my age.

"How old are you?" Geoff asked with sudden curiosity. It was a trigger. I was never sure if the answer was a plus or minus.

"Nineteen," I lied. I don't know why. I was still only eighteen but must've wanted to try out the next number.

"See!" Bowie was thrilled. "Young enough to be honest!"

Since Bowie had fled New York with a lot of suspicions about the money he'd lost to bad business deals, perhaps my age was finally a plus. Perhaps it was a flip side of the incident with Gregg Allman a few years before. Perhaps it was that my ticket into the amusement park had been stamped by Ronnie Wood, forever trustworthy in his Hawaiian shirt with Pimm's cup in hand. Or maybe it was just that I never stopped listening. My orange bag was filled with cassettes. Every night I carefully labeled the cassettes: "David Bowie Interview 1976!" During the emotional chaos and drug-fueled paranoia that followed, there was certainly one thing he could depend on: the constant look of delight on my young face.

The cocaine, it seemed, was always in the service of a project or his latest research expedition. Sometimes it would be a painting, or a biography, or the writing of a song. Often it was carried out with a Chaplinesque sense of whimsy. Sometimes a light layer of paranoia would descend over the proceedings. A ringing telephone might set him off, and he and Geoff would decide that it must not be answered. Or Claudia Lennear might call with a report that Jimmy Page was reading Bowie's thoughts. Or Glenn Hughes might return from a tour with Deep Purple with a report about Roy Nicholas, the Houston drug dealer who'd been stalking him. Nicholas wore thick leather outfits, complete with a cowboy hat tipped just above his Manson eyes. (Manson was another figure who popped up in Bowie's bouts with paranoia.) People had been saying that Roy Nicholas might be Satan himself. Obsessions and warnings flew by. And through it all, the ever-chatty Bowie would encourage me to ask questions.

Do you ever find it difficult to believe in yourself?

I've learned to flow with myself. I honestly don't know where the real David Jones is. It's like playing the pea game. I've got so many shells I've forgotten what the pea looks like. I wouldn't know what it looked like if I found it. Being famous helps put off the problems of discovering myself. That's the main reason why I've always been so keen on being accepted and why I've strived so hard to put my brain to artistic use. In any other profession I don't think I'd survive very long in an established society. I'm gonna have terrific problems one day . . . I get that feeling.

Where do you think rock is headed?

I don't think it is headed. I think it's malfunctioned. I mean, the *pose* is more startling now than the music.

That was the same criticism attributed to you.

Well, exactly. I meant, that's my statement. Music can only be *liked* these days. It can't . . . it's not allowed to have an abrasive effect anymore. It's "Oh well, if the music's, like, *likeable*, what else has it got?" You don't have a choice. That's repression. That's fascistic. And it's right-wing. That's what's happening to me. So there's my view on music. It's dangerous.

Right at this moment. And this evening . . .

Yes, good.

. . . have you been David Bowie or David Jones?

I've been a very emphatic David Jones trying to throw David Bowie at you, as . . . David Bowie as . . .

To throw David Bowie at me or out the window?

No, at you. At you. Give a subject, I'll answer any question. Let's have some fun.

Always, there was a project to tend to. *Young Americans* had been released to significant success. Bowie, who'd told me that he'd retired from rock—"I've rocked my roll"—was now drawing closer to making another record. This was the one that would become *Station to Station*, an album made in the spirit of his new persona, the Thin White Duke. The floor in the next room, by the swimming pool where Satan lived, was sometimes flecked with small pieces of paper, like fortune cookie strips with lyrics. He was writing, he said, in the "cut-out" style he'd

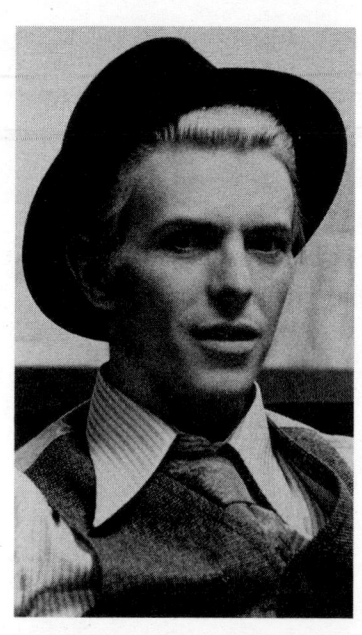

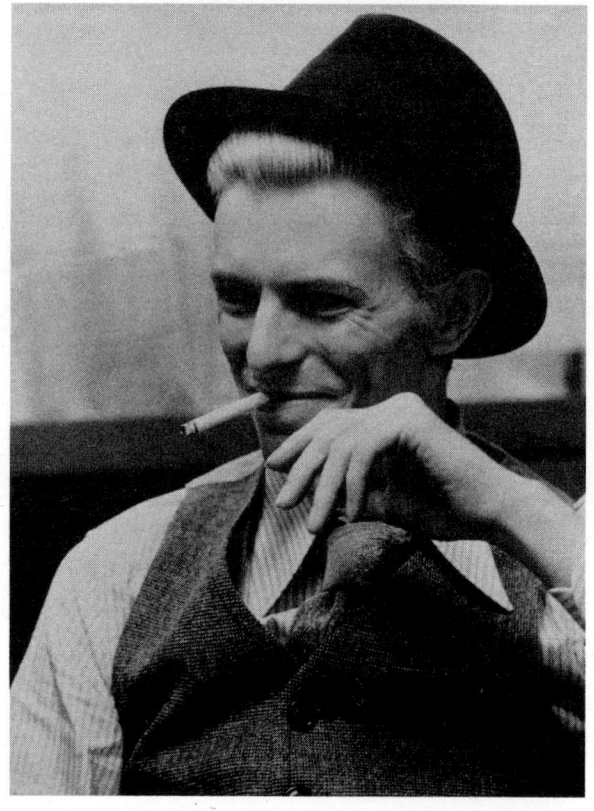

learned from studying the author William Burroughs. He asked me to pitch names of bands I liked

"Led Zeppelin."

He wrote out the words "Led Zeppelin is growing, it erases our minds."

He asked for the names of other artists. I gave him the names Stevie Wonder and Joni Mitchell. He loved both and scribbled down words. He added Ron Wood. Each inspired a line or two of lyrics. He cut up the words and rearranged them on small strips of paper. Soon he had a guitar in hand and was playing a folky progression. Laughing, he began singing a song that sounded like a cousin of "Space Oddity."

Led Zeppelin is growing, it erases our minds
They make us feel stoney, they make us go blind
Hey, Stevie Wonder, there like a wall
So good to lean on, the hardest of all
His face in the mirror, he'll give us a brace
The terminal killer
Oh played in the face
You're played in the face
You've run out of money
You're played in the face

Geoff MacCormack was in the room. "'Played in the face,' that's nice."

"That's the title, isn't it? 'Played in the Face.' No. 'Audience' is the title. Isn't it a nice little tune? Parts of 'We Are the Dead' were written like this. It's how I write now, and I think it will age well. As the mind processes more and more media, the fragmentation is more eloquent than trying to stay linear." He played the song again, adding vocal nuances. "Yes. I might do something with that, actually. I always wanted to do, like, seventies nostalgia."

"Seventies nostalgia?" The decade was barely half over.

"I wanted to do something very cryptic," said Bowie. "I wanted to do something about having a satellite television show and inviting all these bands and then asking them . . . having them all onstage at the same time. And I'd come out with a great big wheelbarrow full of machine guns and say, 'Now, how many of you are going to do anything? How many of you are gonna keep your guitars and how many of you are gonna pick up a gun?' All on television! All being seen all over the place! 'How many of you are gonna say, "Let's change the world. All together. All of us"?' I'd be curious what the reaction would be. Very dangerous. Apathetic . . . or not."

"Well," I said, "what if they wanted to change the world, but not through that medium?"

"Well, no," he said. "It was forced upon them. I don't believe in giving people choices." He put on a heavy English accent. "Totally hypothetical, you understand. And there was sort of other things where they would jam with each other. Elvis would sing with the Stones, and the Stones would back him."

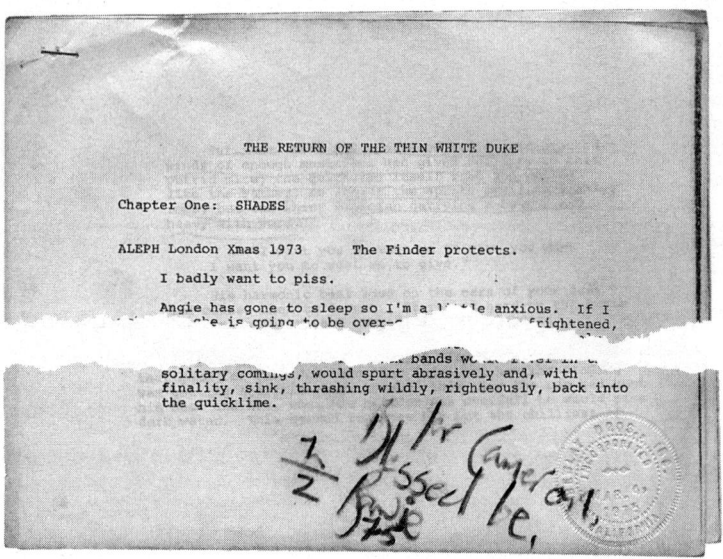

He began playing guitar again. I told him I had more questions. "Oh please! I'm just filling in by playing, I like playing."

Nothing was off the record. He didn't seem to care where I published the story. In our interviews, he began to speak with defiant points of view. It was a new character, a man who sang songs of deep yearning romance but stayed within the bounds of rigid emotion. The interviews became opportunities for him to try out striking points of view, made from bits of books and characters he'd been studying, as if trying on pieces of clothing.

In March of 1975 Bowie called me into his office and gave me the first twelve pages of his autobiography, *The Return of the Thin White Duke*. He'd typed it on thin onionskin paper. He gave me the original copy and signed it—"For Cameron, Blessed Be, Bowie 75." He embossed it with a wax seal. For a few years it was lost in the bottom of a box in my garage. Even today it's a visceral reminder of how I felt when Bowie first handed it to me. I wasn't sure where the adventure was headed. All I knew was that he continued feeding me input, thoughts and feelings. Waiting for the mirror he expected I would hold up to him. It was a journalist's dream.

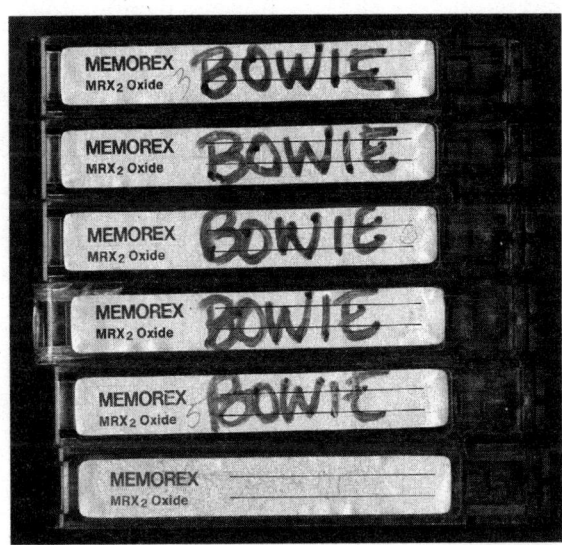

Blessed Be

She was a nursing assistant named Lily. I met her in the waiting
room at Kaiser Permanente, where I'd come with my mom. I liked
her name, and she had little in common with the rock world of Los Angeles. She had a kind face and brown mousy hair with bangs. I was staying at a tiny house in Laurel Canyon and still didn't drive. My world
still consisted of bargaining for rides, augmented by the bus. Lily was
coming to Los Angeles and had the night off. We had a date. I was
nervous and excited. My plan was to leave Bowie's insulated world of
Burroughs and Kraftwerk and half-finished paintings on easels in time
to meet her and go to a movie.

As the clock ticked closer to six, Bowie was on a roll. Working on
songs. Painting. Talking. "Have her come here," Bowie insisted. "I want
to meet her. Don't worry, I'll impress her. I'll build you up!"

I met Lily at the door of her Corolla and quickly told her she was
about to meet David Bowie. It was a secret, of course; he was in a period
of reinvention, transition, a creative rebirth. She nodded, squinting a
little, and I led her inside. Bowie and Geoff were stationed in his bedroom, looking normal, save for the pentagrams scrawled on the curtains.

Bowie held forth valiantly, complimenting me extravagantly, sniff-
ing a lot, and asking Lily about her life as a nurse. It wasn't an act.
He had chosen to be supremely interested in her life. We were sitting
cross-legged on his bed, talking like kids at a summer camp, except our

roommate was a guy with red-and-yellow hair, chain-smoking European cigarettes and listening to the life story of a part-time nurse.

We left a little after midnight and walked to her car. Lily invited me to spend the night in the apartment where she was house-sitting for a friend. Her mattress was on the floor, and we laughed as we recapped the beautiful absurdity of the situation.

"I really *liked him*," she said, "but he's so thin!"

We talked until we ran out of words. We learned how each other's kisses worked. And then came a silence. We both smelled like Bowie's Gitane cigarettes, but the silence now spoke volumes. It wasn't her world, not at all, and as much as I wanted her to believe it wasn't mine either, my excitement over the mission to hold up that mirror to David Bowie and his secret Los Angeles odyssey must have made her want to scurry back at double time to the world of nursing. The next morning, we made promises to get together soon, but it was no great surprise that we were one Christmas card away from falling out of touch, with only a shiny memory of the brief night with Bowie and a love affair that wasn't meant to be.

The product of my eighteen months with Bowie would turn out to be my best work yet, largely because he shone a light for me in all the right places. He'd damn near written the story himself in real time. He was always looking to the future and usually had an impassioned theory about it. One of the last questions I asked him was about his death.

"I'm generally happy," he answered. "Sort of intolerably happy. I'd like to die that way. Let me die a young man's death. Not an old, in-between-the-sheets kind of death. I've now decided that I consider my death precious. If I'm gonna do something with my life, it must be because I'd like my death to be as interesting as my life has been and will be."

We were years away from knowing that he'd just predicted the manner of his own early death.

Bowie would soon mount a world tour in his Thin White Duke persona. He was his own manager now, and signed every check himself. There were those who whispered that he wasn't strong enough, hadn't shed the demons of Los Angeles. Photographer Andrew Kent and I joined him on the West Coast swing of the tour. Angie Bowie was also with him on the tour, as was their son, Zowie. Fans often roamed the hotel hallways pressing their ears to all the doors, listening for an English accent. Angie was often a fan sympathizer. After the show in Seattle, she surprised a gaggle of hallway Bowie hunters by flinging open the door to their suite. The fans were thunderstruck.

"*Angie*," squealed one Seattle glitter child. "*Angie Bowie!!!*"

She was brisk. "Yes, honey. What can I do for you?"

"Where's David, Angie?"

"He's here in the next room," she allowed.

"Can we talk to him?" More fans began to gather in the hallway. "Can we come in?"

"No, honey," said Angie. "But you can talk to him from here."

The fans held a conversation with David Bowie through the door. They peppered him with fervent questions about Ziggy Stardust. Would Ziggy ever return? How was Mick Ronson? Bowie gave them all bright, enigmatic answers. I studied their faces as they listened in the hallway, enchanted with his cheerful, disembodied voice.

"Glam and glitter," he said later, resting his head in his hands. "It's so . . . so 1972, you know. I thought all this had *died*. I mean, didn't it disappear along with T. Rex?"

The next night, in Portland, Bowie slipped off to hide in my room. The *Rolling Stone* cover story was about to be published. An early copy was floating around. It was an important piece of writing for me. He'd challenged me to hold up a mirror to him when we began this exercise in immersive access. There was the mirror, the portrait of him in transition, his harrowing time in Los Angeles, complete with ghosts, bottles of pee, and declarations like "I am the revolution I wanted."

If he'd read it, he didn't mention it. He looked ghostly pale in the light. We talked about the tour, about numerology, and about John Lennon telling him the secret was just to survive. Absent-mindedly, Bowie

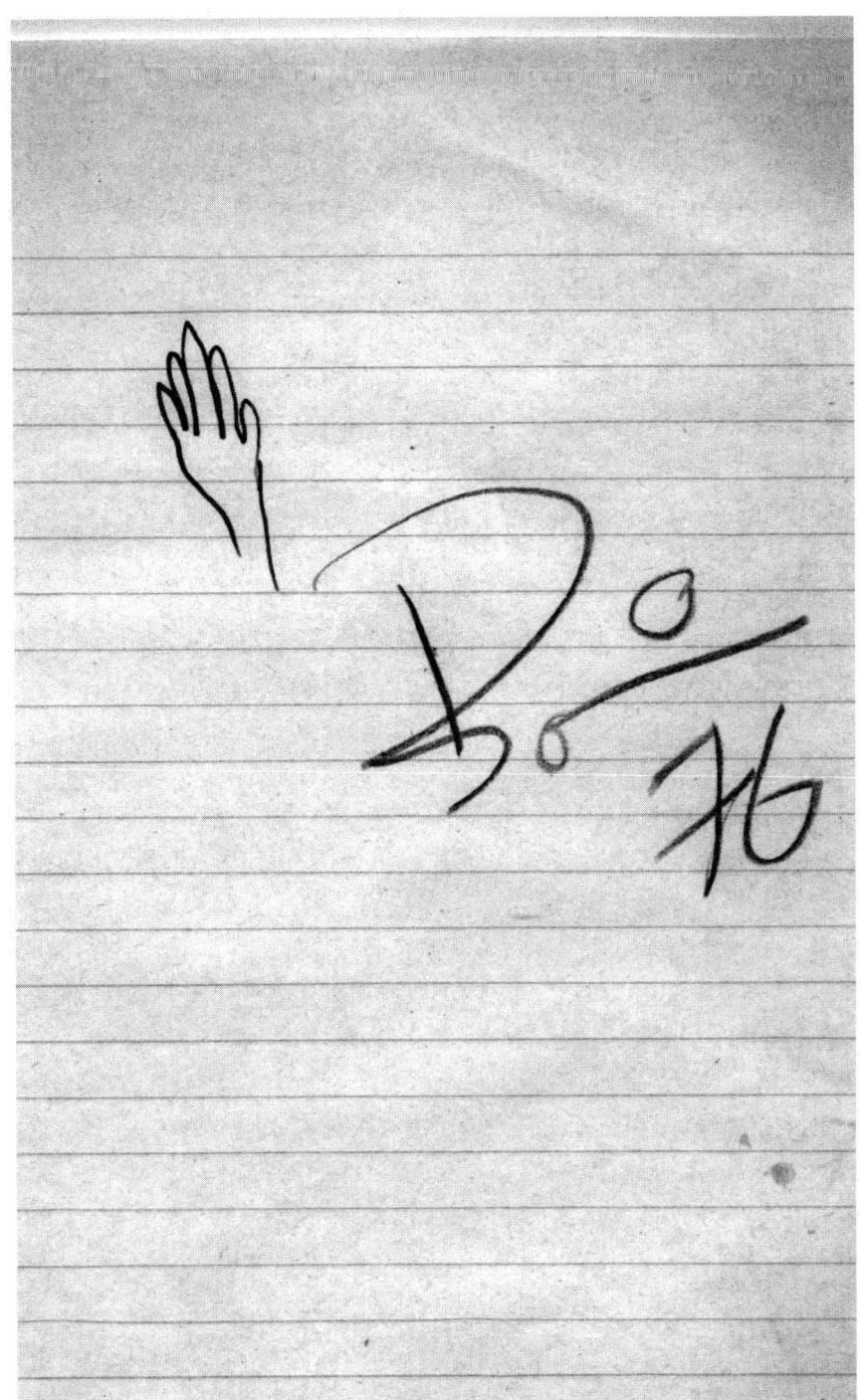

Bowie self-portrait/doodle. Seattle, 1976.

doodled on my yellow legal tablet as he spoke. He turned the page of the tablet.

"Let's play a game," he said. He asked me to name thirty objects. I did. He wrote them all down in two columns. He handed the tablet back to me. I looked at the columns as he recited every object on the list, backward.

"I studied mind control when I was a kid," he said. "I have very good control of that sort of thing."

The hallways were finally quiet. He returned to his room. I looked at my yellow legal tablet. He'd left behind a jagged drawing of an arm, fingers outstretched. It looked like a cry for help. He'd spent eighteen months making a dramatic new album, *Station to Station*, and creating the Thin White Duke.

By the fall of 1977, Bowie had moved to Germany, embraced anonymity, begun shaking off his cocaine addiction, and started recording the groundbreaking trilogy of his Berlin albums. We didn't stay in close touch, but he was always generous in allowing me to use his music in our movies. The earliest versions of the *Almost Famous* script were centered on a storied British publicist, a kind of Derek Taylor character who'd been cast aside by the Beatles. He finds a brilliant new client, Ricky Fedora, with a tragic flaw—he can't say no. Fedora restores Russell Demay's glorious reputation just before the AIDS crisis claims him in the early '80s. I wrote the character for David Bowie to play, but over time his character disappeared and the whole story became a personal story about my family.

I'd always had the hope I could direct Bowie in a movie I'd written. I loved his acting. Even his theatricality was always rooted in honesty. The last time I saw him was at a party Jann Wenner threw for *Almost Famous*. I sat next to Bowie and told him about the origins of the movie and how it began as a desire to write a character for him.

"Write me another one," he said.

A year or two after that, I got a phone call from his assistant, Henry Wren-Mellick. Bowie was looking for a copy of the autobiography he'd started. I'd not yet recovered the original copy he'd given me. Instead, I found a copy deep in the archives of *Rolling Stone*.

We did one more interview, in 2006. This one was on the phone. He was calling from his apartment in Soho, living his fulfilling New York life with his wife, Iman. He was by then famously steadfast about not looking back, so I was surprised he'd agreed to the interview at all. It was for a *Rolling Stone* anniversary issue, and the subject was our 1976 cover story about his Thin White Duke days in Los Angeles. We were to discuss the unprecedented access he'd given me as a teenage journalist, but the moment I heard his voice, all of my professional distance disappeared. The creative excitement of our whirlwind time together came back to me in an avalanche. I couldn't wait to hear if he'd felt the same way.

"I wanted to thank you for finding the autobiography," Bowie said.

"It's great to hear your voice," I said. "And I just want to say, it was an amazing gift to pull me along for those eighteen months, back then. In many ways, it shaped everything that came after. Thank you."

"Well, I'm glad it meant something to you," he said. His familiar jovial voice sounded slightly detached.

"And I remember when you gave me the first chapter of the autobiography. It was at the Bel-Air House, in the blue room."

"I don't remember . . ."

"You mean you don't remember, or you don't look back?"

Bowie laughed a little. He'd tried to revisit the *Rolling Stone* cover story that morning. "I started to read the thing," he said, "but I couldn't finish it. It was probably one of the worst periods of my life. I was undergoing serious mental problems. To me, your article represents the morbid misdirected enthusiasm of a young man with too much time on his hands and too many grams of amphetamine or PCP or cocaine, and maybe all three, in his system."

"Wow," I said, suddenly needing to rally his enthusiasm for the "mirror" I'd held up to him. "I remember it as——"

He interrupted. "I see various photographs of me looking skeletal, which remind me how badly behaved I was back in the seventies. I occasionally look at them and think, *How did I ever get to that state?* I'm absolutely amazed I survived."

"Well, it was the most important profile I ever did," I told him. "The images that you go back to . . . we all go back to the iconic images of that era, but where do you go to in your mind? Is it a blur?"

"I go back to a blur, topped off with *chronic* anxiety bordering on paranoia." He seemed slightly ashamed. "I mean, that was my general state. I just needed to *stop talking*. And come to Europe. Because it was amphetamine talking."

I moved forward pleasantly but carefully.

"Let me read you back some of the quotes," I said. "This was decades ago, and so much of what you saw coming, it came to pass. Here's one. 'We must embrace a kind of empathy with technology. That's what will become more and more important.' Do you remember saying that?"

"I'm sorry, I don't remember," Bowie said.

"'I'd love to be prime minister, but only until they print it, then I'll lose interest!'"

"That's nobody I recognize," said Bowie.

"'I assemble parts of myself like I assemble a robot. The parts that need to be fixed get replaced.'"

"Not the me I know. But carry on."

I pulled his favorite Peter Cook and Dudley Moore routine off the shelf. Surely this would rouse a happy memory. "What's the worst job you've ever had?"

There was a distant chuckle.

"It was a dangerous time," he said. "I needed to completely change my environment and the people I knew. I was doing too much with too small a handful of what one might call normal friends. The rest were dealers. And you." He paused. "It was extremely unhealthy. Stereotypical rock star behavior. 'Rock star dies at an early age.' How sad and typical that would have been. It was probably one of the worst periods of my life. I never fully kicked until the mid-eighties. I've got an addictive personality, and it took hold of my life."

"Okay, one more. This is one of my favorites. You were driving in Nancy Lippman's VW bug, listening to Kraftwerk, talking about Los Angeles, and the Eagles, and the passing of time and you said, 'All of this will be forgotten.'"

"I wish I'd said that."

"You *did* say that."

"I was lost. I'm sorry," he said. "I just don't remember any of it." And in his pause, I knew there was every chance he remembered all of it. He'd just moved on. There was no looking back. I was the last one standing at the shrine to the Great Lost Weekend, the funeral of the Thin White Duke.

"It was a terrible time for me," he said. He sounded grateful to be alive and happy to leave it where it belonged. Behind him. "However," he added, brightening a bit, "I did make some good music."

I ran into Russ Shaw again just weeks before he died in the early days of the AIDS crisis. He was excited about Rod Stewart's newest record. He was always polishing someone's legacy. I made a mental note to credit him if I ever wrote the full story of my unexpected adventure with the Thin White Duke. It never ceases to move me. There's always a hero behind the curtain, so vivid in the day and yet lost in the mists of time. Without that large, plumed collar bobbing through the Indianapolis airport, so much would be different today.

Thank you, Russ Shaw.

The Stuff

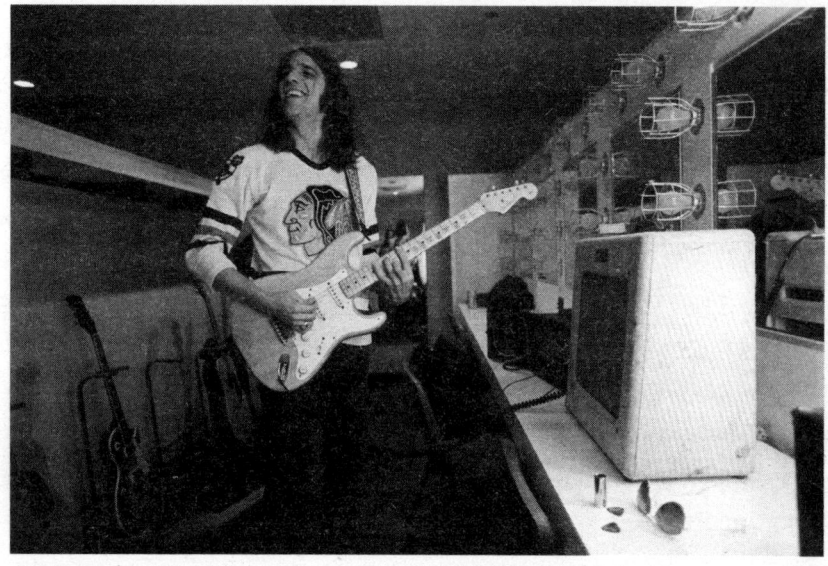

The Eagles were part of my regular beat at *Rolling Stone*. Because we'd met in the earliest days of the band, and I'd planted my flag with them at the very beginning, Glenn Frey and I kept up a long-running friendship. Frey never lost his scrappy player-coach persona, even as the band scaled unthinkable heights of success. He was always quick with helpful little blasts of brotherly advice. Especially when I had girl problems.

By mid-1973, I was smitten with Kathy Kenyon, a willowy California girl who worked at KMET in Los Angeles. Kathy had given me the aw-how-sweet kiss-off. It hurt. For no good reason, I fixated on the song "He's Misstra Know It All" by Stevie Wonder. I knew it was the curse of being younger than everyone else, including her. But when I shared my heartbreak with Glenn Frey, his theory was very different.

"The answer," he said, "is 'Attitude.'" He explained further. "You gotta have 'The Attitude.' When you have The Attitude, you don't live or die with anybody else's opinion. You control every situation if you have The Attitude. If that girl can't *smell* your qualifications, move on! That's *The Attitude*!"

The Attitude didn't work with Kathy. Turns out she was in love with Gus, her super-handsome coworker with the perfect beard. But I never forgot Glenn's Attitude speech. Years later, I quoted his Attitude theory in the screenplay for *Fast Times at Ridgemont High*.

As the Eagles added hit after hit to their body of work, they became a hotter and hotter commodity in journalism. The only problem was that most of the writers were snobs. A collection of rock writers at a party would challenge each other on their musical taste, each one going further and further into the world of the obscure until they'd collectively decided that *Self-Portrait* was Bob Dylan's greatest album and the Eagles barely deserved a record contract. Don Henley, the co-leader of the band, was known to carry a list of writers who'd denigrated them in print. Meeting a new journalist, he'd consult a small notebook in his breast pocket. If their name didn't appear, he'd continue the conversation.

The Eagles had a like-minded young manager in Irving Azoff. Azoff was a mischievous flamethrower who had also studied the tenets of success. Camaraderie was everything. Azoff was to the business what Frey and Henley were to songwriting. Together they were unbeatable. Forward motion was everything. They were sometimes branded as laid-back. Up close, the Eagles were many things, but laid-back was not one of them.

"We want to put the Eagles on the cover," Ben Fong-Torres announced in his jazzy disc jockey voice. It was the summer of 1975. I was eighteen, and this was great news. I'd be able to write the band's first comprehensive profile, drawing from the several years I'd known them. It was another lesson in the world of access in the mid-'70s. There weren't a million media outlets that covered music, and *Rolling Stone*, endorse them or not, was the biggest.

Frey had grown up scouring all the rock magazines to learn about the pitfalls of a career in music. He was not just a student of songwriting, he studied models of success. He had great taste in comedy and records, not to mention bachelorhood and marijuana. The nicknames he gave to everybody weren't simple; they had obscure relevance. He even gave himself nicknames—Teen King, the Lone Arranger (for his talent in arranging band vocals), and more. He also had a bird's-eye view of how the band could be portrayed in the story.

"Move in with us," said Frey.

He and Henley were renting a place where they could concentrate on writing the next album, *One of These Nights*. The house they shared was just off Mulholland and featured a spectacular view of the city. This was Hollywood, with all the glittering promise and craven underpinnings that Henley and Frey's songs would capture so well. Frey dubbed the house "the Eagles' Nest" but the one that stuck even more was "the House with the Million-Dollar View."

There were two main bedrooms on either side of the sprawling single-story home. Henley occupied one, Frey the other. It was a fetching metaphor for their partnership. Under one roof, they were still perfect opposites. They were "the Odd Couple," named after the TV show with Jack Klugman and Tony Randall, one being messy and the other fastidious. Henley was the fastidious one; Glenn was the messier. Little did they know—or maybe they did—that the "Million-Dollar" tag would far undersell the value of the songs they wrote in that house.

My room was in the middle.

At night, Henley and Frey would roll down the hill into Hollywood. They might cruise through the Troubadour bar or the restaurant next door, Dan Tana's. They would collect phone numbers, stories, dates, and fodder for their songs. I would trail along and meet all the fair ladies of the scene, the kicker being they rarely even looked at me. It was ironic that the LA cowboy look would come from two outsiders, carpetbaggers, really. Or as Stevie Nicks would put it many years later: "Skinny, a little underfed, with a look in their eyes like they knew a few secrets. No one wore jeans like them either."

The band was often a push-pull between perfection and looseness, country and rock, fame and anonymity, and the diamond-cutting of Henley and Frey's creative process. The result was greatness.

They worked from an endless supply of yellow legal tablets. With two guitars facing each other, Frey and Henley's nightly ritual involved meticulously sculpting conversational lyrics. (Henley: "More matter-of-fact." Frey: "Watch it happen.") Then the goal might be to land the perfect double entendre, the line that could reward you on a third listen. Always they would add another element—the yearning for romance. They filled in each other's creative potholes.

Years later, at Frey's memorial, Henley would describe the collaborative process as well as anybody ever has. He was the last to speak at the event, an emotional gathering held at one of the band's favorite venues, the formerly titled Los Angeles Forum. When Henley took the podium, he urged everyone to get comfortable. Normally a man of few words, Henley had written a lengthy speech as finely tuned as the best of his songwriting.

"So we took turns," he said. "Sometimes I was the designated scribe, the person whose job it was to document and hold the lantern while Glenn did the digging. Sometimes he kept the notes and held the lantern while I did the digging. What were we digging for? The stuff. Details and clues and images, invention, fresh ideas and melodies and intuitive understanding of people. And I can tell you the holder of the lantern doesn't even know what his partner is digging for half the time. But he knows gold when he sees it. But like an actor or a novelist, you study dialogue. You listen to how people really talk and you learn little by little to take someone's five-minute speech and make it into one sentence without losing anything."

Glenn was a synthesizer; he took from everything and everybody. Prowling Sunset Boulevard in a vintage Chevy, Frey listened to a lot of soul and rhythm and blues songs, like "I've Been Born Again" by Johnnie Taylor or "If You Don't Know Me by Now" by Harold Melvin & the Blue Notes, featuring Teddy Pendergrass. I watched as Frey took the memorable symphonic opening to "If You Don't Know Me by Now" and put it through his own songwriting prism. It became one of the Eagles' biggest hits, "Take It to the Limit."

They collected characters from real life. One night at Dan Tana's, Frey was struck by the image of a girl at a small table, a hint of sadness behind her big brown eyes. Next to her was a silver-haired gent with too many rings. She shared a glance or two with Frey. He drove home and wrote a song-story about all that he saw behind those big brown eyes. The song had too many verses. The words poured out of him, and so did the chorus. He sang it with a twang that was part Jack Nicholson and part George Jones.

I was six feet away, with tape recorder on, as they wrote "Lyin' Eyes," "One of These Nights," "After the Thrill Is Gone," and fine-tuned many other songs, including an unrecorded gem called "When a Bad Boy Meets a Bad Girl in the Night." Though Henley was from Texas and Frey from Detroit, their goal was to capture the national zeitgeist. As they looked out on that glittery horizon, the songwriters kept topping each other with ideas and phrases that could have layers of meaning. "Nothing can just skim the surface," Henley told Frey. The partnership was electric, a guided missile of creativity. I had a front-row seat for their process and wanted the profile to show their chemistry from the inside out. For a notoriously press-shy group, this was way off the grid. They left no doors closed and no avenues off-limits. It was journalistic nirvana, and the Budweiser flowed as we talked for many hours over many nights.

"You can't hiiiide your lyin' eyes . . ." When Henley added his voice, the lyrics sounded like well-worn leather and you could immediately hear what the song might become. Frey was a Vesuvius of images and Henley sharpened them with a clever bite. I would often look over to make sure my tape recorder was rolling. It was.

After *One of These Nights*, the Eagles would make the album that brought together all their influences. The literary-styled lyrics. The humor. The cynicism. The romance. The sweet harmonies. *Hotel California* was a happy/sad musical masterpiece. The success of the album broke the band, and even expanded the size of the music business. After *Hotel California*, there would be more Eagles music. A breakup. A make-up.

The surprisingly early loss of Glenn Frey might have ended the band, but Henley kept his hand on the wheel and his bandmate's Detroit voice in his ear. Even today, I can still feel the reverberation of those young pistons firing backstage in that tiny San Diego dressing room. A few years after he died, Glenn's daughter, Taylor, sent me a copy of that first photo taken by my high school buddy, the four original members with their arms draped on each other. "This was in the drawer of his bedside table," she wrote. "I thought you'd want to have it."

Suddenly Everybody Everywhere Loves Fleetwood Mac

Gibson & Stromberg, the little publicity firm that predicted rock's huge entry into the mainstream, closed in 1975. They were consumed by all that they'd helped create. Once again, Gary Stromberg spotted it early. The young rebels who'd briefly had control of the record business were selling out to big labels and bigger business. Artists like the Eagles and Peter Frampton were about to be headlining stadiums and selling enormous amounts of records. The boomer generation had found their soundtrack. Even Jimmy Carter needed an endorsement from the Allman Brothers Band to secure a victory in the presidential election.

There was always room for a bright new idea. On New Year's Eve of 1974, two struggling young American singer-songwriters, Stevie Nicks and her boyfriend, Lindsey Buckingham, joined the British band Fleetwood Mac. It was an out-of-the-box idea that worked. Big-time. The album featuring Buckingham and Nicks, *Fleetwood Mac*, exploded with hit after hit. By 1976, Fleetwood Mac had joined the multiplatinum parade to enormous notoriety.

Settling into a seat at the Universal Amphitheatre in August, I remember the excitement for the band was through the roof. So fresh was the Buckingham-Nicks lineup that I wondered if most of the crowd even knew that band was nine years and many incarnations down the line. I recently found a note from that night: "Suddenly everybody everywhere loves Fleetwood Mac."

I'd written about the band a lot, including in the *Los Angeles Times*, where Stevie Nicks auditioned names for her all-important second album with the band.

"We've gone through so much drama making the new album," Stevie laughed as we sat in their manager's office, "we should call it *Rumors and Heartaches*."

They settled on *Rumours*, of course, and when the album was nearly finished *Rolling Stone* set the band for a cover story. The group was so eager to talk about the romantic roller coaster of the previous year that the article nearly wrote itself. All I had to do was turn on the tape recorder. The lore is well-known now, but at the time Nicks and Buckingham had broken up, so had keyboardist-vocalist Christine McVie and her husband, bassist John McVie, and the album was rich with potent breakup songs.

On a flight to Indianapolis, each of them discussed the other as soon as they were outside of earshot. Stevie was recently single and eager to make new friends like the Eagles' Don Henley. Lindsey was dating a friend of mine, Kathy Nelson. Christine was dating Beach Boy Dennis Wilson. John McVie was heartbroken. Mick Fleetwood looked on, knowing it had all been captured in the songs. Later he too would enter the heartbreak derby after a brief affair with Nicks.

There was a wistful innocence about the band. They all were on a grand adventure together. They'd all had plenty of experience, but to listen to them talk was to catch the real-time account of bursting out of a cocoon. Like so many of the great recordings, from Dylan to Coltrane to Billie Holiday, the songs were born from breakups and the loneliness of the freedom that follows. On the plane to Indianapolis, Nicks played me one song in particular that seemed to be the perfect audio equivalent of what it felt like being around the band. The song was "Silver Springs," and I was amazed that it had been cut from the album.

"Too many slow songs," she said. She shook her head. "I guess it'll be a B-side."

The song has gone on to have its rightful place as a Fleetwood Mac standard and I think of it whenever I see the classic Annie Leibovitz shot that adorned the cover story. Leibovitz had a way of coaxing artists out of their comfort zone. In this case, she didn't have to do much coaxing. When Leibovitz began the photo session with Fleetwood Mac, they hopped into bed together and created the cover image to match the romantic drama that went into writing and recording the album.

I talked to Lindsey Buckingham about the cover shot and the story a few years ago. It was during Covid, a thoughtful time when all the members were happy to reflect on those early years.

"We were all breaking up and at the same time you're making the most important musical work of your life," he said. "I didn't necessarily want to do good for Stevie. Part of me didn't. But there was a much bigger picture and it had to be pursued. It was a set of decisions that we made. It felt heroic to us. 'Will you rise to the challenge? Will you follow your destiny?' That feeling probably became as much a part of the appeal of *Rumours* as the music itself."

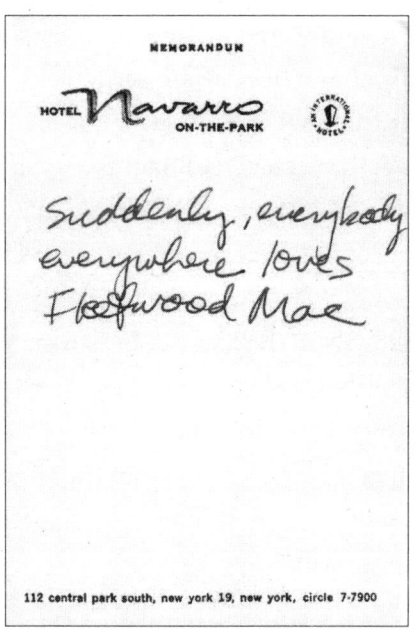

Stevie, who wasn't speaking with Lindsey at the time, agreed. "That's why it lasted," she said. "That's why it lasted from the first day of 1975 until this past January seventeenth [when the band broke up after a MusiCares benefit]. We kept it out of the studio. Most of the time. Even when Mick left me for Sara Fleetwood, his future wife, and she was banned from the studio. I got up and got dressed every day and put on my makeup and my high-heel boots and went into the studio. We kept the trauma out. The studio became the safe place to say all of it."

Mick agreed too. "We were sitting on a bomb that could have blown up or created a huge vacuum. The music would never have continued. And it was like, 'Please, Mr. President, don't press the [nuclear] bomb.'"

Visions of Marley

B y 1976, Jamaican roots rock had broken through to international success. Bob Marley and the Wailers were at the forefront, though reggae had been attempting to flow into the American market for years. Johnny Nash's "I Can See Clearly Now" was a ubiquitous hit in 1972. Jimmy Cliff's film *The Harder They Come*, complete with the hit title song, arrived the next year. Paul McCartney vacationed in Jamaica and wrote some of *Band on the Run* there in 1973. Then came Eric Clapton, who sealed the deal with his big international hit cover of Marley's "I Shot the Sheriff."

Jeff Walker, my friend and formerly an editor at *Music World* magazine, was now working at Island Records, home to Marley and the Wailers. We'd also shared that long-ago unicorn afternoon with Gram Parsons and Emmylou Harris. Along with his photographer wife, Kim Gottlieb, Walker was instrumental in educating the media on Marley and many other Jamaican artists and producers.

Bob Marley was the charismatic face of reggae, the forefront of the movement. It didn't hurt his credibility with the American party crowd that Marley's Rastafarian religion considered marijuana to be a powerful component of the faith. Marley had the looks, he had the songs, he had the spliff in hand. He also had the backing of Island Records, a record company with deep pockets.

In the summer of 1976, Jeff Walker offered me the chance to fly to Jamaica and interview Marley. Also possible were interviews with Marley's original cofounders in the Wailers, the reclusive former members Peter Tosh and Bunny Wailer. Tosh had just released an album of his own, *Legalize It*.

I'd boldly left home a few months earlier and now lived with my first real girlfriend, Mary Beth Medley. Our relationship had certainly grown from that first meeting on the Who tour. We found a condo-apartment on Lookout Mountain Avenue, just down the street from the house where Joni Mitchell once lived with Graham Nash. It was the beginning of America's bicentennial summer when I took off for Kingston, fully prepared to interview Bob Marley and others. I was to travel with Jeff, Kim, and their young son, Ryan. Mary Beth was fully aware of the reputation of Jamaican herb when she dropped me off at the airport.

"Don't try to bring back any marijuana," she stressed.

"I wouldn't dare."

It was well-known that Americans often tried to smuggle some of that legendary Jamaican weed back to the homeland. It rarely ended well. Bags were checked and thoroughly rechecked. The strong-smelling herb was hard to hide. The last thing I needed was to celebrate my nineteenth birthday in jail.

When we arrived in Kingston, we immediately got the report that Bob Marley was not in the country. He was still in New York finishing up promotion for the latest album, *Rastaman Vibration*. We had a day or two to kill, and Jeff knew exactly how to spend the time. We visited some waterfalls, and Walker pointed out the legendary studio where Lee "Scratch" Perry had produced some of the seminal works in the rise of reggae. The next day we traveled to the home of Peter Tosh, where I conducted an interview while standing next to his car.

Tosh was tough and wary in our interview. He knew my questions would lead to a discussion of Marley himself. Tosh first began singing with Marley and Bunny Wailer on the street corners of Trench Town in

1962. By 1976 Marley had risen from the original Wailers to what was already near-demigod status as the front man for a newer version of the band. Tosh was careful in his comments to me about Marley. Between the lines of our dialogue that day was Tosh's clear opinion that Marley had found enormous success with a more populist version of reggae, emphasis on the *pop*. Hard-core followers of the original Wailers liked to cast Tosh as the John Lennon to Marley's Paul McCartney. Tosh and Bunny had left the Wailers several years earlier when Island chief Chris Blackwell refused to release a Tosh solo album. Finally a solo artist, Tosh still had a reservoir of bitterness that made for a tough, fascinating interview.

Marley spent another day in New York, and we used the time to seek an interview with Bunny Wailer. Bunny was a more difficult interview to schedule. He didn't have a phone, said Walker, so it was difficult to pin down an actual time. I asked Jeff about the most reliable way to set up an interview.

"We'll go to the park near the Dunns River Falls," he reasoned. "The way it's worked in the past is—you meditate for Bunny and he'll show up."

We sat in the park and meditated. A local musician friend of Jeff's showed up and offered a puff from what looked like an enormous rolled-up newspaper packed with purple marijuana. One puff was enough. Another hour rolled by as we squinted into the scorching sun and waited for Bunny.

Sure enough, Bunny Wailer appeared. He had the aura of a high priest. He somehow knew he'd been summoned for an appointment. We sat in the town square and talked. His wary eyes sat in pools of dark yellow. Bunny offered some herb wine, which he indicated was powerful. To be polite, I took a small sip from the cap of his jug. It took about ten seconds to travel to the center of my skull. Luckily, Bunny had a lot to say about Marley, destiny, and how he was always meant to put out records himself. I had now interviewed two-thirds of the holy trinity of the original Wailers.

The next day we traveled to Bob Marley's home at 56 Hope Road to wait for his arrival. We camped out in Marley's spartan bedroom, open-air and bathed in sunlight. I briefly fell asleep atop the covers of his bed and awakened alone. Jeff and his family were elsewhere. There was a box on Marley's nightstand, the top slightly askew. Inside I could see several thick buds of highly potent marijuana.

"Well," Jeff Walker announced a few minutes later, "Bob's going to stay in New York."

Marley had been nominated for Best Artist in the 1975 Rock Awards, produced by pop impresario Don Kirshner. Marley had apparently experienced a vision where he won the award. He decided he would stick around in Manhattan to attend the ceremony. None of us were able to wait longer or meet Marley in New York. We made plans to return the next day, happy for the time spent in Jamaica, and the powerful interviews with Tosh and Bunny.

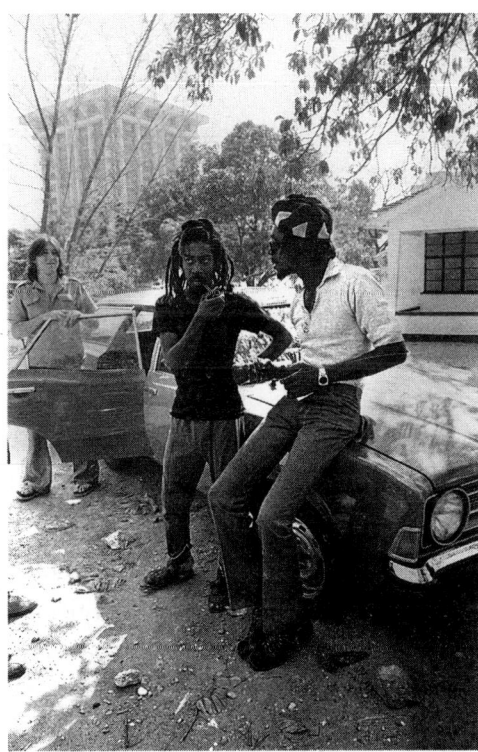

"Meditate and he will show up." With Bunny Wailer and Peter Tosh in Jamaica, 1976.

Later that year, Marley's bedroom was the scene of his near-assassination. Two Datsuns roared up to his home, and seven gunmen poured out, shooting wildly. Miraculously, Marley escaped with only a bullet to his left arm. Two days later he was able to headline the famous Smile Jamaica festival that proved a seminal event in Marley's life and legacy. Peter Tosh was shot and killed eleven years later by an intruder. Bunny Wailer maintained a robust solo career for many years until his passing in 2021, but our brief visit to Kingston marked a time just before the white-hot gaze of mass acceptance would sweep them all into a kind of reggae immortality.

Mary Beth picked me up at the airport and on the way home I shared the highlights. The near-miss with Marley. The interview with Tosh. The town square where Bunny Wailer somehow picked up our telepathic invitation. True or not, it didn't matter. The whole place reeked of magic, and of course, marijuana.

"Well, I'm glad you didn't try to bring any weed back," said Mary Beth.

"Actually," I said, "I did."

She gasped as I showed her a Kleenex packet I'd slipped through customs. In it were a few seeds I'd scraped from Bob Marley's personal stash.

"That was," she said, "so *stupid* of you."

"I know."

Still, having already cheated fate, we decided to grow Bob Marley's seeds in two big pots we kept in the backyard. Three months later, the leafy green plants sprouted flowery buds. One night in November, we invited over several friends to sample the most holy of marijuana strains—Bob Marley's personal stash.

I cannot begin to tell you the strength of the headaches it produced. Karma is a bitch, as they say, and nowhere was it truer than in the result of my thievery from the bedroom of reggae's brightest light.

I never did interview Bob Marley but did indeed see him perform on his last swing through Los Angeles. He was already suffering with a cancer diagnosis, but you'd never have known it from the high voltage performance. The venue's heavy floorboards shook as the audience bounced to the rhythm. Our trip to Jamaica would never disappear from my mind, and as time has now taken all the original Wailers from this earth, I am quietly grateful that I was punished for my sin of trying to import that most sacred sacrament from Bob Marley's bedroom: his seeds.

Dee Dee Is a Punk Rocker

In 1977, Mary Beth was promoted out of tour management and headed into a more executive role with Peter Rudge and Sir Productions. We were still living on Lookout Mountain in Laurel Canyon. My record collection had grown larger and larger; it was now bulging with test pressings and rarities. We had just found our domestic rhythm when she told me that we had to move to New York and begin looking for a place. Her career was skyrocketing.

In New York, my friend and fellow Led Zeppelin tourmate Lisa Robinson told me to look out for a new band that was playing around CBGB's. The Ramones were a sonic blast with something else that few other bands had to offer—a great sense of humor. In their own deadpan way, they were the funniest band I'd ever heard. It was easy to get swept up into their early fan club. They were a palate cleanser in the increasingly self-important world of '70s rock. The average Ramones song was less than two minutes long. I loved "Blitzkrieg Bop," "Judy Is a Punk," and "Today Your Love, Tomorrow the World." Lisa introduced me to the band. We got along well. I was so clearly Southern Californian. They seemed fascinated in the way you're fascinated by a strange animal at the zoo, loaned from another country.

I hit it off with Dee Dee Ramone, the former lead singer and now bassist. We'd often sit on bar stools at the club and talk about what the future might bring for a band like theirs. Slumped in a too-small black leather jacket, he was quietly inquisitive about the path ahead. Just sitting there at the bar, he kind of broke my heart. He knew enough to know what he didn't know, which was pretty much everything. I felt a long way from home myself. As Southern California beckoned, I was scared to tell Mary Beth that I didn't see myself living in Manhattan. These episodes of anxiety were peppered with shows by the Ramones. I could feel their confidence growing. Soon they had a first album, and Dee Dee gave me a copy of the test pressing, signed by the band.

Watching them play their first big-league show at the Bottom Line, I knew I had to say goodbye. More and more, I struggled with how to tell Mary Beth I missed home and my friends and family. I didn't have that special taste for the knife's edge, the dark side of New York. I didn't fit in. I felt suffocated by the cynicism. The Ramones returned to CBGB's with increasing victories under their belts, and as usual, I was catching up with Dee Dee over a couple beers. I visited the bathroom, leaving my wallet on the counter, and when I returned, seventy-five dollars were missing. Surely the money had fallen out of my wallet. Dee Dee helped me look for it. Only later did I realize that the rumors were true. He was struggling with a not-so-secret heroin addiction. He'd taken the money himself. It was a snapshot of everything I didn't want to live with. I knew I'd be cheering for the band from afar.

One day Mary Beth showed up having signed the lease for an apartment that was a whopping $400 a month. She had moved my albums and all my other stuff into the apartment. Having lived through the emotions of others in books and movies and songs, I was utterly unprepared for real life. She was seven years older than me and I wasn't even sure I was truly in love. I panicked and fled back to California without a proper goodbye.

I don't know what happened to my records. Someone told me she dumped them on the sidewalk for anybody to take. I hope somebody grabbed that signed test pressing of the first Ramones album. There was so much left to learn about love. My short romance with Mary Beth lived in my mind like a beautiful insect trapped in amber. I broke her heart.

If I can stop one heart from breaking, I shall not live in vain.

—EMILY DICKINSON

"It's not too late to go back to college," my mom was telling me.

It was summer in 1977 and I was back living at home. She opened her rainbow-colored briefcase filled with articles and course descriptions for the law school across the street. Giving up was not her thing. The living room was still stuffed with books, and at the center was the big chair flanked by the phone that forever rang with needy counselees. The bathroom still had the same framed "I Am Loved" poster on the wall. The same beatific hippie couple faced me as I washed my hands.

My father still commuted back and forth from the desert. He sometimes had late-night talks on the phone with my sister, who barely spoke with my mother. Being home helped with the chemistry of the whole situation. Sometimes the truth is so blinding you don't even see it. My own journey as a journalist gave my mom and dad the emotional glue to stay together.

I was running out of steam. Like a kid in the proverbial candy store, I'd gorged on *Rolling Stone* profiles for years. Lately they'd been taking longer to finish. I spent a long time on an assignment from *The New York Times Magazine* about what Bob Dylan means to '70s teenagers. The article was rejected with a curt apology and a kill fee of a hundred dollars. I didn't know where the road would end for a kid from San

Diego who once had a dream of having a story published in a national magazine. Maybe I needed a new dream.

One day the phone rang. It was John Belushi, from *Saturday Night Live*. More recently he'd played "Bluto" Blutarsky in the big hit movie *Animal House*. I'd met Belushi in New York, at the Blues Bar, which he operated with Dan Aykroyd, as a guest of my fellow music journalist (and future screenwriter) Mitch Glazer. Belushi was playing drums when I walked into the bar, and later that night he'd told me a long drummer joke with an obscure punch line. I loved it. He remembered me and somehow had found me.

"Hey," he said, "I don't know what the problem is, but *Rolling Stone* wanted to put me on the cover, and I asked if you'd be the guy to do it. They told me you were too busy and took too long."

I agreed that it was a busy time. What a shame that I wouldn't be able to do it. Inside, I was dying.

"Just wanted you to know that I asked for you," he added. An intuitive guy, he must have known from my silence that I was hurt. He pedaled hard toward making me feel better. "We'll do something else," he said. "They gave the story to a guy named Charles M. Young."

I hung up and nearly blacked out from embarrassment. I also knew that the sword of Damocles was hanging above me. Chuck Young was a favorite of the staff in New York, and he'd begun asking for the same assignments that had once been mine. Furthermore, he was a revolutionary. He'd stood up to the editors at the magazine and demanded that they cover the style of music that was thundering and thrashing across the ocean—punk. It was everything David Bowie had told me, sitting in that yellow VW on La Brea Avenue. The complacent world of the singer-songwriters was under siege. *All of this will be forgotten.*

The Sex Pistols finally invaded the territory of the '70s rock titans and landed on the cover of *Rolling Stone* in the October 20, 1977, issue. The headline: "Rock Is Sick and Living in London." It was the beginning of the end of the '70s. Chuck Young had won his long-fought battle within the magazine.

On the same evening that the Sex Pistols cover arrived on news-stands, my phone started ringing with worried calls. They were storm cloud calls, the kind of half-confirmed rumors that precede a tragedy. I turned on the television and waited to see if any news had made it to the mainstream. Sure enough, a news report broke in. A Convair CV-240 plane carrying twenty-five passengers, including Lynyrd Skynyrd, had crashed into a wooded area near Gillsburg, Mississippi. There were multiple fatalities.

Had it not been for her promotion, Mary Beth Medley would have been on that flight. Moving to New York saved her life.

The rest of the news was terrible. Ronnie Van Zant died instantly, along with the young guitarist Steve Gaines and his sister. The plane had already been infamous. I knew through Mary Beth that Aerosmith had turned the aircraft down. It was on less than its last legs. A Learjet awaited Lynyrd Skynyrd in the next town, Baton Rouge. They would never board it.

I couldn't help imagining the plane sitting in a swamp in the dark of night. I couldn't escape the feeling that maybe the magic carpet ride that began at the backstage gate of the San Diego Sports Arena was like every great song: it wouldn't overstay its welcome. Everything was ending. Across the pond, a band that could barely play, the Sex Pistols, was making the rock I grew up with seem old and out of step.

I saw Mary Beth again at the funeral for Ronnie Van Zant and the other band members in Orange Park, Florida. It was October of 1977, and the grief briefly brought us back together. We stood side-by-side. I put my arm around her. I could tell she wanted to shake it off but didn't. Our love of Skynyrd had been the glue that first bonded us and held us together in many ways. Now it was all gone. It would be twenty years before we spoke again or I could even listen to Lynyrd Skynyrd.

Near the end of our relationship, Mary Beth and I traveled with Lynyrd Skynyrd to Japan for a series of concerts. We stopped over in

Honolulu for two days before the band continued to Tokyo. Van Zant and I shared a passion for fishing. He enjoyed going after freshwater bass, and I was always extolling the virtue of deep-sea day boats like the ones in San Diego. On a day off in Hawaii, Ronnie surprised me by booking a fishing trip off the Hawaiian coast. I offered to split the cost, but he wouldn't hear of it. He knew I made monthly mixtapes of music, and that was the contribution he wanted.

"Just bring your boom box," he said, "you're in charge of the tunes."

It was a day filled with playful camaraderie. None of us caught a fish or felt a single bite. As any true fisherman can tell you, it's not really about that. It's about the memories. There were plenty from that day.

On the trip I was able to give Ronnie Van Zant a surprise cassette tape from Neil Young. Though the band had playfully chastised Young in their song "Sweet Home Alabama," they were actually admirers of each other. Van Zant loved Neil Young's defiant creativity, and Young was taken with the band's three-guitar attack. It reminded him of his own early band, Buffalo Springfield. While I was covering Neil Young on his *Rust Never Sleeps* tour, he'd given me the tape of three new songs he wanted me to share with Van Zant for Lynyrd Skynyrd to potentially cover for the band's next album. ("Captain Kennedy," "Powderfinger," and "Sedan Delivery.")

A couple decades after the plane crash, I was randomly listening to old mixtapes in the kitchen. I'd always made monthly cassettes of my favorite songs, and listening to tapes now was like reading an old diary. I didn't realize I was listening to one of the mixes I'd played on our Hawaiian fishing trip. It was right in the middle of Paul McCartney and Wings' "Beware My Love" when there was a sharp clicking sound on the tape, and the music stopped. Suddenly I heard the voices of Skynyrd guitarists Gary Rossington and Allen Collins, laughing on the high seas, and then there was Ronnie making a joke about us not catching any fish. I'd pressed the wrong button on the day and recorded over some of the music by mistake. But for the next two minutes, time rewound to that January day when Skynyrd were still a complete unit and everything was possible. The sound of their voices was the best kind of music. And after two minutes, *click*, it was back to the mixtape. I stood in my kitchen, listening to the end of "Beware My Love." I had already been crying but hadn't even realized it. I dried the smear of tears off with my T-shirt. Within a few weeks I was able to listen to their music again.

Use it or lose it.

—ALICE CROWE

After the funeral, I returned to San Diego a beaten man. In several years, I hadn't stopped to gather my wits. Back living in my old room, I looked at an old Eagles poster on the back of the door. It had all gone so quickly. My time at the magazine was ending. I still had a few more cover stories to finish. Joni Mitchell was one of them. Mitchell had been my dream profile subject from the beginning, but she rarely did interviews. Her songs, she felt, spoke for her.

One night back in 1973, my sister Cindy and I were interviewing Bonnie Raitt in the Troubadour dressing room. Mitchell swept in and joined the interview, praising Bonnie and asking a few questions. I was delighted at my good fortune. The next morning, I received a phone call from her manager, Elliot Roberts, telling me that her participation had been off the record.

"Joni doesn't do interviews," he said. "Maybe one day."

In 1978, Mitchell was contacted by jazz great Charles Mingus. Mingus invited her to collaborate on some of his final melodies. The legendary bassist-bandleader had been quietly battling Lou Gehrig's disease but still had a boisterous and often gruff spirit. They both clashed and clicked together, and the result was Mitchell's most adventurous album yet. Her record company was wary about how the album—a hybrid of spoken word and jazz—might sound to a rock audience. Miracle of miracles, the word got out that Mitchell wanted to sit for one interview to help explain *Mingus*. She chose me.

Joni Mitchell was famously a *Rolling Stone* disbeliever. In 1971, they'd cheekily published a graph of her boyfriends and dubbed her "Old Lady of the Year." The wound was still fresh when we sat down at the Sunset Boulevard office of her manager in the early summer of 1979.

"Let's turn the tape on," she said, looking at my cassette recorder, "I'm ready to go."

She spoke with third-draft precision, sometimes searing in her honesty and other times rollicking with laughter. She also wore her sensitivity proudly, and in one of our conversations, she defended the work that had cost her a significant chunk of her pop audience.

"Here's the thing," she said forcefully. "You have two options. You can stay the same and protect the formula that gave you your initial success. They're going to crucify you for staying the same. If you change, they're going to crucify you for changing. But staying the same is boring. And change is interesting. So, of the two options," she concluded, "I'd rather be crucified for changing."

I might have been crucified if anyone had found out what happened next. Mitchell asked if she could see the article before it was published. I knew she was worried about *Rolling Stone* tinkering with the piece. I agreed to show her the finished manuscript before publication but asked that the arrangement stay between us. I left the manuscript with her overnight. The next day she returned it with some notes. There were a few sentences she said I'd left out. With the precision of her schoolteacher mother, she instinctively knew when I'd edited some of her answers internally.

Before I left, I asked her to sign an early copy of the *Mingus* artwork that featured one of her paintings. She signed it: "Thanks for the co-operation, Joni Mitchell." I knew instantly I could never put it where a fellow journalist might see it. Famous for her honesty, she had outed me as a collaborator. I didn't mind. What might have been considered criminal to some journalists was a key to her comfort. From the comfort came something that has stood the test of time.

The interview was as intimate and honest as her best work and still stands today as my personal favorite for the magazine. Though I'd delivered another key artist who'd always turned them down, the editors still left my name off the cover. There was no mistaking the message. My time at *Rolling Stone* was all but over.

"I'm twenty-one," I told my parents, "I'm washed up."

I'd raced through my own Catholic school education. I never really had the time to do the things that most kids my age did—to fail, to waste time, to spend summers on the beach. I'd jumped into the ocean of adulthood and ultimately got caught in a riptide. I hadn't even gone to my own prom, much less law school. All I had was the high school diploma sent to me in the mail. My sister Cindy was right all along. I skipped too many grades. I skipped adolescence. I'd traded it for a backstage pass.

I'd always had a nagging desire to write a *Rolling Stone* piece about the kids that I'd sometimes meet in the parking lots outside the concerts I was covering. Each one had an odyssey to share. How they got the tickets, who they'd invited from school, the romances that consumed them, and more. It was one of my back-pocket theories. Every life was an epic tale if you knew where to look. I wanted to write an extended story about the characters I might meet at a typical American high school.

I drove around my own neighborhood looking for a high school that might possibly take me in as a reporter. My own former Catholic high school was already merging with another school across town. I was set on a public school. My mom was in the car when we came upon the school that would become "Ridgemont High." She had teacher connections to the school's vice principal. She set up a meeting with him, and he listened to my pitch with wary eyes. I wanted free rein to attend classes and document the school year.

"This will get me fired," he said.

I told him that I wouldn't identify the school. I showed him some of my articles and he stopped at one.

"You interviewed Kris . . . Kristofferson?"

He was an enormous fan. I told him about my early encounter with Kristofferson. I told him about the red leather chairs, the angry maître d', and my lucky shot at becoming a writer for *Rolling Stone*. I wouldn't have had the same career, I told him, if it hadn't been for Kris Kristofferson.

He approved of the idea and set me up with four teachers who would know about the project. Luckily, I still looked young enough to slip into the jet stream of modern high school life. I was barely prepared for how much had changed in the few years since my own high school experience.

Mind Over Matter

More than ever, I missed the girlfriend I'd met before leaving Los Angeles. Molly was a popular record company publicist for obvious reasons. She had an effervescent personality and exquisite taste in music. She'd turned me on to British new wave protopunk long before it even reached our shores. I'd mistakenly taken her for granted in the pursuit of work. Now that I was off that fast track, I was left with late-night thoughts of how much I missed her.

I kept replaying her breakup speech, examining it for inflection and veracity, and decided that she didn't mean it. One Friday night after school, I raced back up to Los Angeles hoping to see her. She wasn't answering her phone. I drove past her first-floor apartment and parked outside.

The light of a television was inside. Molly didn't answer the door. I tried a soft special knock, the one that signaled *It's me*. This time I heard another guy's voice, whispering something. Then her own *shhhh*.

I must have tried to write about that very specific, very epic pain a thousand times or more. It's that moment when the trapdoor of love opens and you go tumbling downward. The breakup scene that comes closest is in *Say Anything* . . . when Diane Court breaks up with Lloyd Dobler in his car. In my case, Molly's breakup gift wasn't a pen, it was a rare checkerboard UK edition of Elvis Costello's debut album, *My Aim Is True*. When someone breaks up with you that well, believe them.

I returned home. Many of my new friends were now the people I'd met in high school. It turned out to be a seismic year, culture-wise. The eighties were just around the corner. The cost of a modern teenage lifestyle had skyrocketed during Jimmy Carter's economy. Clothes, concert tickets, gas prices, dating—everything was more expensive. A seventeen-year-old looking to keep up with the lifestyle needed a job. Many balanced schoolwork with fast-food jobs. The newly completed mall nearby was the hub of all social activity.

Even on the school's lunch court, I could see the same kind of social hierarchy that would await them as true adults. Those who worked at the higher-end fast-food places tended to group together at the better lunch-court tables. The low earners sat on the outskirts. Then there was the increased prevalence of sex, and with that came even more emotional pressure. The conversations around me could often ping-pong from work politics to taxes to the specifics of sexual prowess.

Kids were becoming adults at younger and younger ages. When did adolescence even end anymore? Eleven? Twelve?

One fine spring day, a student in a big puffy jacket came into journalism class and announced his hero—Ronald Reagan. A new definition of cool was emerging, and it was a long way from the shaggy hippies I knew at the *Door* house. Now there was a new kind of teenager, a young Republican who savaged the perceived naïveté of liberalism but also really liked rock.

One student had a friend who worked in the ticket office for the Sports Arena. He'd heard that Led Zeppelin were going to tour in the coming year, with a concert set for San Diego. The tour was ultimately canceled due to the death of the band's drummer, John Bonham, but the anticipation of the show coming to our town colored most of the school year.

By the end of the second semester, I'd sought out the students I knew I'd want to write about. Some of the characters would be composites, I explained, but the overall story would be true to the year gone by. As I was sitting in the bedroom of a pal from the school newspaper, an announcement came over the radio that the legendary actor John Wayne had died. He shrugged. He didn't know or care who John Wayne was.

Two days after graduation, I drove past the high school that had been so filled with color and characters the past two semesters. It was a ghost town, as lonely as a swimming pool in winter. The school's army-green dumpsters were filled with the emptied contents from all the lockers. I decided to have a look. Inside those dumpsters were the discarded souvenirs of the entire year. Here was all the angst, the romance, the failures, the yearning poems, the folded notes, the disastrous test papers, the emotional artifacts of the two semesters gone by. All of it, thrown away in the delirious celebration of a brand-new feeling—*freedom*.

Back home in my room, surrounded with all my research and these dumpster treasures, I was overwhelmed by the huge emotional lives of the teenage *adults* I'd gotten to know during the year. In the weeks ahead, I would seek out more students I hadn't yet told of the project. We agreed that some of the secrets should never be told. But the overall story of that year—*go for it*.

All I wanted was to write something they could read later and maybe even grace it with the ultimate seal of approval: *That's what it felt like.*

Whatever you can do, or dream you can, begin it.
Begin it—now.

—JOHANN WOLFGANG VON GOETHE

Two months later, a year of research and writing had amounted to a tall stack of yellow legal tablet sheets in search of a guiding principle. All trees and no forest. I sat in the living room and read the chapters aloud to my mom and dad. It was my mom's idea to divide the stories into small chapters. Sitting in the living room at Friars Village, working with my mom and dad, I whittled it down to succinct chapters. It became a family endeavor.

I decided to call the book *Stairway to Heaven* in tribute to the Led Zeppelin tour that had never made it to San Diego. I sent the manuscript to New York on a Monday and didn't hear anything for two weeks. Then came the first report. A senior editor known as the "Warrior King" of publishing read it first. He lived up to his name. His withering response: "I don't know what it is. But I know what it's not—it's not *Catcher in the Rye*."

Eventually the manuscript fell into the hands of a younger editor named Susan Bolotin. She found it surprisingly funny. The book that began as an experiment in documenting the secret lives of teenagers, the life I hadn't lived myself, finally found a champion. One of the higher-ups felt my title *Stairway to Heaven* would be confused with the 1939 movie of the same name. Soon we had a new title, *Fast Times at Ridgemont High*.

When the first few hardcover copies landed on my doorstep, I packaged one up in a big manila envelope. I had acquired the address of J. D. Salinger's post office box (32) in Windsor, Vermont, where he picked up his mail. Salinger loathed those who tried to find him, but I took a shot and wrote a long letter from my heart that included a Hail Mary request for an interview. I was so happy with the letter; I was sure it would win a response. Ten days later, my package was returned unopened. On the postal sticker, in the box marked "Package Refused," was J. D. Salinger's scrawled initial: "J."

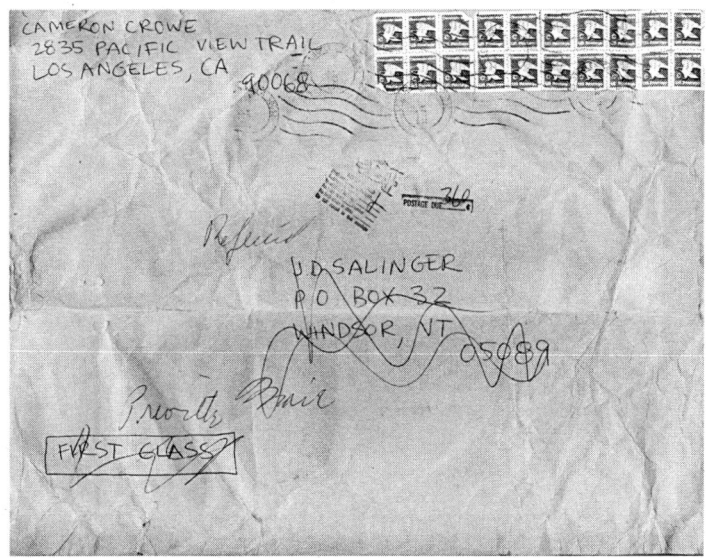

It was almost as good as a yes.

J. D. Salinger's rejection sent me on a jag of sending letters to important cultural figures. Mostly I sent a copy of their own autobiography along with a request for an inscription. Richard Nixon immediately returned my copy of his book *RN*, lavishly dedicated and signed with what I thought was "Love, Richard Nixon." (I later realized I'd read his penmanship incorrectly. It was actually "Yours, Richard Nixon.") Others who returned their books personally signed: General Alexander Haig, Jimmy Carter, Gerald Ford, Woody Allen, Seymour Hersh, and Ronald Reagan. James Brown sent back a card from prison, signed "GFOS" (Godfather of Soul). Eerily, Sammy Davis Jr.'s *Yes I Can* arrived on my doorstep with an upbeat dedication a week after his death.

Meanwhile, *Fast Times at Ridgemont High* was optioned for a movie. The producer was Art Linson, a former rock manager I'd met when he managed Nils Lofgren. Linson had a renegade spirit and a rock and roll heart, and was part of a new wave of younger filmmakers that included Hal Ashby and Jonathan Demme. Knowing I was the least expensive option, he suggested the studio hire me to write the screenplay. For months, Linson showed me the screenwriting ropes. His background in the world of rock was a huge plus. The script had a beat to it. I even had a small office on the studio lot, where the front-gate guards would examine my credentials with suspicion.

Finding a director for the film was not easy. The studio first suggested a young director who'd made a horror film, an art house favorite. David Lynch was his name; the movie was *Eraserhead*. I was excited but curious about the studio's choice. What was it about his macabre masterpiece that said *high school*? I'd met Lynch before. He was the brother-in-law of the actress Sissy Spacek, whom I'd profiled for *Rolling Stone*. This time I met Lynch at Bob's coffee shop in the Valley and gave him the script in a crisp manila envelope. A few days later, he drove over to my office in a white VW bug. We had a friendly meeting on the sidewalk.

"I like it," he said, returning my script in the same manila envelope. I wasn't positive he'd even opened it. "I'm not sure it's . . . my . . . I don't know . . . my . . . I don't know what you'd call it, but . . . uh . . ."

"Your thing?" I offered.

"Yeah," he said, savoring the phrase like he'd never heard it before. "My *thing*."

It was Art Linson who found Amy Heckerling, the up-and-coming director who'd written and shot a prizewinning short film called *Getting It Over With*. It was a wonderful story about budding sexuality told from a woman's point of view, and it addressed many of the same emotional issues as *Fast Times*. Linson sneaked the movie through the system. Even

the front-gate guards were barely aware we were filming our mischievous little film about kids from a kid's point of view. The big movie filming next door, the one everybody was talking about, was Burt Reynolds
and Dolly Parton's *The Best Little Whorehouse in Texas*, directed by the
writer of *Harold and Maude*, Colin Higgins.

Linson and Heckerling included me in the casting and the filming
of the movie. I was there every day, and Amy was very protective of my
script. She loved the idea of the movie, a story about kids with almost no
adults in it at all. Just like in my book, most of the action was set around
the local mall. Because there were then few movies for teenage stars, we
had our pick of all those who were of age—from Matthew Broderick
to Scott Baio. Amy was very impressed by Nicolas Coppola, the quietly
charismatic and extremely shy nephew of Francis Ford Coppola. In the
end, he landed a small part as a fast-food cook. (He later changed his
professional name to Nicolas Cage, and now as an Oscar-winning actor
plays more significant parts.) The two young leads played by Jennifer
Jason Leigh and Phoebe Cates became the center of *Fast Times*. I was
worried that my favorite character, the surfer-stoner Jeff Spicoli, would
be played by someone who didn't get the joke. The Spicoli *type* had
become omnipresent around Southern California but nobody had put
him in a movie. I was obsessed with getting it right.

Don Phillips, the casting director, was an excitable character who put his
whole heart into finding new faces. He was interested in a kid who'd come
in to meet him named Sean Penn. Penn's father was a successful director,
and Sean had known many a surfer from the beaches near his home in
Malibu. When Sean was called in for a second meeting, Amy and Art and
I were all set to be in the room. I was slightly late and racing to the meeting
when I was almost hit in the parking lot by a short-haired kid in a Camaro.

Minutes later, the driver of the Camaro entered the room. Sean Penn
had only been cast in one movie but had the confidence of someone
who'd already been in ten. He sat down and spoke about the character
like a young scientist.

"I know this guy," he said.

We asked him to show us his take on Spicoli as part of an audition. He politely refused, but his level of confidence was rock-solid. It was as if he were holding uranium and couldn't remove it until absolutely necessary.

Miraculously, we gave him the part. For the entire shoot of the movie, he asked to be called only by his character name. It was a bold Method acting choice for an actor with so little experience. (Sean's nickname was "Sean De Niro," named for the Big Dog himself.) He had a crush on an actress playing a cheerleader, Pam Springsteen, sister of Bruce, but was too shy to approach her as himself. After a day of shooting, we'd often go have a pizza at Little Tony's, near the studio. I kept asking him to try out the line that I felt was key to the whole movie—the moment his character called his nemesis, the history teacher Mr. Hand, a dick.

Nothing I could say or do would cause him to try it out for me.

Finally, the day arrived, and my friend Kelly Curtis and then-girlfriend Nancy Wilson were crouched behind the camera with Amy. The first shot was an angle on Ray Walston, who played Mr. Hand. Walston was a beloved film and TV icon best known as the star of *My Favorite Martian*. Walston had a wonderful calming spirit. On breaks, you'd often see him riding around the studio lot on his bicycle, offering a beatific smile for all who recognized him. I was worried that Penn might wilt in his scene. Dueling with a wily pro like Walston wouldn't be easy. When the time came for Sean's off-camera reading of the "You dick" line, he surprised us all, especially Ray Walston.

"Hey, bud," asked Sean, off camera. "What's your problem?"

"No problem at all," said Walston sharply. "I think you know where the front office is."

"You red-faced . . . old . . . *motherfucker*," Sean said from behind the camera.

Walston's eyes narrowed. His rosy face indeed grew red. Everyone in the room froze. Ray Walston, TV legend, stood with teeth gritted for a beat and then exited the frame.

"Cut," said Amy. "Print it."

Walston immediately took Amy aside and for a full minute all we could hear were snatches of words like "lack of respect . . . what in God's name . . . how dare he." Everybody's favorite Martian was fucking *pissed*. I watched Sean. He was expressionless, still in character. Such was Sean Penn's knowledge of the craft. The take was a keeper, beyond perfect. Finally, Walston returned to the scene. I could see his nostrils flaring from twenty feet away.

It was time to shoot the other side of the scene. Spicoli's side. Now all we needed was the line I had been waiting months to hear. The scene began. Walston looked at the young upstart actor with a fiery expression. He performed the scene off camera with relish. In Major League Baseball terms, Walston was throwing fastballs at the young actor's head.

"Sorry I'm late," said Spicoli, now on camera, offering his class attendance card. "It's just this new schedule is totally confusing."

"Mr. Spicoli."

"That's the name they gave me."

Walston ripped up the card and let the shreds fall on Penn.

"Hey, bud," said Penn, "what's your problem?"

Walston advanced defiantly, now two inches from Penn's face. "No problem at all."

"You . . . *dick*."

It was a five-course meal of a delivery. Everybody behind the camera could barely hold back the guffaws. Amy let the camera roll and finally ended the take.

"Cut."

The room exploded in laughter. I'd never heard anybody in a movie call a teacher a dick before, especially not like that. Somewhere in that camera was a small miracle. As for the rest of the movie, who knew? It all felt like something we were all doing while the adults were out of town or not paying attention.

Anyone who doesn't believe in miracles isn't a realist.

—DAVID BEN-GURION

S omeone wrote a memo to the head of the studio. "This movie is pornography." To top off their lack of appreciation for our movie about teenagers where parents were only spoken about and rarely seen, the studio's research had told them that a movie about high school kids would not do well.

"Kids don't watch movies about themselves," they told us. "If you want the movie to be a hit, you need nostalgic adults. You need a story set in the past, like *American Graffiti*."

At the last minute, the studio cut the number of theaters set to play the film by three-quarters. There was one last test screening set to take place in conservative Orange County. We met at the home of one of the studio executives. The producer, the director, and a few other execs sat on the porch and sipped drinks as the sun went down. Our post-production executive was Verna Fields, the esteemed editor who'd shaped *Jaws* for Steven Spielberg. The success of *Jaws* had been so great and Fields's editorial hand so assured with the young maestro Spielberg that she was already a legend. Everybody hung on every word of her prognosis for *Fast Times at Ridgemont High*. Soon it was time to leave for the screening.

"Well," said Fields. She sounded like a weary card dealer clearing the table of a bad hand. "Let's go to the funeral."

It was a punishing screening. All our plans to gather on the September night of the movie's release, so we could proudly travel together to theaters, evaporated with the bad response an audience of adults gave us that night. As the release day approached, with no one to visit local theaters with me, I made plans to drive to Arizona with my good friend, the journalist-screenwriter Judd Klinger for our fellow rock writer Mikal Gilmore's wedding.

It was mid-August and the temperature was cresting around 112 when we decided to pull over at a mall in Tempe, Arizona. *Fast Times at Ridgemont High* was playing at a multiplex, and we decided to check out the damage. The lobby was empty, so we poked our heads into one of the theaters.

It was packed.

Suddenly the movie that played like a funeral to an older audience was embraced by kids themselves. By the end of the first weekend, audiences were already watching it multiple times, cheering, and wearing checkerboard Vans like Spicoli.

It was a miracle. The studio didn't kick me out of my office. I heard that the head of Universal, Sid Sheinberg, had even addressed the executives on the Monday after opening weekend. "We fucked up on *Fast Times*," he said. There was a silent moment at the meeting. No one wanted to take the blame. He announced that the lesson of *Fast Times* was that they'd uncovered a new movie audience. Now he wanted *more* movies about young people. The *next* time they'd be prepared.

The big winner might have been Vans, the company that made the checkerboard shoes that Penn showed up with for the character. They couldn't make them fast enough. The shoes saved the company, built it into a footwear empire. Today their Checkerboard Fund helps finance nonprofit organizations that promote inclusion. All because Sean showed up with them the first day, asking everybody to call him Spicoli, and never took them off. On the last day of filming, he walked onto the set in a brown corduroy jacket and, in a soft voice, said, "I'm Sean Penn." And he gave Amy, Art, and me each a lacquered checkerboard Vans shoe. He also promptly asked Pam Springsteen out on a date.

John Hughes would soon arrive with scripts for an assembly line of teen movies. He was given the office above mine. We saw each other in the hallways and nodded. Actors like Molly Ringwald and others would pop into my office and ask where Hughes's office was. He was often surrounded by a young fleet of hopefuls as they swept in and out of the building. We came from different career paths. He'd come from the world of *National Lampoon*, home of ruthless and highly educated comic writers like Doug Kenney and P. J. O'Rourke. I came from Lester Bangs and *Rolling Stone*. Were we competitors? Were we supposed to be friends? I was never sure.

I liked working on Saturday, my favorite day of the week. The studio was empty, and I felt free and unwatched. One Saturday night I noticed that there was someone else working upstairs. John Hughes's car was in the parking lot. We were the only two still working in the empty office. It was about ten at night when I decided to visit him upstairs. I wandered to his doorway, where he sat at a humming row of databanks and a green semi-oval screen. His office looked like a police station monitoring city crime. He heard me at the door and turned to look.

"Hey," I said.

"Hey," he said, his eyes wide behind his oval glasses.

"I hear you have a computer," I said.

"It's actually a word processor," he said. "I'll show it to you."

He carefully pointed out the ins and outs of the exotic new computer. I felt like my father inspecting the first telephone answering machine. It was a glimpse of the future. What would writing be like when it was performed on machines like this?!

"I write all my scripts on this," Hughes said. "It's called an IBM Displaywriter. This is an early model. You can save your scripts on one of *these*." He showed me a four-inch-square floppy disc, and flicked it with his finger so it made a funny wobbly sound. "One of these can hold all ten scripts you're working on."

Ten scripts? I knew he was prolific, but . . . *Woah*.

We talked about music. He talked about Chicago. I talked about San Diego. We talked about P. J. O'Rourke. And for the next half hour, we abandoned the natural suspicion that writers have about each other. It was the last time we spoke. After that, there was a slight smile on each of our faces as we passed in the halls. We were from different cliques but had secretly crossed the Rubicon. It felt just like high school.

It also struck me, even sitting there in his office: Here we were, two guys writing our stories about inclusion and popularity and cliques. Two guys with robust opinions and a supposed knowledge about culture, and what was happening and what wasn't, both with no other place to go on a warm Saturday night. A secret meeting of the Uncool.

"Good luck," I said.

"You too," said Hughes.

Out of the ashes of a sputtering career as a music journalist came this new path as a screenwriter. If I could document life the way I documented musicians, maybe I had a chance. James L. Brooks. Billy Wilder. Hal Ashby. Mike Nichols. These writer-directors were my new heroes. It was the next frontier.

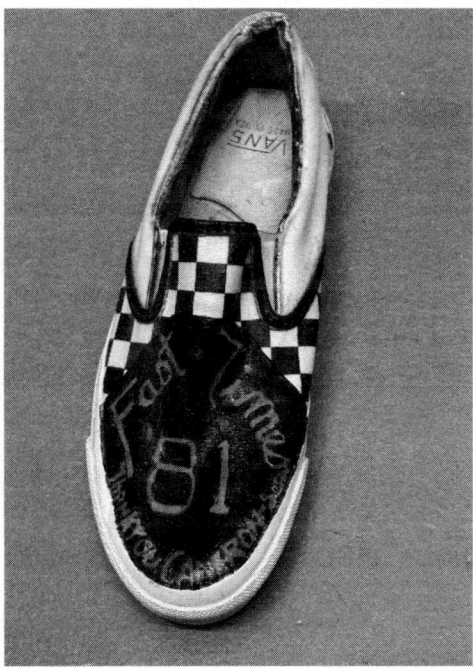

Hey bud, here's a shoe, *Fast Times*, 1981.

Only paranoids survive!

—ALICE CROWE

The director Martin Scorsese has said that he doesn't get nervous much anymore. He's met enough stars in his long and bountiful career as a modern film maestro. But occasionally, he's said, if he's around someone he revered as a teenager, meeting them as an adult could make him feel queasy . . . self-conscious . . . inadequate. In other words, *teenage*. Why? Because they existed in a time when our lives were largely made up of waking dreams. The people we encounter before eighteen, says Scorsese, will always remind us of those hugely emotional days, when everything seemed possible or nothing seemed probable. Some of those faces belong in the past, or in an old yearbook, or in our memories as part of the awkward latticework that made us who we are. And some we meet again.

As I drove to Del Mar, California, with Neal on a muggy June day in 2015, all those feelings were swirling in the air. It had been forty-two years since our *Rolling Stone* adventure with the Allman Brothers Band, and now we were heading to the fairgrounds where Gregg Allman was playing an afternoon set with his touring band. It wasn't far from San Diego, where that early tour had begun, and we were busy recapping those days as Neal pulled into the half-filled parking lot.

It was a lengthy walk through the shooting gallery, the Ferris wheel, the dunking machine, and the many stands featuring exotic food combinations, like bananas and butterscotch fudge, fried of course. The whole place smelled like burnt oil and caramel, and I can't say it didn't smell great. We would have stopped if we weren't a touch late. The performance area was at the end, an unglamorous general-seating area with rows of bleachers better suited to a drag race.

We were looking for Chank Middleton, Gregg's tour manager, and we found him in the small courtyard near the artist trailers. He slapped us with passes, just like the old days, and said Gregg would be ready to meet us in a few minutes. Standing in the afternoon heat, waiting for Gregg, we were clearly on a mission to see what remained from our roller-coaster time with the Brothers a mere four decades earlier. Like a historian of the heart, I was thirsty for details: the feel of his handshake, the look in his eyes. Chank signaled to Neal and me—*Come on in.*

Gregg Allman was in a small trailer near the stage, and when we hiked up the steps and walked inside, he was standing with two guests. His posture was different, of course. In subsequent years, Gregg Allman had grown into a different body. He carried himself less like that sleek rock god of the early '70s. These days he looked more like a biker on a pit stop, or the owner of a downtown bar where somebody got hurt every night. At sixty-seven, Gregg Allman had little vulnerability on display. He smiled to see us. His grip was firm. He no longer seemed ghostly or light as a feather. He looked smaller, a touch burdened by the past, or possibly it was the many layers of necklaces around his neck. It had been forty-three years since we'd shaken hands.

"Good to see you," he said. His voice was lower now, a box full of rocks. He was wearing Ray-Ban shades and I couldn't see his eyes.

Neal had brought a green photo box filled with prints he wanted to give Gregg. He'd also brought a Sharpie so that Gregg could sign a couple photos for us. We made some small talk and Gregg took off his sunglasses to examine Neal's prints. I took a good look at his eyes and thought of something I'd once heard about Frank Sinatra. A drummer had joined Sinatra's road band and had been playing onstage with him for a couple weeks. The drummer knew Sinatra's set of hand signals, visible from behind. Though they'd still never officially met, he and

Sinatra had learned their own musician's shorthand. One night the drummer finally asked his road manager if he could be introduced to Sinatra. The road manager declined his request.

"Frank," he said, "has met enough people."

I wouldn't say that Gregg Allman had met enough people, but he didn't seem like he was looking for a bunch of new friends. Allman moved to a lamp to see the sumptuous prints in better light. The first photos were of live shows from 1973. One was the moment in Arizona by the pool when I asked Gregg for our first interview. He was standing in cutoffs, considering whether to take the time to answer my questions. As I looked at the photo now in his weathered and tattooed hands, it occurred to me that the entire goal of *Almost Famous* had always been simple—to capture that moment of promise. To write about the music I love, and maybe even free Allman to discuss the happy/sad story behind the great creative victories of the Allman Brothers Band.

He silently flipped to the next photo. Gregg paused briefly on a gorgeous shot of himself with Dickey Betts and moved on. The next was a photo of Gregg and his brother, Duane, onstage at the Fillmore East. There were three more prints in the box, but Gregg stopped flipping through the photos on that shot, the one with his brother.

"I . . . I can't," he said softly. He closed the Pandora's box of memories.

Chank Middleton, Gregg's longtime road manager, instantly knew it was time to pull the plug. "All right, let's clear out," he announced.

"We'll see you after," said Neal. Allman looked at both of us, and we could see the stage beckoning in his demeanor. Gregg stood up straighter, puffed his chest out a little. The rock star in him was taking up residence. Not much had changed in four decades, except everything. It was showtime.

We found a spot in the wings and watched as Gregg walked slowly up a ramp to the stage, out of sight from the crowd. The band took their places—they looked psyched to be there—and when I looked back to watch Gregg take the stage . . . his posture had straightened, his shoulders were thrown back, and he walked to the Hammond B-3 organ and took a seat. They began playing "Statesboro Blues." Then or now, there is nothing like Gregg Allman playing "Statesboro Blues." The crowd shook to life and the fairgrounds filled with the sound of his voice. The elixir was potent, burnished with time but elemental in its power.

He was no longer the golden-haired little brother with the big bluesy voice. He was a man who'd had seven wives, a fleet of children, enough heartache to fill several lives. He'd earned the voice he'd always had, and I doubt it had ever sounded more authentic than it did that day in June.

The show finished with "Whipping Post," the Allman Brothers Band's early career standard, and when it was over, Allman rose and walked gallantly offstage, waving to the crowd. As soon as he was out of the eyeshot of the crowd, his rigid posture sagged. Neal and I watched as he moved very slowly down the ramp toward the dressing room. I snatched a set list from one of the amplifiers. We traveled back to say goodbye to Gregg.

He was already packed up and ready to go. Saying goodbye to some friends, he turned to us, and I couldn't stop staring at his hands. I had never seen so many miles on a pair of hands. I could have studied them for hours. He knew the show was good; he seemed spent but happy. We looked at each other. It was time for one of us to make some kind of reference to our long-ago adventure.

"Thank you for *Almost Famous*," I said.

"You're welcome," he said.

We posed for some photos. I put my arm around him. He shook it off. Instantly. It felt like a matter of pride, but I couldn't quite figure it out. He readjusted things quickly so that his elbows were on both Neal's and my shoulders. Looking back, I suppose it was a matter of his not wanting to appear frail or beholden. Or maybe Gregg Allman just wasn't built for social media bro-posing. But for that one moment, we both knew. He was reminding us he was no charity case. This was the road, baby. He'd known many an adventure like ours. *Brothers.*

Walking back to the car, I couldn't stop thinking about his hands. I asked Neal: Did you see *the hands*? Neal handed me his camera and showed me the last photo he'd taken. The hands. It's one of his best photos. Less than two summers later, Allman died of liver cancer. I treasure the day we got to say goodbye. And I'll always remember those hands, the same ones that had signed the contract for my tapes, the same ones that had strummed that guitar in the hotel room and played "These Days."

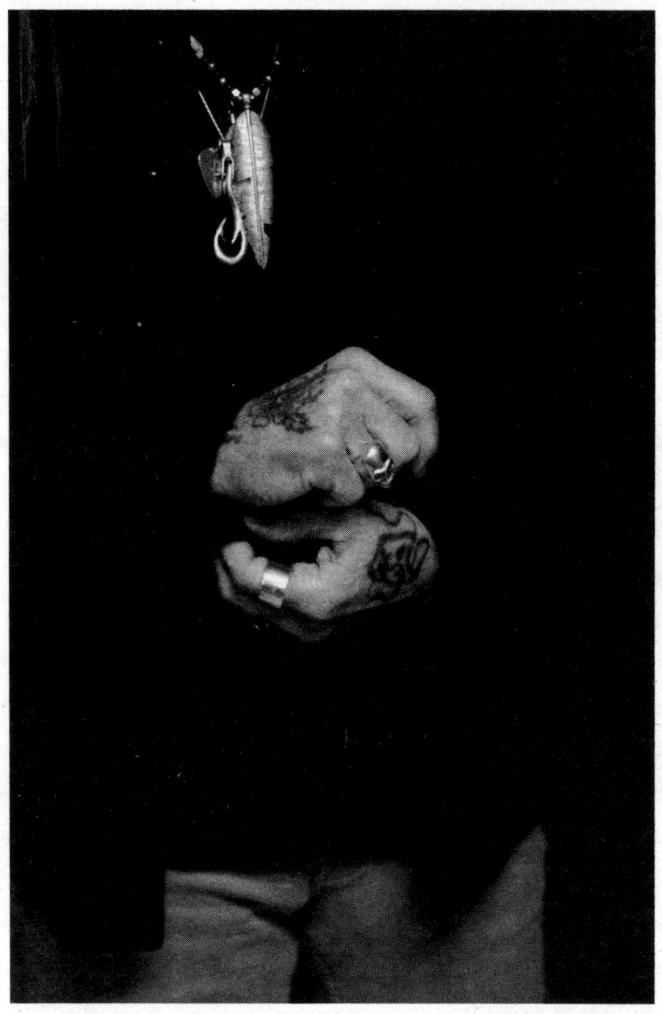

Count your blessings. Leave the funeral!

—ALICE CROWE

The end of *Rolling Stone*, as we knew it, came in early May 2019. Sitting in Jann Wenner's office, looking out on New York, was a quietly emotional hang. It was a coincidence that I was already there, rehearsing *Almost Famous: The Musical*, when the word came that this was the last day the magazine would be in the New York building where their modern reputation had been built. The magazine had been sold to new owners, but Jann remained as a consultant. Jann was quiet and gentle, happy to be alive, I think. We were joined by his son Gus, who'd taken over the magazine with real verve. He looked like his father did on the day we'd first met, when I was a nervous teenager, thinking about what Lester Bangs had told me about the magazine. He'd never really gotten over being fired by *Rolling Stone*. Now, many decades later, Jann was combing through his past and working on his own memoir. He pointed over to a humming laptop in a small room adjacent to his office where he'd been writing in chronological order. He was up to 1971.

"Lester Bangs was good, wasn't he?" Jann mused. "A step above the others, wasn't he?"

Somewhere in another dimension, I could hear Lester's generous laugh, full of joyful derision. *Then why did you fire me over a Canned Heat review?* he was chortling.

"Yeah, he was," I said. "Better than all the others."

"Why?"

"He led with his heart."

Jann nodded. We talked for a while longer, and I headed back to the *Almost Famous* play rehearsals on Forty-Second Street. I couldn't wait to share the story with Rob Colletti, who played the part of Lester Bangs with his whole heart. We laughed at the irony and went back to work on the musical. We were soon to open *Almost Famous: The Musical* in San Diego, my old hometown, but also auditioning for a later run on Broadway. There was a rehearsal later that day, with several potential investors attending.

A pink-faced man in a blue suit sat in the front row. He was from one of the big theaters on Broadway. After the plaintive opening song, "My Name Is William," I saw him shift his large frame to be more comfortable. After three more songs, his head bobbed and fell on his shoulder. All I could see was a fleet of exuberant actors and the back of his slumped head several feet in front of them. Later I asked the actors if it had been hard to perform with a sleeping man snoring in the front row.

"Oh, that happens a lot," Anika Larsen explained cheerfully. She was playing Elaine, the character based on my mom.

"Yeah, that's nothing," said Chad Burris, who played the uber Led Zeppelin fan Vic Nunez. "They have a couple drinks at lunch, it happens. You just concentrate on the ones who are awake."

"You'll see what happens when we open," Anika predicted. "Something happens when a real audience is sitting there. It's an X factor you can never predict. You'll see things that never happened in rehearsals." She paused to tell me a secret. "It's all we wait for."

They were connoisseurs of emotion. Theater actors are different from movie and TV actors in an important way. Sometimes in directing for film, the actors will want to give less. That big glowing camera can be intimidating. Some leading men don't even want to say, "I love you." *I'll show it to you in my eyes.* The actors in our musical were always anxious to find ways to give more. They wanted that live audience, and every rehearsal, every director's note, was just a matter of biding their time, waiting for the X factor. The live audience.

Act as if.

—ALICE CROWE

"Getting old sucks," my mom said. "Make an old lady happy and tell me you'll have three seats at the back for me at every performance."

It was eleven. Rachel Maddow was over. My mom the cheerleader was open for business. We were getting ever closer to opening night.

"You have three seats at the back for every performance," I said.

"How was it tonight?"

I showered her with a few minutes of basic anxiety, nothing she hadn't heard from me many times before. "It's just very, very difficult."

"And you *love it*," she'd say. "You wouldn't have it any other way."

"I just want it to be good."

"It will be."

I groaned.

"You were such a happy kid," she said. "What happened to you?"

Mrs. Kellerman, the fortune teller from Yucaipa, had been right about her long-ago prediction. My mom's third act had been joyful. She was an active grandmother to my sons, Billy and Curtis. Her love affair with her husband Gary Johnson had been a good one until recently. I wish he liked me more. I can't really say I blame him. The house was filled with souvenirs from my career. Posters from my movies were on the walls. He must have found it suffocating. Often I caught him staring at me, like a lumberjack considering where to make the first cut with his chainsaw.

Once, when the three of us were out to dinner back home and my mom started to ask about the musical, Gary took out a book and wordlessly began to read. He had a tricky personality, with a river of rage that sometimes came out on the freeway when another car darted in front of him, or when I asked him how he was doing. His answer was always the same.

"Not bad for an old guy."

The musical was my mom's dream come true, a dream she'd harbored since she was a young girl passing through New York City and happened upon Marlon Brando on Broadway, when he was performing in *A Streetcar Named Desire*. Or listening to Mike Nichols and Elaine May's comedy albums. She was always thirsty for stories about the musical, Gary's boredom notwithstanding. He knew the stories made her happy.

"Relinquish your fears," she chirped now. "Thoughts are actions."

The movie of *Almost Famous* was similarly difficult to get just right. I was discouraged when I first showed a cut to my mom, all four hours. Her response was, "There's a masterpiece in there." She'd always been my best editor, and along with Joe Hutshing and Saar Klein and Mark Livolsi, we found a version that clicked and told our simple story. The movie didn't do well in the theaters, but it had developed a following over the years. And now, here we were, testing the gods again.

She didn't like to talk about the problems, just the solutions. My mom's brain was strong, usually sparkling, but sometimes her body would rebel. She would need to be taken to the Kaiser hospital, where she had many fans, and once I saw her medical file. It was more than a stack of paper; it was the mother of all medical reports. With all the multicolored sheets of paper and forms, it looked like a small maypole. Being married to her was a commitment and I think Gary was worn out. My mom was worried about his health. Kellerman had told her years earlier that she would outlive two husbands, and she fussed over Gary, who was twenty-two years her junior, like a lovesick teenager. Now he was gone. When I went fishing for details, the answer was always the same.

"I don't talk to the two of you about each other."

We spoke carefully about my sister Cindy. My sister and my mother had stopped communicating regularly. "Love me as I am," my mom had said, with chin upraised, "or don't love me at all." In 1989, my father passed away unexpectedly while visiting friends and family back home in Kentucky. A heart attack claimed him while he was staying with his brother in Lexington. He was only sixty-five. There was so much more time we were all meant to spend together.

Say Anything . . . had just come out, and Siskel and Ebert rescued it from obscurity with a pair of rave reviews. I was grateful my dad lived long enough to see me become a director. Still, his death upset the fragile chemistry of the family. The job of taking care of my mom only grew more difficult, and soon it became a wedge in my own relationship with my sister. Cindy was a wonderful mother to three girls, Kaitlyn and the twins, Kristin and Kimberly. She and her husband, Kris, had built a strong and beautiful family. All three girls were enormous fans of musical theater too. And so it was that I returned to our old neighborhood with a musical about our old neighborhood.

*Doubts are traitors and make us lose the good
we oft might win by fearing to attempt.*

—WILLIAM SHAKESPEARE

Almost Famous, the movie, was a surprise success. It was a love letter to family and music. A script I put in my drawer, too personal to ever be made. But when my prior film, *Jerry Maguire*, found success, I pulled *Almost Famous* out of the drawer. If there was ever going to be enough goodwill to get my script made, now would be the time. I was supremely fortunate that Steven Spielberg, then head of Dreamworks Pictures, agreed. He read the script and responded simply, "Shoot every word."

A curious thing happened while making the movie. My personal story of searching for soulmates, and ultimately being sent back home to my real family, had attracted a cast of actors who were seeking the same thing. Life imitates art that imitates life that becomes truth. We bid each other a tearful goodbye on the last day of shooting.

The movie was a failure at the box office but gained fans through home video. By the next January, my sister and mother and I were all sitting together at the Academy Awards, where the movie had been nominated for four Oscars. We were all rooting for Kate Hudson, as Penny Lane, who was tipped to win the award for Best Supporting Actress. I was nominated for Best Original Screenplay, my favorite category, but had no chance. Another movie had won the screenplay award at every single ceremony leading up to the Oscars. Let's be honest. The true miracle had already happened. The movie had brought my mother and sister together, if only briefly.

I was in shock when I won the Oscar for Best Screenplay. Public speaking terrifies me. Tom Hanks must have seen the look on my face. He spoke to me with the calmness of St. Peter at the gates of heaven as I approached the podium. "Very happy you won this," he said in a voice you might be able to imagine. "Just turn around, say a few things, and I'll be right here when you turn back around."

I wished my dad were there too. And, of course, Cathy. They were both in every frame of the movie. I'd even ended *Almost Famous* with a Beach Boys song. I hope, somewhere, Cathy smiled.

There were no empty chairs at the Oscars after-party as we sat together, what was left of our family. The Oscar sat on the table before us. Finally, my mom spoke, with absolutely no sense of irony.

"It's not too late," she said, "to go to law school."

When my friend Lia Vollack, who'd become a formidable theater producer, later suggested *Almost Famous* as a possible musical, I was beyond superstitious. Why tempt fate after our much-appreciated fan-built success? Lia was effusive about the theater community. I felt her enthusiasm and began to meet people interested in helping introduce me to the world of adapting my own autobiographical film for the stage.

Which brings us back to that warm San Diego night in early September, the smell of gardenias in the air, and my voice echoing through the courtyard, battling back the aphorisms of Alice Crowe. In less than a week, the first paying audience would fill the theater to see *Almost Famous: The Musical*.

You cannot afford the luxury of a negative thought.

—PETER MCWILLIAMS

September 2019. A shadow had fallen across Alice Crowe's plans to be present for every performance of *Almost Famous: The Musical.* My mother had rebroken her hip. She wanted to be sparkling for her arrival at the Old Globe, the theater she'd loved and attended so much when we first lived across the street from the park. Now, more than the pain of her injury, it was the visual that haunted her. I was trying to convince her that it was okay to attend the play in a wheelchair.

Sitting in her bedroom, I implored her to keep the hospital appointment with her doctor early the next morning. Many months ago I'd planned to take the musical's production designer, Derek McLane, an accomplished sportsman, on a sportfishing day trip in San Diego. Jeremy Herrin, the director, was also going to join us. The fishing trip now conflicted with the doctor's appointment.

"Don't cancel the trip," she said. "I won't miss the doctor's appointment. Ruthie (my mom's caretaker) and her son can drive me." She paused and added soberly, "I'm not going to die. I'm worried about Gary. Remember what Kellerman said, 'You'll outlive two husbands.'"

I wondered why she was worried more about the odd, angry man who'd callously left her two months earlier, the man she still loved. It was off-limits for conversation, a closed door, not unlike Cathy's death. The Monday appointment information was carefully written in thick

Sharpie script, taped to the wall next to her new hospital-style bed. She looked content but tired. She wore her favorite soft-pink cotton house gown festooned with tiny flowers. She was surrounded by her pills and aphorisms, with a red phone at her side.

"Did you read the card from the actress playing you in the musical?"

"No," she said. Though it was open and positioned on the table next to her, I wasn't surprised that she'd never read it. She probably thought it was a sympathy card, and therefore kryptonite. She didn't carry herself as a weakling. She didn't want sympathy.

"Let me read it to you."

She steeled herself as I read Anika's sweet and soulful card. "'We haven't met yet,'" I began, "'but I'm the actress who's playing your alter ego in *Almost Famous: The Musical*. I heard about your fall, and I wanted to send some love and good thoughts your way. I and everyone at the Old Globe Theatre are cheering on your recovery. We can't wait for you to see the show! And I can't wait to meet you! It is a thrill and an honor to play such an extraordinary woman . . .'"

She smiled. "All right, you can go."

"Do you want to meet Anika?"

"Not like this," she said. She needed to go the bathroom, I sensed. She didn't want me to see that everything was growing more complicated. "Go and don't eat too late. Those boys need you healthy." She paused. "Don't worry. I'm not going to die. I'll never leave you."

"Mom," I said, "when the play is over, we'll figure it out. Meanwhile, you have your three seats for every performance."

"You're *sure*?" she said. "I want *three* seats at the back of the theater so I can get in and out easily."

"Three seats at the back of the theater."

Now she switched topics. "I wanted to live with you. You didn't want me."

"We'll figure it out," I said.

"I've outlived everybody's desire to be around me," she said softly. Without self-pity. Just a student of human behavior.

"That's not true," I said. "Cheer up. The play will be going for two months. You'll be there for however much of it you want. If you want, go for the last few weeks. You'll be there for the homestretch." I added the woeful truth. "Trust me—*I need you there*."

Then I switched gears.

"I will not let you go to a nursing home," I said. She seemed worried about any avenue that would lead to her being stuck in a home with "a lot of old ladies waiting to die." She saw conspiracy around every corner. I wasn't sure of the long-term solution. I wanted her to hear it and remember. "I will not let you go to a nursing home."

"You go fishing," she said, "you need it."

"Okay."

"All right," she said.

"I love you very much."

She squeezed my hand. We were two wounded warriors for optimism. "Take care of the boys. They need you." She added a kicker, one of her favorites. "Call me anytime," she said. She loved quoting Philip Seymour Hoffman as Lester in *Almost Famous*. "I stay up late."

I wasn't thrilled about going fishing. I wasn't happy about the ragtag way my mom was conducting her life with Ruthie, who was feeling increasingly ill-equipped as Mom's body failed her. Strong painkillers, bottles with horse-sized pills, were lined up on a brown table beside her bed. Besides a light dose of Ativan, she didn't take any of them. She was frail. I was very happy she was going to see the doctor first thing on Monday morning.

The sky was still black when I arrived at the Seaforth Sportfishing dock. Jeremy and Derek soon followed, and we talked in the early morning darkness about our high hopes for the play. We picked up some Dramamine too, just in case. Soon we were steaming out for the two hours it would take to get us close to Mexican fishing waters. Before long, Jeremy began to turn green. The waters were choppy and though Derek and I were okay, Jeremy spent much of the day puking. I felt for him, hanging on to the boat's railing for hours, trying to look at the horizon, helplessly chewing on Dramamine pills. Nobody caught much save for Derek. The captain stayed out longer than the three o'clock return time, still looking for fish. It was almost five as we pulled back into the dock. My cell phone, out of service on the high seas most of the day, pulsed with a call.

The screen read: RUTHIE.

This was never a great sign. Ruthie was not one of those people who liked to make good-news calls. The Ruthie calls always began with a careful account of how she and Mom were able to surmount the latest obstacles involving health, finances, national politics, or hair color. Ruthie was, after all, an expert in nails and hair. Her love and fandom of my mom made up for whatever chops she might have lacked in hands-on medical experience.

I answered the Ruthie call as the boat docked. But it wasn't Ruthie. It was the emotionless voice of a paramedic. Just doing his job.

"Is this Mr. Crowe?"

"Yes, it is." My heart was already pounding.

"I'm here with your mother and she's stopped breathing," he said. "She's had a cardiac arrest. Do I have your permission to administer lifesaving services to her?"

"Yes."

Ruthie took the phone and spoke in half sentences. She sounded like herself on helium, stammering and not making sense. "I was taking her, taking her, to the, to the bathroom, and she . . . and she passed out."

"What happened with the doctor this morning?"

"She didn't go."

Of course. Now I needed information. "They're taking her to a hospital?"

"Yeah, yeah," said Ruthie. "Sharp hospital."

"All right, I'm on my way."

I jumped onto the dock as the boat pulled in and found my car on wobbly ocean legs. I called information to find the address of Sharp hospital. There were four Sharp hospitals. I took a shot and drove to the one closest to her home.

"I'm looking for new admissions," I said. "I think my mother is here."

"That would be the next building."

I sprinted to the next hospital building, past the stony-faced families of the patients within. Something about a hospital at night. Anybody healthy enough to go home has gone home. All that's left for the evening is the netherworld of unknowing. Battles with hopelessness. Maybe it was just me.

"May I help you?" The woman at the front desk wore an unmistakable expression of *Whoa whoa whoa*.

"I think my mom is here. Alice Crowe."

"I don't have her name. Are you sure she's here?"

"She's at Sharp."

"There are four Sharp hospitals."

"I know. I started with this one."

She shook her head, looking at her screen. "Wait," she said. "Cardiac arrest?"

"Yes!"

"Okay, she came in as a Jane Doe. She's in ICU." Ruthie had been in shock and unable to give the proper identification to the paramedics. "Seventh floor."

A woman in a half-crescent kiosk sat perched outside the two swinging doors marked ICU. I gave her the information. The details matched. She invited me to wait in the lobby. I sat in a yellow chair and did what the others were doing, staring at the monitor playing a soundless CNN. We blankly watched the crises of others, trying not to think about our own. *Is she dying?* A kid with a swimming noodle stared blankly at me. His father was still wearing his clothes from a barbecue. Something had happened at a pool party.

"Crowe?"

"I'm here to take care of things," I said.

I heard myself sounding different. A strange nobility can take over in situations like this. Suddenly, you are the righteous hero of your own movie. You take a little bit from Gregory Peck in *To Kill a Mockingbird*, or a lot from a hundred television shows, and you combine it with the best version of yourself. I figured out a name for it. Hero Adrenaline.

"Okay, she's just coming out of some X-rays," said the receptionist. "It'll be about ten minutes. You're welcome to some coffee."

I took a cup of sad hospital coffee and joined the others in the waiting room. We looked at each other blankly, acknowledging each other's places here in limbo. The barbecue dad yawned. A woman in a flowered dress kept rearranging the hem over her legs. And the little kid with the noodle kept staring. I wondered how many were thinking what I was thinking. That this was all a mistake, that it was someone else behind those swinging ICU doors. That Jane Doe wasn't my mom.

"Cameron?" A nurse with dark hair and a green smock scanned the room. She had tattoos up and down her arms.

I rose with my Styrofoam cup and drained it before following her. "Dr. Levin is going to come talk to you." She led me not to my mom, but to a small room outside the X-ray station. I sat for a moment, looking up at another monitor, as the same nurse returned with a concerned-looking Dr. Levin. He introduced himself and the three of us sat facing each other. The tattooed nurse was holding another Styrofoam cup.

"Would you like some water?" he said.

I said I was okay. But it wasn't a question, not really. She extended the cup. They knew better, I'm sure. I took the water.

"Your mom is not doing too well," the doctor said.

I nodded.

"Do you have any brothers or sisters?"

"One sister."

"Is she nearby?"

"She's about an hour away."

"Do you want to call her?"

"We're estranged."

"Well, you might think about calling her."

"How is she?"

"She stopped breathing for about nine minutes, and we were able to bring her back, but it's hard to know about the neurological damage." I drank the water. "I've got some X-rays, and we should look at them. She's got a lot of fluid in her lungs. And she appears to have pneumonia."

"She missed her appointment at Kaiser this morning."

"Well, do you want to see her?"

I nodded. My mom was resting, on a ventilator, still wearing her flowered house gown. The paramedics had ripped it aside, making room for the work they'd done to pull her back to a faint heartbeat. It was at this moment that all my fantasies of mistaken identity vanished. *This was real.* A number of nurses were around her, looking at her with fascination and respect.

"Your mother," said one of them, "is a fighter."

I had seen her in rooms like this before, surrounded by impressed younger types, drawn to her charisma. In that moment I could see that, even in a coma, as a Jane Doe, she had pulled together a fan club who admired her tenacity. By all rights, she shouldn't have still been breathing. As we waited for the X-rays, I found myself telling the room who she was, and that there was a play about her, and our family, getting ready to debut just a few miles away. The tattooed nurse explained that she was a singer-songwriter, and she patterned herself after Joni Mitchell and Bonnie Raitt. My mom rested calmly, her chest rising and falling as if she were sleeping. It was the kind of room she would have liked, younger people talking about their future. A nature show was on the television. Thank goodness it wasn't the president. We stood together, regarding her. Even unconscious, she gathered fans out of strangers.

I drifted home for the night in a zombie state. I peeled off my soiled clothes as the adrenaline wore off. The strong smell of fish was over-whelming. Clearly I'd stunk up the ICU. I didn't know if she'd make it through the night. I loaded the washer with the fishy clothes and tried to eat the remains of a burrito. A stress headache was building. When I woke up around 5 a.m., there had been no call from the hospital. I drifted off to sleep for a bit more and then checked in. She had made it through the night and was resting comfortably.

Become the most positive and enthusiastic person you know.

—H. JACKSON BROWN JR.

I called Cindy and let her know the news. She was quick to arrive, and she brought my niece Kimberly for support. They sat quietly by my mother's bedside. From time to time, Cindy reached out to hold Alice's hand.

I'd written to our actress Anika Larsen the day before to let her know my mom had rebroken her hip. Anika asked if she could come by and meet her. I let her know that the woman she was portraying in our musical was now in the ICU. I was sorry they wouldn't be able to meet. Anika wrote back. She still wanted to meet her, even if Alice Crowe was now in a deep coma. Could she come and sing her the songs from the musical?

I typed out a message: *How about this afternoon?*

She wrote back instantly. *How about lunchtime?*

I left Kimberly and my sister and raced back to the theater to pick up Anika. She bounded into my car and we raced up the I-5. Traffic was heavy, and as the minutes ticked away, I could tell Anika was growing worried about making it back in time for the rehearsal. As we wheeled into the parking lot, I could feel a billowing dark cloud advancing on us, but waiting for us on the third floor would be a force who'd spent a lifetime in battle with the darkness. It was time for Alice to meet the woman who had been speaking her words on stages from New York to San Diego and back again.

"Are you ready to run?" I asked Anika.

"You bet," she answered.

"We're going to be in a Beatles movie now," I said. I took off running, crisscrossing through the wide hallways. We raced past wall-sized admonitions—GET YOUR FLU SHOT! Turning pain into beauty, or at least laughter, was a specialty I'd learned from my mom. Giddiness in the face of darkness. It was perhaps her greatest lesson. We tore through the hospital toward my mom's room like we were in Richard Lester's *A Hard Day's Night*.

Cindy and Kimberly were sitting there, and we rushed in and I introduced Anika to my mom. Anika, who had two little boys of her own, talked to her with a tone that sounded like mother-to-mother. She cued up the music on her phone and began singing her three songs in the show, one by one. The first was "He Knows Too Little (And I Know Too Much)," the second was "Listen to Me," and the third was her showstopper, "Rock Stars Have Kidnapped My Son." She sang them, in that small room, with all her heart. I looked at my sister's face. Cindy was juggling a lot of feelings, and I was grateful that her own daughter was there for support.

Somewhere in the distant recesses of her mind, I knew my mom heard. She'd heard the songs once before, when I shared the latest ver-

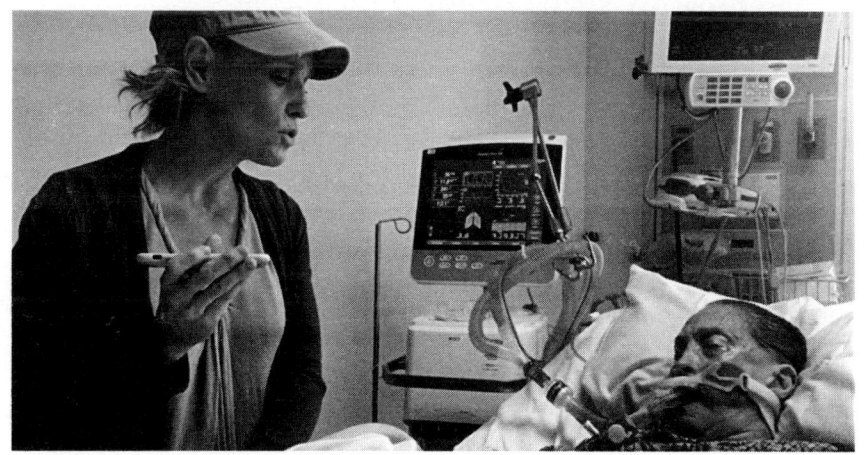

sion of the play with her. She had studied Anika very carefully at the time, with a frozen smile of delight. Now, with her mouth slightly open, resting peacefully, she heard them again.

"Well, Alice," Anika said, "it was a pleasure to meet you and sing for you."

We raced back to the car and had a wonderful conversation about Anika's own life and career. Anika had retired from theater, at least for a bit, to raise her sons. When the part of Elaine Miller came along, she made an exception and joined our workshop for the still-gestating play. Anika knocked it out of the park and never looked back. She innately understood my mom, her passion and her humor, and today they'd finally met. We were both high with Hero Adrenaline.

As we talked my phone was pinging but I ignored it, loath to disrupt that feeling in the car. Surely there were only blue skies ahead for all of us. I dropped Anika off at the theater. Pulling back onto the freeway, I listened to the phone messages. It was time to return quickly to Alice Crowe's bedside.

I arrived to find Cindy sitting ramrod straight, along with Kimberly, studying the machines surrounding Alice. None of the information was promising. It was just before midnight on September 11. Cindy reached over and held our mom's hand. "I love you," she said softly.

"She's gone," the nurse said.

Alice Crowe had left the building.

I looked at her, peaceful and still, and realized that she was now experiencing what she'd been preparing for her entire life. She'd escaped a Hawaiian tsunami, survived the loss of a daughter, battled crippling depression with laughter, thrown herself into a life of service and metaphysics, and even been given the gift of prophecy. All that she longed to know about the unknown, she had the answer now. I also knew this: somewhere, she was *pissed that she was going to miss the opening of the show*. Those three seats she'd sought would be empty.

Everything was in the folder she'd left for me marked "If I Die in San Diego." She'd already picked out her mortuary and paid the deposit.

I was soon sitting in the faux Southern mansion that housed the funeral home. We were still within a two mile radius of the theater. The morti-cian was named Clarence. He was on the young side but well practiced at the art of solemnity. Clarence explained the details of my mom's cre-mation in a soft Southern voice. He offered coffee that had been brewing since early morning. Next to it, the requisite stack of white Styrofoam cups. Where turmoil and sadness live, Styrofoam follows.

I told Clarence that there was a play in my mom's honor. It was about to open at the Old Globe, just across the street. He was from a family of funeral directors and was disappointed at how franchised it had all become. As we worked through the various papers, he was increasingly impressed to find that my mom had already signed most of the appro-priate paperwork. She had prepared it all, years earlier. *I know it will be hard for you, so I wanted to make it a little easier.* She didn't want me to experience the same lost-in-space dread that sent her spinning when my dad died suddenly, without leaving instructions.

"She sounds like a very memorable person," Clarence said. I felt that I'd punctured his professional demeanor a bit. He'd had no idea there was a movie and a play about her.

I slipped into the theater. In the darkness, nobody noticed me taking my usual seat. The actors were rehearsing. All I knew was that inside the musical, struggling to get out, was an authentic *feeling*. It was the very thing that had kept me from being the next J. D. Atkinson, that had kept me from crossing the street and entering *the finest law school in California*. It was the emotion of growing up with complex feelings and finding true meaning in a song. It was the power of happy/sad.

It was time to let go. Every opportunity to bail out of this experience had disappeared. *Something* was going to be on the stage in two days. There were fans coming from Australia, England, and New York for the first show. There would be reviews on social media. It would all be in print within days.

Showtime

I watched from the courtyard as the first ticket holders arrived. First came the subscriber crowd, some of them in their seventies. Then came curious fans of the movie. Then the smatter of cosplayers. Quite a few young women were wearing faux-fur-collared vintage coats like the one Penny Lane wore in the film. It wasn't hard to feel removed from the show now; I was powerless to control it. The courtyard filled as the audience of all ages waited for the doors to open.

I pressed the code on the side door and buzzed myself into the empty theater. The actors were climbing into stage clothes. In the lobby, a group of ushers had gathered in a circle to receive instructions from the house manager. She was telling them how to hand out programs, when to seat late arrivals, and how to describe the show to those who asked.

"It's about a young journalist who goes on tour with a rock band, and his strict mother," she told them.

"Excuse me," I interrupted. "I'm the writer of the play and I want to thank you for being here. This . . . this is the story of our family." Why was I doing this? Why did I suddenly feel like I needed to be a *host*? I started to sprout tears, and it was instantly embarrassing. "My mom passed away three days ago, and her dream was to see the play, and I know she's here with us."

There was a silence. Then light, dutiful applause from the small group of ushers. I shrunk off to hide in the courtyard. I wanted to find the emotional clown I'd become and shake some sense into him. And then I recalled my mom's own behavior after my father had died. She too had felt compelled to grieve with strangers. She'd even tried stand-up comedy for a few weeks.

Soon the first paying customers were filing through the doors. The theater programs were handed out, along with a map of all the locations in San Diego that corresponded to the show. It was a hometown production. There was a buzz in the air.

Our idea was that as soon as you entered the theater, you were in 1973. The houselights were still on when the show began with Rob Colletti, the inventive actor from Chicago. He was already in character as Lester Bangs, stalking the aisles, jousting and discussing music with the audience members. If you mentioned anything after 1973, he'd stare through you like a member of the King's Guard at Buckingham Palace.

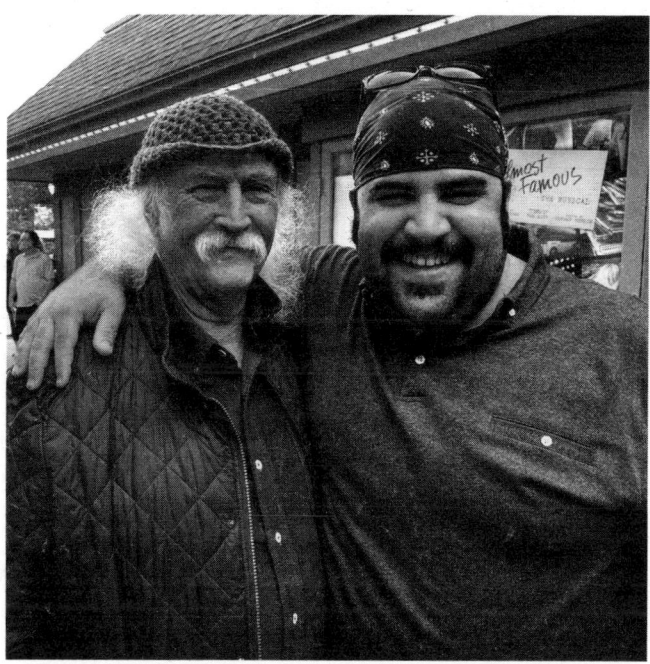

Forgiveness: David Crosby meets Rob Colletti, who plays Lester Bangs in *Almost Famous: The Musical*. Bangs gave Crosby's first solo album a bad review in *Rolling Stone*.

Soon the lights dimmed, and *Almost Famous: The Musical* began its first public performance.

The show flowed from one emotional peak to the next. Our charismatic kid at the center, Casey Likes, exploded with energy. The cast lifted the story and the songs onto their shoulders. It was that extra element that an audience brings, the one the actors had always talked about. *Just wait until there's an audience here.* Anika Larsen stole every scene she was in. By the ending stage call, set to "Fever Dog," Casey was racing across the stage and even dove into the raucous audience, like a young Eddie Vedder. Life strikes again. While I'd been off wrapping my head around my mom's surprise-twist exit, Tom Kitt created a feast of a musical banquet. The room was filled with sonic texture and feeling. And Kitt had even composed a glorious hard-rock reprise of "Fever Dog" that sent the audience home on an explosive 1973-style high. Out of sadness came the ending I'd been longing for.

I stay up late.

—ALICE CROWE/LESTER BANGS

The show was honed over the next two weeks. Every night was sold out, and the actors continued to double down. A theater full of living, breathing humans was everything they'd been waiting for. Feeding off a particular audience's personality, hearing every laugh or sigh in the room—this was an actor's joy. I soon realized that they were making every show a tribute to my mom. Her early exit was exactly what they used for emotional fuel.

I was at every performance. Each one was slightly different. It was like following around your favorite band. *They did something different at the Philadelphia show!* Afterward, I'd hang out in the courtyard and listen to the reactions. Often, I'd feel a hand on my arm and turn to see someone I'd never met but who knew me. "I'm a friend of your mother's," they might say. "She counseled me for years. How is she?"

And I'd have to tell them the story. She might have left early, but Alice Crowe was alive every night and twice on weekends. Many of the people who introduced themselves were former counselees, older now, but they often recounted her advice, word for word. Time had given them the gift of understanding what was most important in the world—to be heard. And here they were, watching her character onstage, meeting her again, and laughing. Standing in the courtyard, I learned that over time the details fade. What lasts is the way someone made you feel.

On the official opening night, Joni Mitchell traveled from Los Angeles to see the show. Her song "River" appeared at a pivotal part of the musical. I'd written about her often. She had been in a wheelchair since suffering an aneurysm several years earlier. She was wheeled in by her friend Marcy Gensic and two of her faithful helpers. She wore a sharp-looking red hat and was beaming. She was given the seats at the back, the ones I'd held for Alice Crowe. It didn't feel like a coincidence when I saw Joni Mitchell's hat peeking out from the crowd, sitting in my mom's opening-night seat. Even during the height of Alice Crowe's war on rock, she always loved Joni Mitchell. "Both Sides Now" was her favorite.

Afterward, Joni rolled onto the courtyard and declared the musical better than the movie. Jeremy was nearby, nodding and chuckling.

I laughed too. "Who am I to argue with Joni Mitchell?"

"You mustn't," said Jeremy.

A few minutes later, I felt a hand at my shoulder. There was an awkward moment. I recognized the person but couldn't place from where. He must have noticed the quizzical look on my face.

"Clarence, from the mortuary," he said.

"Clarence!"

My mom's funeral director had shed his professionally solemn demeanor. Clarence had a drink in his hand and was effusive. He introduced me to his partner, a man with extra-long earlobes, who pumped my hand. They'd bought tickets on a whim and loved the show.

Across the way, I spotted my sister looking quiet. Her three daughters were nearby, enthusiastically chatting up the actors. Kimberly, Kristin, and Kaitlyn would become the show's favorite audience members. Cindy had the look of someone who'd boarded a ship with the wary fear that it might be the *Titanic*. I knew the look because I'd seen it in my own mirror for months. I raced to her side.

The show had won her heart.

The movie, she said, always reminded her of a more difficult time. For a long time, she'd felt disconnected and abandoned by me. Many emotional waves had hit us over the years, and Cindy made a strong decision to focus on raising her own beautiful family with her husband, Kris. My mother and she hadn't spoken in years. For better and mostly worse, I'd ceased trying to be the peacemaker. The film summoned a lot of dark feelings. But now it was just us, and her three theater-loving daughters, and a cast that had spent so much energy bringing our family story to the stage. It was a chance to finally celebrate each other as brother and sister, and the music we loved. And she loved the musical.

"The music," she said, "always helped me stay sane. It was ours together and separately. But I spent a long time feeling like I'd lost my brother." She squeezed my hand. "It was very lonely."

"Maybe we found each other again," I said.

"I hope so," she said. It was a powerful moment for us both. "We lost a lot of time."

Every night I would encounter theatergoers of all ages in the courtyard. Sometimes I felt like a Jim Carrey character, a big grin on my face, pumping all their hands like a madman. Who were these people who left their homes to see this story about ours? I was determined to talk to every one of them. They were all pieces of the story, and the story was my family. It turned out that many of them were coming in the hopes of being reunited with their favorite counselor, the one who spent so much time hearing about all the romantic intrigue, the angry lows and the giddy highs. They came to see her again.

"You don't remember me," said one who approached me. She was a silver-haired woman in a professional pantsuit. At her side were a handsome husband who looked like a golf pro and two twentysomething children.

"I think I do but tell me."

She leaned close and offered a single word. *"Gloria."*

She introduced me to her husband, Dennis, and her two kids. "We heard about the play and flew in from Florida," she said. "I've been trying to get in touch with your mom!" She turned to Dennis. "We were best friends when Cameron was the guy in the play."

"Good job," said Dennis.

"Do you remember what happened the last time I saw you?" she asked.

I wasn't sure how much she remembered about painfully exploding all my deeply held parental myths, boldly revealing the two flawed people I loved so much, only to then cry and try to make out with me.

"You go first," I said.

"I was visiting his mother, and he stabbed his waterbed with a pen and the water went everywhere! We spent two hours cleaning up the mess!" I will never stop marveling at the power of people's memories and their ability to turn a gaping wound into a tall tale with a punch line. "How is your mom?" she asked. "Why isn't she here?"

"She's here almost every night," I said.

"Give her my number." She pressed a piece of paper into my hand. "Tell her Gloria said, 'She saved my life.'"

"I will do exactly that."

Soon everyone was gone and I was alone in the courtyard. A door slammed. It was the last crew member to leave. Abby, the costumer, who'd heard me yelling on the phone to my mom. *I want my old life back!* She nodded to me as she lit up a cigarette. I nodded back to her. Sometimes the best conversations are the silent ones. Her sneakers snuck away, and the night was over. Gloria was right all along, of course. Life is a trip.

Not long after, we got a rave review from the *Los Angeles Times*. The show was extended and broke all the records of the Old Globe Theatre, the very theater where Alice Crowe had force-fed me Shakespeare and said, "One day you'll brag about it." And here I am, doing exactly that.

"Ting" went a sound in her head.

——RUMER GODDEN

I'd been waiting all week for the book to arrive. Researching the early days of my family's time in Palm Springs, I'd been combing through newspaper archives from the *Desert Sun*. One article in particular caught my eye. My dad had been part of the gold rush to the desert, and his oldest daughter, Cathy, had participated in the Palm Springs Public Library's Wednesday-afternoon "Story Hour" gathering in May of 1957. ("And remember, the only admission required is 'Imagination Unlimited.'") The children were to choose their favorite books from a previous meeting. I was still stirring in the womb at our often sweltering home on Pasatiempo Drive, two months away from being born, and Cathy brought back a book she'd read. It was called *The Fairy Doll*, by Rumer Godden. "This is my favorite book of all," she declared to the reporter.

The cover was a caricature of Elizabeth, a young girl with unkempt hair and a curious expression. She was seven, a year younger than Cathy when she'd first read the book, but the character spoke in a voice she must have recognized. Eight years old was the age when my sister began to be called "different." "Different" was a different distinction then. "Otherness" was less celebrated. "Different" wasn't a club for cool kids. "Different" was different.

In *The Fairy Doll*, Elizabeth, the youngest of four sisters, was unlike the others in her family. They were skinny; she was plump. They could ride a bike; she could not. They recited math problems; she got confused.

Even her teacher, Miss Thrupp, derided her. Her mother tried to help with only fitful results. Elizabeth soon withdrew until her great-grandmother guided her to a special gift that might help her diminished confidence.

The gift was a fairy doll that had mysteriously turned up one year and that the family had come to place at the top of their Christmas tree. In the off-season it resided in a cedar chest. The fairy doll made Elizabeth feel understood, especially when it began to make a noise, a "ting" that resonated within her. The ting gave her answers that no one in the often-critical real world did. Whispering in her ear, the ting guided her through the obstacles that had caused all the criticism at home and school. Things began to change.

"What's the matter with Elizabeth?" asked her older brother, Godfrey. "She's not half such a little duffer as she once was."

The family began to trust Elizabeth with tasks they'd once thought beyond her. As her confidence grew, Elizabeth even learned to ride a bike, with the fairy doll positioned on the handlebars like a guiding force. *Ting.*

Soon others began to taunt Elizabeth again. Perhaps it was just the fairy doll who was succeeding, not Elizabeth herself.

"Try without her and you'll see," said her jealous sister, Josie.

Elizabeth set the fairy doll aside and subsequently lost her. Before long she was the butt of jokes again. Her great-grandmother returned and held Elizabeth's tear-stained face. Somewhere she heard a distant ting. It had to be her imagination. The doll was lost. The cedar chest was empty. But sure enough, she began to hear the tings anyway, and her personal confidence returned.

"Were the 'tings' me all along?" she asked her great-grandmother.

"How could they be?" asked her brother. "It was just a doll."

"A *fairy* doll," corrected her great-grandmother.

But the doll was still lost, and the following Christmas the family decorated the tree, wondering what to put on the top. Elizabeth studied the empty cedar box and the blanket where the fairy doll once rested. She'd learned to live without the help of the ting, but oh how she missed the boost it gave her, just when she needed it. It was then that she heard a noise not unlike the ting, but stronger, different, almost like the whoosh of a magical wand. Elizabeth closed her eyes and felt a great sense of herself and all she could be in the real world. She held out her hand, and when she opened it, the fairy doll had returned.

The family began to function the way it should, with the youngest daughter a cherished equal. The fairy doll lived in the cedar box again, and even though Elizabeth had a new doll, a baby doll, that she loved, whenever she passed the cedar box, she placed her left hand on it and could almost hear a distant noise, the ting that had given her guidance in the face of all who had dismissed her as *different*.

Holding the book today, on a sweltering afternoon so many summers later, I can only imagine how the character of Elizabeth spoke to the soul of my oldest sister. In May of 1957, Cathy was only ten years away from the dark July when she left us. She had to have imagined what a ting sounded like. To a girl who looked like the frazzled heroine on the book's cover, living with the prejudice of the label "different," that sweet pop music she loved must have sounded like a ting. Why else would she have worked so hard to play those songs for me, her face smiling contentedly as Brian Wilson sang "Surfer Girl" or the Tremeloes sang "Silence Is Golden"?

Music was an emotional beacon for all three of us, Cathy and Cindy and me. From the Beach Boys to Todd Rundgren to Joni Mitchell, it was the happy/sad songs we loved the most. It was already there in the records she'd ordered from Custom Classics, our musical outpost in the desert. It was surely there in the last package my dad picked up the weekend after she died. My music was her music.

It was our ting.

Follow That Dream

Nnovember 1982. I was working on a documentary about Tom Petty & the Heartbreakers with a couple friends. It was a video profile, and for the first time I was conducting interviews with the band members on camera. The camera was intimidating, but I did my best imitation of Dick Cavett. One Saturday morning we were headed to the desert in a Winnebago to shoot the video for their new song "You Got Lucky."

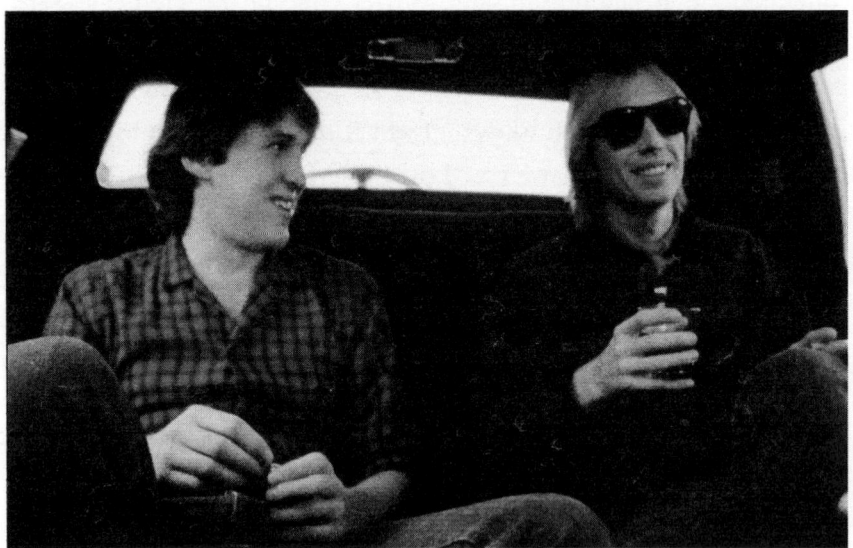

Filming *Heartbreakers Beach Party* with Tom Petty, 1982.

Tom Petty sat on the back sofa playing an acoustic guitar. We'd had a running conversation centered around our mutual appreciation of Elvis Presley's movies, a kitsch fascination fed by the fact that Petty had actually met Elvis, on the set of his 1962 movie *Follow That Dream*. We were connoisseurs. Elvis movies shared wonderful similarities—a vague plot, a ridiculous character name for Elvis, and a few new throwaway songs. (In *Follow That Dream*, the King played a beach vagabond with an exquisite name, Toby Kwimper.)

What made *Follow That Dream* special was that it was filmed near Petty's hometown of Gainesville, Florida. Petty was ten, his uncle worked on the set, and he'd been presented to the King one afternoon. He remembered Presley as tall and orange, thanks to the movie makeup. Our documentary was called *Heartbreakers Beach Party* in honor of the beach-blanket spirit of all those Elvis movies. On this morning, rolling toward the video shoot, Petty began playing "Viva Las Vegas," the title song of Presley's movie with Ann-Margret, and soon he was playing a lesser-known ballad with a Bo Diddley beat, "(Marie's the Name) His Latest Flame."

As I sat listening to Petty bring such clarity and feeling to the song, it was clear that so much was ahead for Tom Petty. The band was sensational, one of the great American groups, but I sensed there was a budding poignancy to the creative trajectory of their leader on this early-morning ride. Just like Ronnie Van Zant years earlier, an artist can throw off sparks that give you a sense of the bonfire that's coming. I could tell what might be ahead. Songs like "I Won't Back Down," "Learning to Fly," "Wildflowers," and more. The band would rise up on the shoulders of Petty's personal songwriting. It was all ahead, that early morning as we rumbled toward the desert. He could see I was moved by the song he'd just played.

Later we were talking about some of the prejudice he'd felt growing up in Gainesville as a kid with long blond hair. The stereotype he sometimes endured was that he was young and dumb, a version of the Spicoli character in *Fast Times*.

"Pick up the camera," he said, "I've got a song for you."

A large camera was at my feet, but the video director was now elsewhere. "I'm not a director," I said.

"Pick up the camera and shoot," Petty instructed. He had a lopsided grin. He clearly enjoyed the mischief of pushing me into someone else's territory. "Put it on your shoulder."

I lifted the camera and steadied it. I pressed the record button, and he began playing directly into the camera. The song was called "I'm Stupid." Watching from the other end of the lens felt electric. I'd been a music journalist, translating time and place for others to savor. This was an exercise in cutting out the middleman. It was like writing but without a pen. This was something new—writing with my heart and a camera. It was electric. I felt like I was capturing life and music and feeling in real time. And it was funny as hell.

Kris Kristofferson had tried to explain this to me years ago, sitting in that leatherette chair in the El Torito. This was the *elixir*. Music, image, feeling, story, life. All at once. Petty finished the song, and I

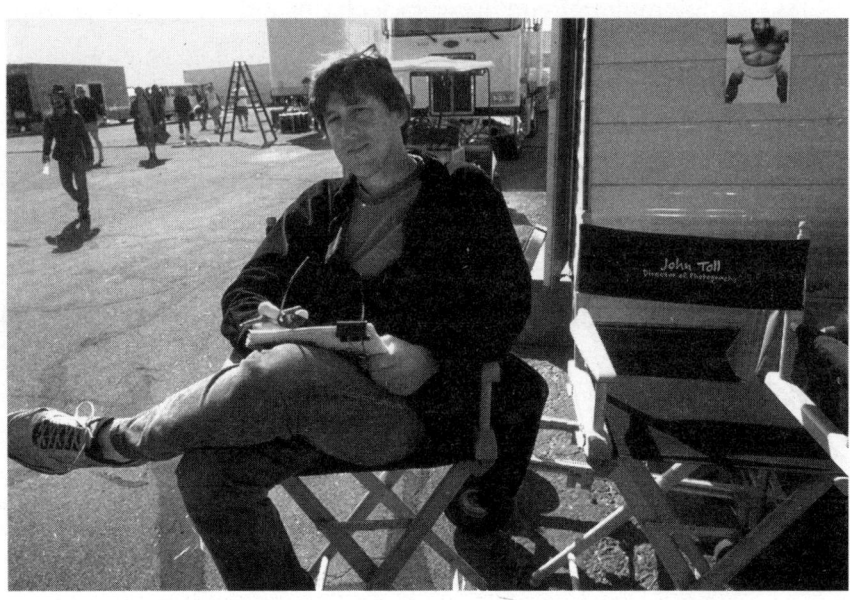

set the camera down. A whole chapter of my life was now instantly in the rearview mirror. My hobby—disappearing into the lives of others—had now opened the door to a new life. Now I wanted to tell my own stories.

"Congratulations," said Tom Petty, "you're a director."

*In the depth of winter, I finally found that what lived within
me was an invincible summer.*

—ALBERT CAMUS

I still hear my mom's voice all the time. She's still teaching. It's in her voicemails and in the many notes and faxes and letters and emails. I kept everything. She was a world-class packrat. I am but an amateur who lives in her shadow. Like any true packrat, I never throw things away. I just move them into different piles. In all the piles, and all of the notes, are her aphorisms. She was known for them, of course. I've included them throughout this book. You might find they tend to arrive at the perfect time.

Tucked into the nearby shelf filled with her old self-help books is a velvet burgundy bag. Inside it is a tub of her ashes. We paid extra for the actual ashes, and holy shit, there are *a lot* of them. She didn't want a grave. She wanted her ashes spread throughout our garden, amid the Spanish pots and the colorful flowers, where the hummingbirds buzz by daily.

With the help of Heidi Giovine, the beloved house manager at Broadway's Bernard B. Jacobs Theatre, where our musical finally landed in the winter of 2022, we were able to make some of Alice Crowe's big dreams come true. Heidi was the first face that ticketholders saw when attending *Almost Famous: The Musical.* She stood near the front door, dancing and playfully announcing to all, "Welcome to *Almost Famous!*" Though the show has moved on, my mom is still currently on Broadway. Don't tell anybody, but my mom's ashes are spread throughout the entire theater. Alice Crowe is currently appearing in the curtains, among the seats, on the wooden planks onstage, and even on the roof, where she landed in big puffs across the marquee reading: *Almost Famous: The Musical.*

Thank you, Heidi.

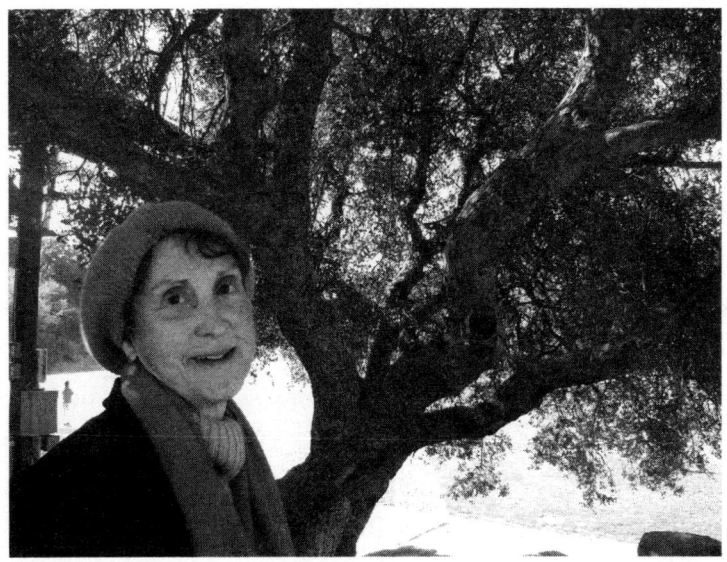

"C" I love you! Gracias for a Great Visit!!! "M"

—NOTE LEFT ON THE KITCHEN COUNTER, 2018

December 31, 1973. My heart was still somewhere on the road with the Allman Brothers Band. The band was ending the year with a show on New Year's Eve at the Cow Palace in San Francisco, the same city where Gregg Allman had snatched my tapes and nearly capsized all my dreams. New Year's Eve was always a special night at the Cow Palace. Bill Graham, the famous promoter who pretty much defined the modern rock concert experience, always put on a special New Year's Eve show for the fans. The Grateful Dead usually played, but this year Graham had invited the Allman Brothers Band. The Brothers' shows were often a spiritual cousin to the free-form concerts put on by the Grateful Dead.

At midnight, Graham would usually swing down from the rafters dressed as a baby, alongside the Dead's Jerry Garcia, dressed as Father Time. The show was to be broadcast live on the radio, and I was torn between staying home and recording it, and heading up the street to Sharie's house, where my friend Chuck was throwing a party with kids my own age. I wanted to go. My parents were teetotalers and had planned a quiet night watching TV and trying to stay up long enough to see the ball drop in Times Square.

I set up a tape-recording system by the stereo in the living room. The whole year had been an enormous transition. I was operating a journalism business out of my downstairs bedroom. I knew my parents were worried, disappointed that I was heading in the complete wrong direction from law school. I wasn't sure either of us was right. I thought about how easy it had been for the Allman Brothers Band to cast me aside. It was my first glimpse of what it would be like to be thrown from the horse, this dangerous passion of writing about my heroes. Suddenly, on New Year's Eve, everything felt like a crossroads.

Somewhere around 2 a.m. the woozy crowd at Sharie's began to empty into the now-quiet streets of Friars Village. I'd only had a couple bottles of Miller High Life and I was wide awake. Walking home, I wished I'd stayed home and recorded the show, knowing my road buddies were there, Twiggs and Red Dog, along with Richard "Dickey" Betts and even the ghostly high priest himself, the surviving brother, Gregg.

I slipped the key into the lock and turned it quietly so as not to wake up my mom and dad. The door eased open and I saw motion in the living room. It was my father in long pajamas, hovering over the tape player with a small stack of cassette tapes.

"I don't think I missed much," he said. He had been tending to the recording of the Allman Brothers Band's concert, and it was a long one. They were still playing. He'd been carefully feeding tapes into the machine, turning over each cassette every forty-five minutes. My mom had long since gone to sleep.

We both knew what this evening meant. My dad taking my hobby seriously felt like the end of something and the beginning of everything. All the things he had chased in his own life of business, from real estate to the answering services, had proven challenging. The ease of his early military life had been elusive in later years. To watch things fall into place for me might have caused resentment in other fathers. Not James Crowe. Success, he explained in an interview I discovered years later, given to his hometown paper on the eve of his own death by heart attack, was defined by something he learned from his own dad. *Did you bring joy to your community? Did you put something back into the world?*

We both knew that soon there would be another assignment, and then another. There would always be a suitcase ready in my room. People might even get accustomed to home answering machines. Jim and Alice had a life and a marriage to reclaim. The path was stretched out ahead of us both. It was a grand conversation we had in those early hours of 1974, most of it unspoken.

I set down my backpack and hugged him. He was always up for a hug. We used to hold hands when I was little, something his own dad never did. I had spent this New Year's Eve trying to be a kid again, living a teenage life with kids my own age. It was already too late, and we both knew it. I'd had a taste of an adult's life and there was no turning back. He knew my heart was still somewhere on the road with the Allman Brothers Band, and all the tours and adventures that might follow. He was right.

He laughed. Over the years, the laugh would become mine, along with the hug that I now give my own kids. It always confounded me that there were so many undemonstrative parents. Years later, I would be fretting loudly about *Almost Famous: The Musical*, the show just up the road, the one about my family. It would bring laughter and tears and standing ovations, but nothing would resonate quite like that single hug in the early hours of New Year's Eve. The lonely passion of the Allman Brothers Band and those dizzying guitar journeys in the dark gave way to a promise for the years to come. We both wanted to be perfect for each other. It was impossible, of course. Music was the gift my older sisters had given me.

So much was waiting for all of us. Just last fall my own two sons, William and Curtis, were joined by a little sister. Vivienne Crowe is the result of a wonderful new love in my life, Anais Smith. And though Viv was still three months away from being born, she managed to meet Brian Wilson at a dinner party Wilson and his team had thrown for friends and family. We asked Brian which was the favorite of all his songs, and on that day his answer was immediate.

"Surfer Girl!" he yelped.

Wilson then offered her a tiny serenade of Cathy's most beloved song. Who would have imagined it, standing there with my father in the early hours of 1974?

"Dad," I said, "I want to tell you something."

"Shut up and deal," he said.

"I love you."

The Allman Brothers Band's four-hour-long concert was still going, complete with special guest Jerry Garcia. The song was "Mountain Jam," and Dickey Betts's and Garcia's guitars were dancing recklessly into the future. My father had stayed up to capture the whole thing on the tapes carefully stacked next to the stereo-cassette player-recorder.

"I love you too, son," he said softly.

My father and I both knew the truth. I wouldn't be crossing the street to the finest law school in California. I might never be the youngest or longest-practicing lawyer in the country, just like his grandfather. But I would be an affectionate father, with his laugh, with tonight's unspoken understanding that our lives were like those two guitars. Reckless and beautiful and unpredictable. Music was everything to me, then and now, but all I knew for sure on that early morning were James Crowe's words that I'd never forget.

Nothing beats the sound of the human voice.

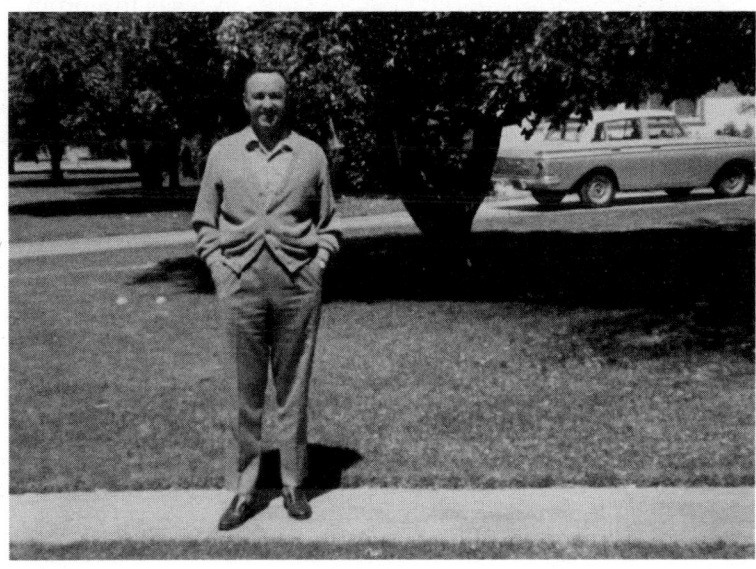

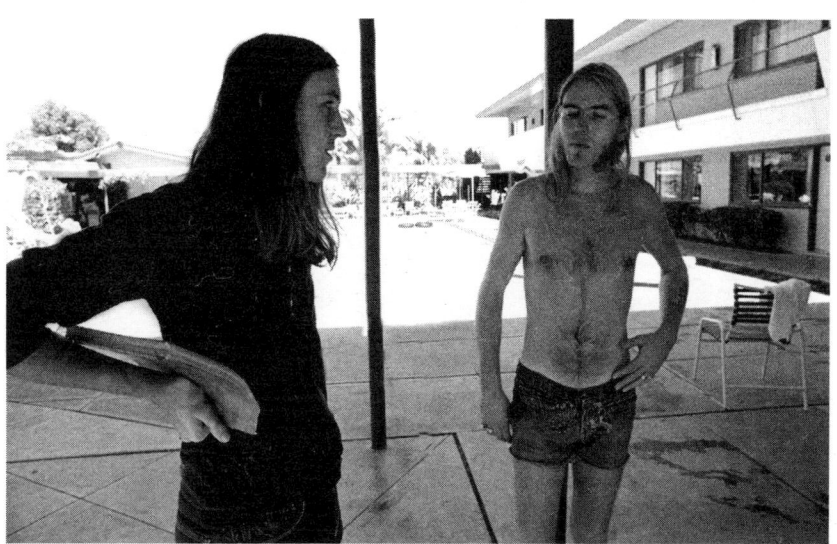

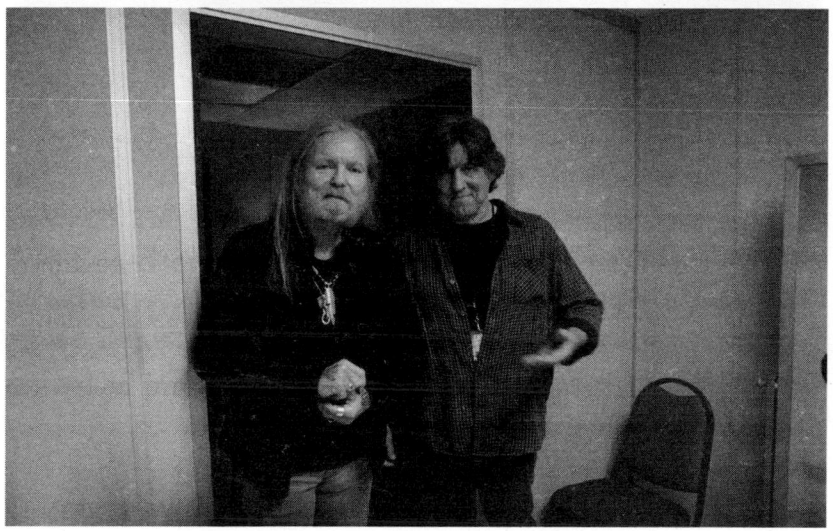

Then and now: Gregg agrees to the interview, Arizona, 1973 . . . and then offers one word of reminiscence, Del Mar, 2015.

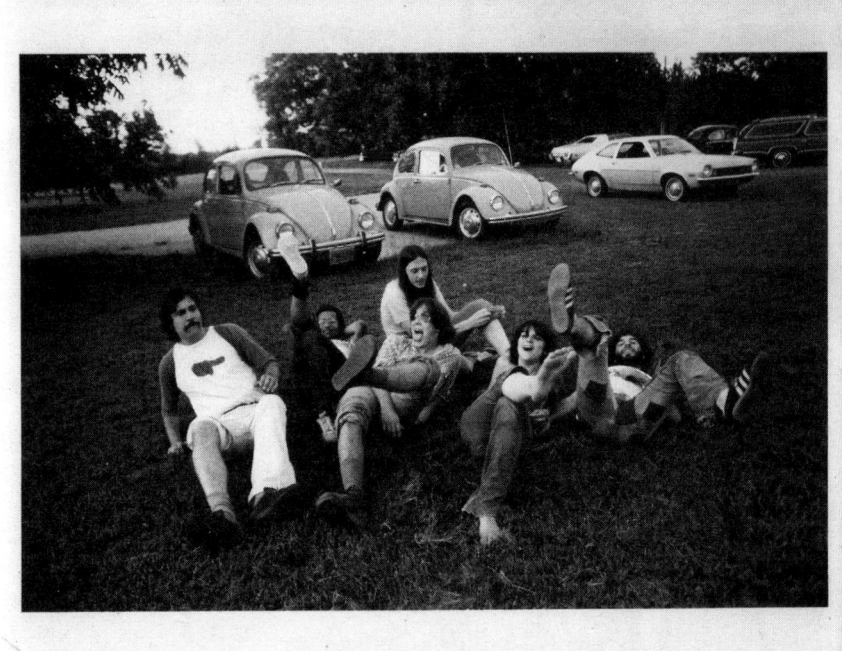

Lester Bangs, Gordon Van Buren Fletcher III, Mike Hyland, me, Jaan Uhelszki, and Neal Preston at the Capricorn Records barbecue, 1973.

A message from Alice Crowe taped to my bedroom door.
She is talking about *Fast Times at Ridgemont High*. San Diego, 1980.

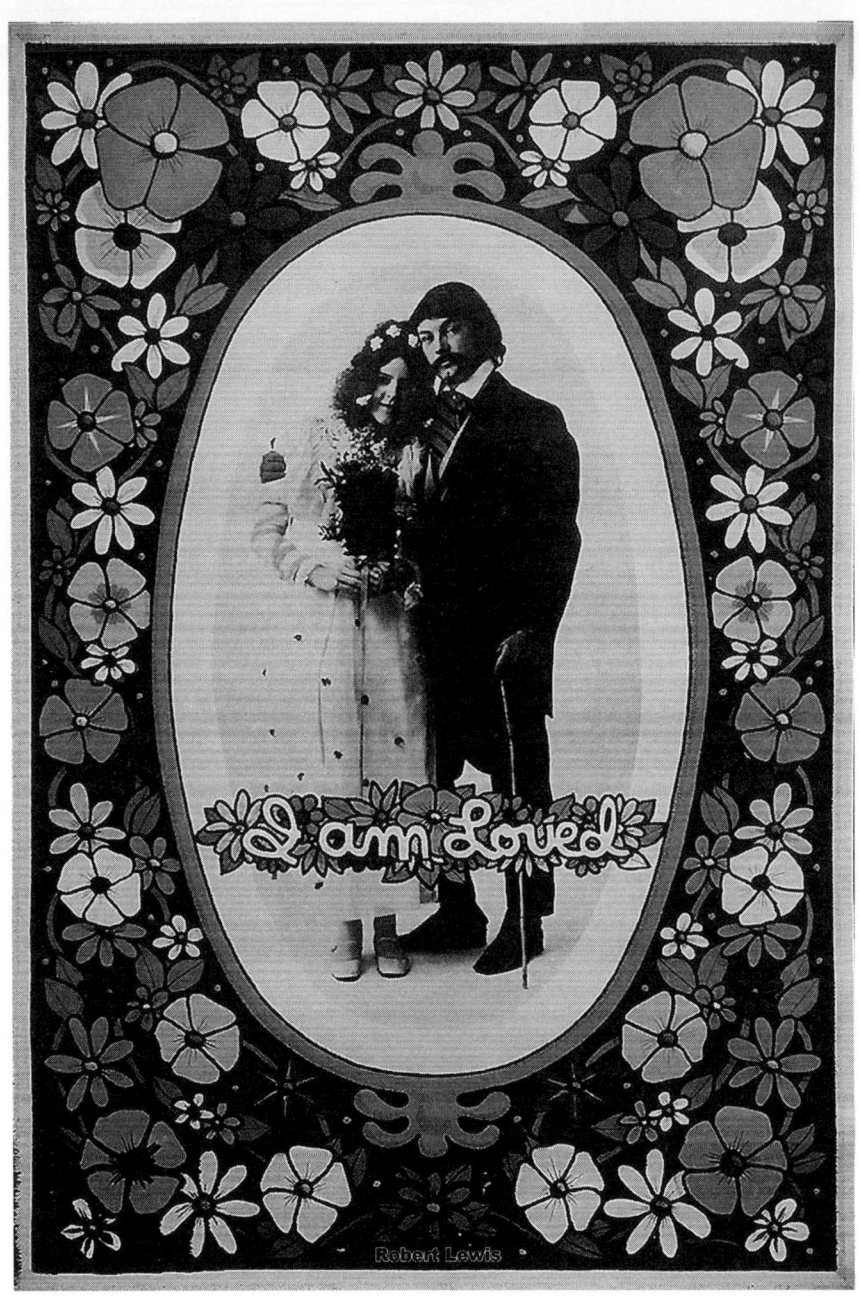

"I am Loved"

Acknowledgments

I tried to write this book without using the phrase "I remember." (Failed a few times at that.) Mostly it was important to write a story that felt as present as those days still feel to me. The feeling of wishing there were more hours in the day to chase the wild dream of writing about what I loved . . . Music, life, family, characters who might feel so real they jump off the page? That's a passion that's never left me. Thanks to all those who opened a door, or pulled me onstage for a better view, or shared an adventure sealed with my favorite look, the one that says: "Can you believe this is really happening?"

With love to my cherished fellow adventurers: Anais Smith, Neal Preston, Joel Bernstein, Vince Compagnone, Kim Gottlieb-Walker, Andy Kent, Gary Elam, Greg Mariotti, Albert Lee, Eddie Clemens, Charlotte Perman, Sam Solomons, Jofie Ferrari-Adler, Jonathan Evans, Alison Forner, Allison Green, Jonathan Karp, Dave Kass, Carolyn Kelly, Eva Kerins, Carly Loman, Heather Musika, Aja Pollock, Joshua Cohen, Jessie McNiel, Alexandra Silvas, Clay Smith, Meredith Vilarello, Katya Wiegmann, Nicholas Poser, Louise Haines, Victoria Pullen, Hope Butler, Naomi Mantin, Jonny Geller, Natalie Beckett, Viola Hayden, Melissa Chinchillo, Georgie Mellor, Ethan Schlatter, Eric Stoltz, Frank Gironda, Wynter Mitchell-Rohrbaugh, Ali Harnell, Kristen Foster, Klaus Whitley, Jann Wenner, Martha Durazo, Adria Petty, Will Botwin, Gary Stromberg, Tracey Jacobs, James L. Brooks, Leslie Morris,

Marcy Gensic, Heidi Giovine, Wes Anderson, Richard Sakai, Eddie Vedder, Maggie Rogers, Clay Griffith, Harry Styles, Karen Johnston, Stevie Nicks, Kellianne Murphy, Cindy Weber, Kaitlyn Weber, Kristin Weber, Kris Weber, Tom and Rita Kitt, Nancy Wilson, Shelli and Irving Azoff, Mom and Dad, Nicole Dale, Vivienne Marie Crowe, Curtis Crowe, and William Crowe for the Green Chair Sessions.

Most of all, this book is for my two sisters, Cindy and Cathy, who showed me the power that still lives inside those vinyl records.

Tiburon, California
August, 2025

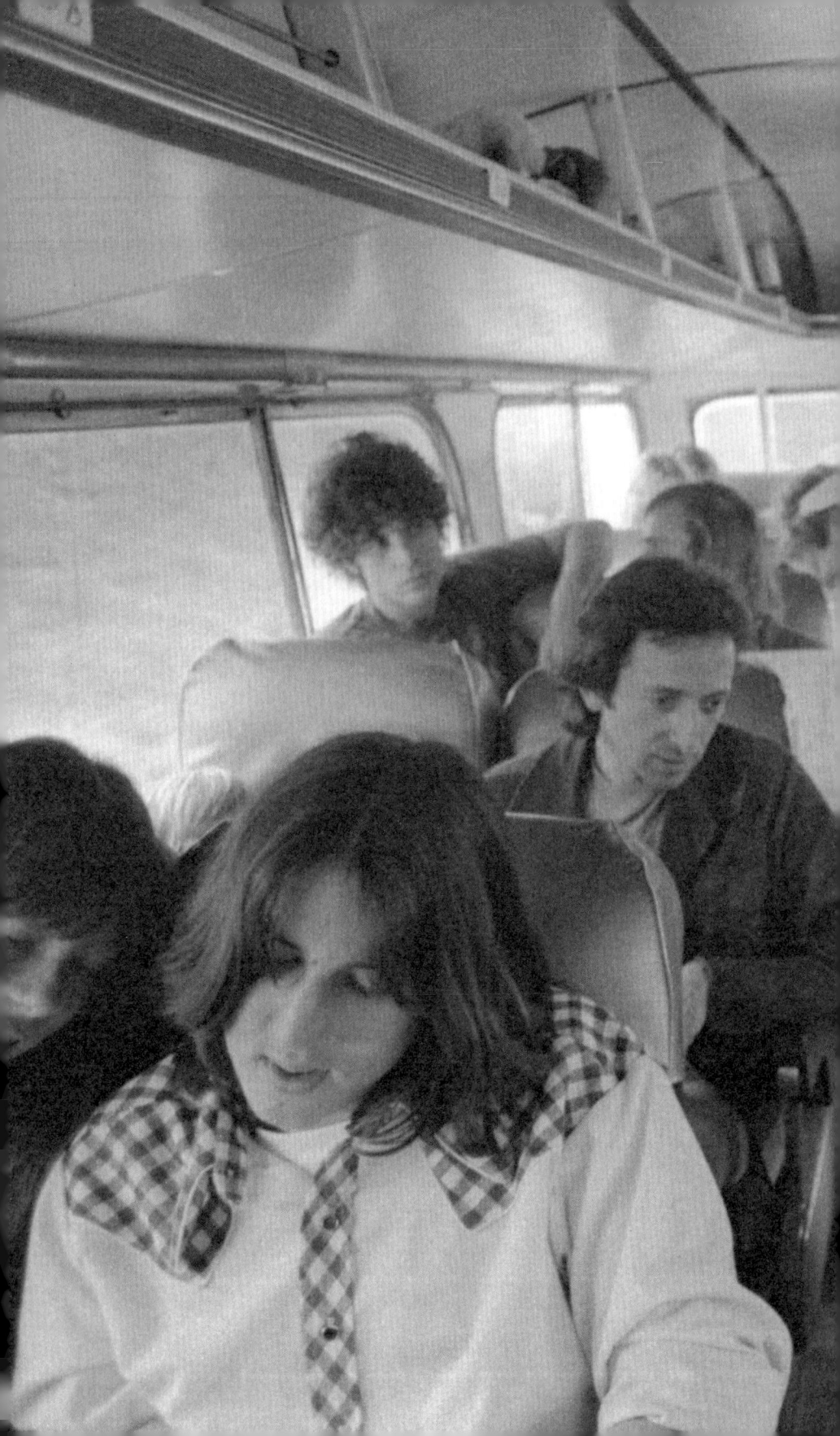